# ABOUT THE AUTHOR

**Christina Slade** is Associate Professor of Philosophy and Communication at the University of Canberra, and Head of the School of Creative Communication and Culture Studies. She received her Ph.D. in Philosophy from the Australian National University, was a Harkness fellow at New York University, and has been a visiting fellow at the Université de Québec à Montréal, at La Universidad Ibero Americana, and at the ITESM in Mexico City. In addition to numerous articles, she is the author of *Critical Communication* (with Glen Lewis).

# The Real Thing

Toby Miller
*General Editor*

Vol. 4

PETER LANG
New York • Washington, D.C./Baltimore • Bern
Frankfurt am Main • Berlin • Brussels • Vienna • Oxford

Christina Slade

# The Real Thing

## Doing Philosophy with Media

PETER LANG
New York • Washington, D.C./Baltimore • Bern
Frankfurt am Main • Berlin • Brussels • Vienna • Oxford

P
91
.S54
2002

LIBRARY OF CONGRESS CATALOGING-IN-PUBLICATION DATA

Slade, Christina.
The real thing: doing philosophy with media / Christina Slade.
p. cm. — (Popular culture and everyday life; vol. 4)
Includes bibliographical references and index.
1. Mass media—Philosophy. 2. Philosophy. I. Title. II. Series.
P91 .S54    302.23'01—dc21    2001018606
ISBN 0-8204-5555-5
ISSN 1529-2428


DIE DEUTSCHE BIBLIOTHEK-CIP-EINHEITSAUFNAHME

Slade, Christina:
The real thing: doing philosophy with media / Christina Slade.
—New York; Washington, D.C./Baltimore; Bern;
Frankfurt am Main; Berlin; Brussels; Vienna; Oxford: Lang.
(Popular culture and everyday life; Vol. 4)
ISBN 0-8204-5555-5

Cover photograph: Horacio J. Hernandez Alvarez del Castillo photograph of Puebla,
Puebla, in ed Alcázar, C. (1999) La Coca-Cola de México Fernando Porrúa, Mexico City
Cover design by Lisa Dillon


The paper in this book meets the guidelines for permanence and durability
of the Committee on Production Guidelines for Book Longevity
of the Council of Library Resources.

© 2002 Peter Lang Publishing, Inc., New York

Printed in the United States of America

# CONTENTS

# PREFACE

This book arose out of the overwhelming sense that debate about cinema, television and new media such as the Internet does not do justice to the philosophical complexity of the ideas that are being juggled for our entertainment. Movies such as *The Truman Show, Pleasantville,* or *The Matrix* are products of the late 1990s, taking as their theme the problem of reality and truth in the mediated world. The very title of *The Truman Show* reveals the problem. Truman, the eponymous hero, discovers in his twenties that his entire life has been designed as a television soap opera, with all the events scripted for everyone but himself. The horror of his discovery about the truth of his life and his subsequent attempts to escape and find "true love," "true life," and the real world become the plot of the soap opera, while the producer of the series becomes the evil genius, the maleficent demon of an updated Cartesian meditation. Finally, given the generic demands of both the modern movie as well as the soap, the hero wins out and escapes the soap opera for the outside world.

Here we have reality and truth and its distortion through the media giving both the plot and the twist to the movie. The *frisson* a viewer feels is not merely the sense of superiority of the soap opera viewer, who knows better than the actor what is going on. It is a reflexive and self-conscious sense that we, too, might be deceived about the reality of the world. Reality as filtered by the media is not an enclosed world for us as it is for Truman, but neither is it possible for us to escape. Truman's world resembles Plato's metaphorical cave in which the ignorant see only shadows of the real world. Truman, like a truly wise man, can escape and see the objects as they are. We cannot. We are left with the movie-induced stereotypes and a sense of unease.

In *Pleasantville*, two late-1990s teenagers unwittingly enter the world of a 1950s television series, which has been set in a small and conservative U.S. town. The movie breaches the borders between the televisual world, the black and white harmony of a small U.S. town in the '50s, and that of the viewers. This is a familiar plotline but is exploited as a moral tale, as an evaluation of two cultural and ethical orders. With the entry of the teenagers, the two moralities conflict. The small town learns about sex and, in the process, goes into full technicolor; the rebellious modern teenager learns the virtues of reading and consistency. Trite although the plot appears, it plays on the reflexive twists of the viewer seeing the act of viewing portrayed in the media. The story engages through a series of moral questions. What are the structures of fulfilling family relationships? Should artists be free to transgress social norms? Is sex before—or even after—marriage desirable? The moral questions resonate precisely because the two moral universes—the televisual and the world of the viewer of the television series—are in conflict. We, the viewers of the movie, then make our own metalevel assessment of the moral space of the movie, implicitly understanding the tension between our own ethical beliefs and those of the movie itself.

*The Matrix*[1] moves on from the world of movies and television series to the contradictions of virtual reality. Here we find a technological version of Cartesian doubts about the existence of the external world, this time transposed into the realm of cyberspace. What if the world as we know it is just a computer program, run by anonymous interests, and apparent acts of will are just programmed choices? What if people are just robots, being programmed to believe they are living satisfying lives in the real world? The success of the film is partly dependent on the generic characters—the young hero, the older guide, the good woman, the forces of evil in trenchcoats—all combined with a *Star Wars* mythic structure. Good wins out, a satisfactory conclusion reached through whizzes, bangs, and demon fig-

---

[1] The science fiction stories of William Gibson (e.g., 1984) whose ideas contributed to the central themes of the movie, have been immensely influential in the development of the popular and scholarly notions of virtual reality. It was Gibson who created the word, cyberspace, which has taken over from the notion of virtual reality in everyday language. I owe this observation to Annabel Beckenham (2001), whose thesis deals with the issues of cyberfeminism.

ures. But at another level, the film has been unexpectedly successful because it confronts the philosophical problems that haunt those who play
video games. How do cause-effect relations work across the virtual-real
interface? Can an action later than another also be its cause, as it appears
to be in the movie? Can the death of one's correlate in virtual space cause
real death? Could our whole life really be an illusion?

Of course there is nothing new in the interweaving of truth and reality
in fiction or games on philosophical themes in fiction. Julian Barnes'
(1999) *England, England* both ridicules and undermines a conception of
historical reality in a baroque tale in which an England theme park in the
Isle of Wight takes over as a tourist destination from the real thing, the
unpredictable and inconveniently spread-out England. England, its economy faltering, turns its back on Scotland and Wales, on Europe and on
economic rationalism, and recasts itself as the dim and chilly land of the
post-war childhood of those who created the theme park. The reader is left
to ponder in what sense the new Britain of the economic miracle of the late
nineties is real....

My aim in this book is to demonstrate the philosophical depth and
complexity of the materials of our mediated world. I argue that there is
depth and complexity, but that it is up to us, the viewers and consumers of
the media, to explore this complexity in a rigorous and philosophically sensitive way. Our mediated world is interpreted and reinterpreted; the bodies and private lives of celebrities flaunted in weekly television magazines;
the significance of the events of soap operas and real princesses played
over interminably. But—outside a very few in the academy—there is very
little attempt to spell out and interrogate the philosophical ideas of television and the newer media. Certainly, there is a paucity of material that attempts to engage those who consume the media in the philosophical
debate. Academic analyses of, say, *Dallas, Party of Five* or the coverage of
the death of Princess Diana are not written with the fan or everyday
viewer in mind. However, viewers are intensely interested in the mediated
events, not merely at the level of gossip but also at the level of philosophical debate. For some 10 years, while I have been working with school and
university students, colleagues and friends, debating the philosophical
questions inherent in soap operas, news reports, advertisements, cartoons,
films and web sites, there has been a sense of unforced interest and ex-

citement. "Noone had ever asked me what 'Just Do It' meant before," one
child said. Another said, "I have always been worried that I might just be
dreaming. How can I be sure I'm not?" He was amazed to discover that
Descartes had raised the question before him.

This book is designed to show how we can develop philosophical debate among those who use the media. I concentrate on television which, 50
years after its introduction, scarcely qualifies as a new medium. Nevertheless, it is a *newer* medium of communication than talk or books or radio,
and we are still learning how to assimilate and discuss its impact. The new
medium of the Internet has been an integral part of the project I describe
here, and I will at times discuss its impact as well.

The book is also a report of the exchanges and means I developed in
order to begin fostering philosophical debate among students using the
*Reason and Media* web site—developed with the aid of funding from the
Australian government and with assistance from the Bertelsman Media
Workshop New York. Between 1993 and 1996 I made brief videos to encourage debate, and by 1998 I had launched the web site, which took
snippets of television products and paired them with discussion pages and
spaces for users to respond. By its nature such material is transient, depending on current trends and the interests of viewers' peer groups. But
the issues and the value of discussion persist through changing forms.
What is important is to begin with questions that viewers themselves find
interesting. From that point it is possible to go on to metalevel debate
about the impact of the media and deal with questions such as those raised
toward the end of this book on the notions of the public and private in the
media. However, the starting point should not be an *a priori* philosophical
position about the impact of the media, but the philosophical debate that
surges forth in reaction to the media and the implicit plea for a framework
in which to cope with the inchoate reactions we all have to media.

I draw on a number of sources. My greatest debt is the work of Matthew Lipman who, as the founder of Philosophy for Children, alerted me,
among many others, to children's longing for and skill at philosophical debate. With his brief texts, and the manner of teaching philosophy for children which he developed with Ann Sharp, he showed how to precipitate
philosophical questioning among children. Instead of starting with a
metalevel description of, say, the problem of other minds, they describe a

child struck by the problem. The aim is to open up a debate between children and teacher as joint participants, not a debate in which the teacher is the source of knowledge. The teacher's role is to encourage the debate, by putting up a superstructure of reasoning and by remaining sensitive to the philosophical possibilities children raise. Gareth Matthews, as well as those in the Philosophy for Children movement, have shown us just how illuminating such debate can be. Although Lipman was highly skeptical of the value of television, we worked together on this project and he has supported my attempts to develop web sites using the Philosophy for Children corpus. It was he who taught me that philosophical debate should not be reserved for the philosophically literate. A good philosophical debate, rather than a debate in which participants quote and interpret the ideas of others, is one in which they show the ability to think clearly and critically about issues, to search for assumptions and presuppositions, and to evaluate reasons.

In terms of theoretical orientation, my second debt is to active audience research, which valorizes the actions of television viewers as critical and intelligent beings who transform meanings. My own introduction to this tradition came in 1990 through Patricia Gillard, then a colleague at the University of Canberra; through the work of David Buckingham; and in 1996–1997, through the work of JoEllen Fisherkeller, a colleague at New York University.

My training was in the philosophy of language and formal logic, from within a broadly Anglo-Saxon tradition. Formal models are not always easy to apply to "real" arguments, although, as I have long argued, everyday argumentation is much more logical than critics have supposed. In taking a detailed approach to argumentation in television and the media, I draw on the work of the pragma-dialecticians, such as Frans van Eemeren in Amsterdam. I discuss the model in chapters 5 and 6. It is essential to my project that we assume that the great majority of human interaction is rational and that it is susceptible to coherent analysis. Also, unlike the many critics of television and the new media, I assume that the media are reasonable.

This philosophical orientation sets me apart from many of the media theorists whose work I call on, and indeed of the late twentieth-century qualitative investigation of television. The work of Ang (1996), Buckingham (*passim*), Ellis (1982), Palmer (1986), Radway (1984) and Sartori (1998), a few on whom I draw, is underpinned by a European philosophical tradition and employs the approaches of hermeneutics, phenomenology and the broader orientation of the postmodern or cultural studies portmanteau. I have learned an immense amount from the perceptive analyses within these traditions and have a great respect for the philosophical tools used. My own battery of tools, however, is quite different. I should like to see myself as contributing in a small way to what has been called analytic film theory, as practiced for instance by Richard Allen (in Allen & Smith 1997). Maybe there will one day be a discipline of analytic television studies. This analytic orientation does not mean, however, that my arguments keep to the analytic tradition, or that they would be acceptable to analytic philosophers of language. I have drawn on a range of sources that leave me marooned between the intuitions that guide various arguments. I have done my best to sort through those intuitions and arguments fairly.

For instance, I suggest, controversially, that pictorial images may serve as arguments and that there is reasoning inherent in, and subsumed in, much imagery. Here I draw on the work of Gunther Kress and his application of Halliday-style systemic systems to images. I reject entirely the opposition between creative and reasoned analytic thought and argue that good creative thought is as reasoned as analysis. I also reject the opposition between emotions and reason. Emotional reactions have their reasons.

This book was written while I was based in three widely different places: Canberra, the capital of Australia, a small city of roughly 300,000; New York, more precisely Manhattan; and Mexico City, a megalopolis of 20 million. This has led to a somewhat idiosyncratic mix of examples as well as erratic spellings, as some reviewers have noted. While some may think that the unusual mix of examples may detract from the consistency of the argument, I believe that it adds to the plausibility of the claim that I am looking at a global phenomenon. It is not only in the United States that the media are calling out for philosophical attention, but also in at least two other regions, Australasia and Latin America. More seriously, my strategy for dealing with the media has been enhanced by the fact that it has been tested in three such widely different regions.

I was fortunate to have a year with the Media Ecology group in the Department of Communication and Culture at New York University. I learned much from the neo-McLuhanism of the program and the detailed work of scholars in the department in plotting the impact of technologies of the media. Neil Postman, Chris Nystrom, Mark Crispin Miller, and Todd Gitlin each encouraged me in my view that it is a prerequisite of a democratic society that we are able to engage with and criticize the media. My way of engaging with the media is not one these scholars necessarily approve, but I should be proud if the current work could be seen as a small part in their larger endeavor of urging social responsibility for the mass media.

I should here acknowledge the support of a number of institutions. The first and most important of these is my own institution, the University of Canberra, which gave me the chance to apply philosophical training in the area of communication and which has supported me while I have been a fully engaged teacher at the university at best only sporadically. I note in particular the support of the Vice-Chancellor, Professor Don Aitkin, the Pro-Vice-Chancellor, Professor Peter Putnis, and my Head of School, Professor Warwick Blood. I am also grateful to the Harkness Foundation for granting me a midcareer fellowship at New York University in 1996–1997 to work on these topics, and to professors Neil Postman and Toby Miller at New York University, who provided me access to a variety of fruitful sources. Professor Ingrid Volkmer of Augsburg University allowed me to use the data gathered as part of the Global Media Generations 2000 Project in this study. I thank her and those I interviewed for permission to use the data. All names are fictitious.

I should like to thank the Australian government teaching grant fund, then named the Committee for University Teaching and Staff Development (CUTSD), which allowed me to develop the *Reason and Media* web site, as well as the support of the Bertelsman Media Workshop in New York in implementing that site. Throughout the book I include student responses to this web site dealing with these issues. Most of the student responses are those of first semester first-year students in their first weeks of university courses in communication. They are virtual "virgins" in the theoretical approach to television, and, were we talking of olive oil, what we might call "extra virgin" in logic and philosophy. The sophistication of their remarks on the web site, or the lack of it, owes nothing to academic training. I am grateful for permission to cite responses from students at the

University of Canberra from 1998–1999; as I am to those of students from the Instituto Tecnológico de Estudios Superiores de Monterrey (ITESM) in Mexico City over the same period. I also quote students from New York University over the period 1996–1999.

Earlier versions of several chapters of this book have been given as conference papers, published in conference proceedings, and in some cases published as journal articles. I thank the editors of the new Sage journal *Television and the New Media*, in which a version of chapter 3, "Why not lie?" appeared (2000: 419-430); and the editors of the Kluwer journal *Argumentation* in which a version of chapter 5 "Reasons to buy" will appear. A very early version of chapter 1 appeared in the proceedings of the Communication Research Forum, Canberra, 1998; a newer version will be published in the second volume of *Spiel*, 2001. An ancestor of chapter 2 appeared in the Proceedings of the Ontario Society for the Study of Argumentation for 1997. A version of chapter 7 is forthcoming in a volume edited by Karen Ross, entitled *Mediated Identities*. I have made every effort to seek permission where appropriate for the use of these articles and for the illustrations I have selected from the media. I apologize for any unwitting breach of copyright.

Finally, I should like to thank my family, who have watched television and surfed the net in my stead while I have been engaged in the earlier technologies of writing and talking about the media.

# ADDENDUM

As this book went to press with Peter Lang in Manhattan, the world sat riveted to the television, watching attacks on the World Trade Center and the Pentagon on September 11, 2001. In Australia the reports began just before midnight. A neighbor reported flicking off the television in disgust at what he took to be a rerun of a low quality movie. Reality only sank in with the repetition of the cataclysmic images each fifteen minutes or so. One movie director explained that if he were trying to give a sense of verisimilitude he would have insisted on close ups. The distance shots just do not seem real.

This book is about what is real, what seems real and the ways television seems more real than reality. Tragedy and violence are the stuff of television fiction and the lifeblood of television news. In New York and Washington last week, images were causally connected to shocking events in the world. It was not fiction; it was truth. It reminded us of the horror behind the images, not just in this case, but also in other reports of violence on television.

The production manager at Peter Lang, Lisa Dillon, replied immediately to an email inquiry I made less than a week after the attacks. I am very grateful to her and to my editor, Sophy Craze. In the year I lived in Manhattan, I learned to appreciate the professionalism and vitality of the city. It is in many senses the real thing.

Canberra, September 18, 2001

# WHAT IS REAL?

## Ontology and the Media

Coke is the real thing. But what do we mean by real? Is an artificial flower real? A toy elephant? Your reflection in a mirror? A photograph of a person? A legal contract? A nightmare? The blue of a blue flower? The blue of the ocean? A rainbow? The number 7? Beauty? Love? Quasars?[1] There are no easy answers here. A toy elephant is a real toy but not a real elephant; your reflection and a photograph are real images but not real people; a legal contract is binding; a nightmare can have vivid effects; colors can be perceived, even if, as with the sea and rainbows, the colors do not inhere in the objects. The question is more complicated when we talk of the number 7, love and beauty, or scientific constructs such as quasars. Is the number 7 real, and if so what does it refer to—a set of seven objects perhaps?[2] Is love real and if so what is it? Are quasars real or just scientific constructs, created to explain physical facts?

Debates about what is real are ontological debates. Traditionally, on-

---

[1] This list is based on an exercise devised by Matthew Lipman as part of the Philosophy for Children project. Several of the items are mine, as is the method that I found works best in presenting the exercise—a plastic bag with the objects, or cards describing the objects, in it. The exercise is then to discuss with a neighbor whether you judge the object real or not and whether it seems real or not. (Lipman & Sharp 1984: 4)

[2] Frege (1950) answered the question about numbers with an adroit suggestion that a number could not refer to the objects—since there is nothing numeric in the concept of chairs when we have seven chairs—but about the concept all groups of seven objects have in common.

tological debates are philosophical debates about the objects that there are
in the world. Philosophers seek to establish what is the ultimate furniture
of the universe, or what things are there. What are the objects that are
properly called real? There are many answers to this question, each of
them complex. In fact, to say that Coke is the real thing is to say something
very complicated indeed. The concept of reality is philosophically loaded
with complexities that advertisements quite intentionally play on. Coke is
remembered as the real thing, partly because it is so patently not real water, not real lemon juice, not real anything but what it is: Coke. It is no
wonder that the advertisement was so successful since it focused on an issue that was—whether consciously or not—at the heart of mediated experience. Television as a medium and the plethora of advertisements and
shows we see on it often appear more real, in some sense, than the world
they describe.

This chapter deals with the ontological issues viewers of television and
users of the Internet confront every day, then turns to the ways children
and adults talk about the issues of reality. There is a vigorous debate about
the media that has been going on for the whole of the twentieth century—
the century of mass media.

### TELEVISION AND VIRTUAL REALITY:
### MORE REAL THAN THE REAL THING?

At first blush, it is easy to make a distinction between the real world
and television. The real world is *out there*, it is what is, or to use a slightly
more technical phrase, it is "what is the case."[3] What we see on television
is a representation, an image of what is the case out there. The natural extension of this idea is that a representation that we see on television is more
or less *realistic*, depending on how well it corresponds with what is the
case. The more it corresponds with the world out there, the more realistic
it is.

In the second chapter, I argue that the first pretheoretic idea of reality
is not far wrong. However, this idea has been assaulted by philosophical
skepticism for centuries. How can we be sure that what is out there is
really out there, and not imagined? How do we even classify what is out

---

3    This is of course the phrase of the early Wittgenstein [1921] (1961,§1) of the *Tractatus*.

there? How can we measure the correspondence between what is out there and a representation, without begging the question about what is out there? Which comes first, the representation or the reality? In recent years, postmodern theorists have urged these sempiternal philosophical debates in a new guise, using television and the new media as rich exemplars of the uncertainty about representation and reality.

Television has turned what is real into representation while representation has displaced reality. The process is one that Baudrillard describes, saying that simulacra replace and displace the objects they are designed to represent:

> [The image] bears no relation to any reality at all: it is its own pure simulacrum. (1983: 11)

For Baudrillard, the televisual image has become more real—what he calls hyper-real—than the object being depicted. His argument has a certain force. An event that is not represented on television, or does not fit the narrative pattern of television, is not taken to be real, since its very presentation lacks the conviction of familiarity. Reality is not real unless massaged into a reality package. A soap opera generic style taking as its model not reality but fiction has become the norm of television.

Baudrillard's problem can be illustrated using a story by Henry James (1963) called "The Real Thing." In this story an illustrator of note began to use "the real thing"—decayed gentlefolk whose weekends were spent in the houses of the aristocracy—as artistic models for his ladies and gentlemen. As a result, his illustrations grew more and more wooden until, shamefaced, he returned to his original cockney model, who could portray aristocratic characters more vividly. She was, in short, more real than the real thing. At one level this is only a play on the various senses of the word "real." To be a real object is not the same as being the basis of a "realistic" image; just as a real elephant is not the same as a real toy elephant. That is not a philosophical problem. What made a real lady or gentlemen, at least for Henry James was, among other things, birth, consideration for others, manners, and the ability to move in certain circles. Obviously, what characterizes the drawing of gentlepeople on paper cannot, in a two-dimensional illustration, be birth, consideration for others, and manners. Instead, the image or the symbol through which the many characteristics of a gentleman are represented in a drawing will be comprised of features of the superficial presentation of the class. In James' story, this consisted of a certain style, which the cockney model possessed, of holding herself still—that is, not in motion. The genuine lady had not been trained to act as a model of her own characteristics. There is no contradiction here, merely two different aspects under which the notion of a real lady or gentleman is assessed. Nor is there any question of priority; we would not have the secondary notion of the aristocratic-seeming model without there first having been the social class.

At another level, the point is that representations of people, or of social classes, take on their own life, so that the outward symbols become more important than the original criteria mentioned above. Being a lady or a gentlemen reduces to little more than taking on the outward appearance. When Henry James draws attention to the superficiality of the appearances of being a gentleman, he is calling attention to the problematic ethical issue of which complex social practice is right or should be aspired to.

The notion of a "real gentleman" has in this century become something for show; a brand name. As with products, the real and the fake are only differentiated by cost. For instance, Land's End, the mail-order company, when advertising its denim, says that it is "the real stuff." They know, as we do, that there are many sources of real denim. What Land's End is suggesting is that their denim is better. Much the same is true of "real" gentlemen. There are many who have the manners, the clothes, or the look of gentlemen. The force of the "real" then acts as a form of discrimination between types of gentlemen who cannot otherwise be separated. To call someone a "real gentleman" is shorthand for approval. This approval may have little basis in reason. When we buy "real" brands, not copies, we pay more just for the label, often knowing full well that only the label differentiates the two. It is possible that a real gentleman is just a brand name, identical in all important respects to the rest.

Baudrillard's objections to simulacra are also objections to the process whereby the real is dispensed with in favor of the representation. The film industry and television have accelerated the process of dissociation, to which James was referring, between the object in its full physical complexity and its representation. This is precisely because the representation is more complete, more lifelike, more entirely like reality than ever. However, it is too facile to say that we have lost touch with reality. There is an ambiguity in the sense of reality. When Baudrillard talks of the image or simulacra as hyper-real, he is often playing on that ambiguity. He speaks of a televisual reality that in both presentation and criteria of assessment is not in competition with the reality it represents. There is a clear difference between the football game on the field and its presentation on the screen, even though how a football game is now played is in part these days determined by the way television presents it. The game seems more vivid on television, since we have a much sharper view of events than we do as a live spectator, but there is no ambiguity about which causes the other: the televisual image is caused by the football game.

But Baudrillard's comments must also be read at another level. In terms of the broader social practices, the superficial presentation of events typical of television has come to dominate our interpretation of the world. We prefer to interpret as real those events that resemble events seen on television, and thus television has given us a blueprint for interpreting the world. The televisual world influences our understanding of social mores and democratic processes. As Sartori (1998) points out, democracy is being undermined by the blending of reality and fiction. As voters, we no longer know how to interrogate television; to find out what is real, beyond what is given to us. The hyper-real of the television is undermining the possibility of social change by removing us from a sense of what is real as opposed to what is represented.

In effect, Baudrillard is gesturing at the second sense of the notion of "real," in which to be real is to be valuable, approved of, morally sound. That meaning is very strongly present in the Coke advertisements, where there is an implicit suggestion that because Coke is real it is good. Here the suggestion is not just that Coke tastes good but that it is morally preferable. To be real is not to be fake; not to be a cheat.

Virtual reality is even more complex. Turkle (1995) quotes a user of the Internet as saying:

> Well, hasty judging people might say that the escapists are weak and can't stand the reality—the truly wise see the other side of the coin: there must be something wrong with reality if so many people want to escape. (Turkle, 1995: 242)

The assumption made by the user is that the Internet offers an alternative "reality." This metaphor has become fossilized in the notion of virtual reality. It is a metaphor: we have no difficulty distinguishing between real death and virtual death. But, as Turkle's studies make vivid, the participants are living and acting out multiple identities on the Internet, so that the most important and valued part of their lives is that which takes place online. For the commentator, "real" as a moral term is taken over by the virtual space.

The association between what is real and what is good itself has a venerable philosophical history, and can be traced at least to Plato. As Alex Nehemas (1988) points out, Plato also outlines a version of the modern argument that reality can be usurped by its representations and the concerns of modern critics about the effects of the media. Plato's reasons for excluding poetry from the ideal republic (*The Republic*, Book X: 595b) are closely linked to the arguments put forward by many media critics. For Plato, poetry is dangerous not just because it is representational, but because it leads to shameful behavior in the young. It distorts reality by failing to represent depth, while at the same time pretending to transparency. Unlike visual art, poetry pretends to portray the world directly. It encourages the error of thinking that the poet knows the truth. Television does the same, according to Nehemas. Television gives the illusion of real life, in a way that paint, or even photography, cannot. Just as for Plato those who take poetry literally may be led to improper behavior, so for Nehemas those who mistake the televisual world for reality run the risk of behaving badly. Fictional love stories, images of violence, and representations of the world in news stories have equally the appearance of reality. Indeed, according to Nehemas, it is the claim of transparency that is the identifying mark of popular culture. Fine art shows its hand, admitting that it is only a representation, whether by style or convention. Popular culture aims to deceive, to make us, the consumers of the culture, unaware of the devices that induce a sense of realism. If we accept Plato's reservations about poetry, television should be banned precisely because it seems more real than reality.

That television claims to represent the real world transparently is for Baudrillard a danger. For viewers of television, however, it should be seen as the beginning of a debate. The rise of "reality television" is a sign that the debate has entered the sphere of television itself. When real crimes become part of an entertainment show, or when television filming glitches are the theme of their own program, transparency is no longer being taken for granted. Viewers are aware of the medium and are playing out philosophical problems as they watch.

### METHODOLOGICAL ISSUES: THE ACTIVE AUDIENCE

It is a startling fact about television research that, while millions of dollars are spent on ratings surveys and the promotion of television and we know within days just how well the most recent quiz show is being received, we know little about the extent to which we see television as real.[4] We are told, repetitively and with little evidence, that fictional portrayals on television or in pornography guide the behavior of criminals; that children identify with television characters; that kids cannot tell advertisements from content. We know how the conventions of television require certain formats for news, others for quiz shows, and how the framing of shots and playing of laughter contributes to the sense of the audience "being there." But there is little systematic investigation of the underlying questions about the ways reality is represented and how those representations are interpreted. The difficulty is that the philosophical issues about reality are not obvious targets for traditional or new research methods in communication.

Ratings research dominated the early days of television. Recently, there has been much funding given to research that seeks to measure how viewing violence impacts on society. Ratings are predicated on the belief that the important factors about television viewing can be captured by numbers. The assumption was, and still is, that all the data necessary for advertisers to decide when to sell their products can be garnered with these methods. Diaries were used to establish who was watching television—yet diaries are notoriously unreliable for who tells the truth about

---

4  Chandler (1999) gives an overview of the evidence about the extent to which children see television as real. There is a body of developmental evidence, evidence relating to how kids identify themselves with television characters and some philosophically sensitive analyses which I cite in the next section. Buckingham (1993) is the most philosophically sensitive analyst of the problem. In his recent work (2000a: 108-115) he also summarizes and criticizes the evidence. In proportion to the massive bodies of data on and using quantitative models of television, the reality factor is much under-researched.

what they watch? Later, "people meters" were designed to filter misleading diary entries. The meters only need to register each new viewer as they enter the room, by clicking the name on a box by the television set, and their program choices are then automatically registered in terms of what is showing on the set. However, even people meters fail to monitor attention or the ways in which the television is used. Television is part of a cultural complex. The ways we make sense of the world, and its televisual representation, are interwoven. Ratings research makes the unwarranted assumption that all there is to study is how *much* we view.

The quantitative and reductive models common to ratings research are driven by commercial factors. For instance, the ratings companies are happy *not* to monitor what most viewers do when an advertisement comes on because they are well aware that their customers, the advertisers, would be appalled to discover how little attention their advertisements receive. By emphasizing quantitative data and describing viewers as "subjects" or demographic units (e.g., middle class, female, in their twenties), the research abstracts away from the fundamental issue: how are the viewers actually viewing?

Such oversimplification can be found in a number of studies concerning the impact of television in the "effects research" tradition. In this tradition, the assumption is that we can measure the impact of television by isolating factors and measuring change. The work of Bandura *et al.* (1967) on the question of the impact of violent television on behavior is a much-criticized case. The researchers measured how children reacted after being exposed to a violent cartoon showing children hitting a bobo doll—a bounce-back punching bag designed to be hit. The technique used to measure the impact was to show young children the television program, then put them in the room with a bobo doll. Not surprisingly, the children, having just had an effective lesson in how to play with the toy, went on to hit the doll. However good the statistical sampling in such research may be, the research failed to differentiate between children's play and real violence. This point was one made by the researchers themselves, but it alerts us to the limitations of laboratory work when television effects are being investigated.

There are important empirical studies of the ways that children's viewing behavior alters as they grow; of the impact of visual and auditory queuing devices; and of the correlation between hours of viewing and anti-social behavior.[5] Such research is fundamental to a proper understanding of the medium and, well managed, can be used to sustain or reject some of the more common claims about the effect of television. Nevertheless, such research methods are insensitive to the cultural context of television.

The most convincing models are based on what is called "active audience" research.[6] Active audience research concentrates on the role of the television in the home; how it is used, whether as a background noise, children's entertainment or concentrated adult viewing; and the social circumstances of television users. This style of research tends to identify the role of television in a culture or subculture and to locate the viewers as an active audience, not just as passive receivers. Viewers actively interpret the content of television, with interpretations far removed from those intended by broadcasters.

It is not easy to develop a holistic research methodology that is sensitive to the ways people actually use television. The active audience tradition remedies the worst excesses of earlier research by focusing on ethnographic research methods. The researcher endeavors to enter the culture of the viewer and extract, through extended analysis of the ways that viewers react, an account of how television is used. Rather than treating the viewer as a "subject" to be calibrated, ethnographic research treats viewers as part of a culture. The research has brought out the deviant or resistant ways in which audiences interpret television and has shown the ability of the viewers to use television for their own purposes.

Quantitative methods limit the sort of information we have been accustomed to receive about television. If we look for crude behavioral reactions to television, such as simply turning it on or hitting bobo dolls, we are unlikely to notice the phenomenon of viewers engaged in philosophical questioning. On the other hand, however fully spelled out an account of television culture may be, it is still descriptive. An ethnographic study

---

5     Gunter & McAleer (1997) provide an overview of evidence.

6     E.g., Alasuutari (1999), Buckingham (1993, 2000a), Livingstone (1990, 1992); Morley (1986), Nightingale (1990), Palmer (1986). Buckingham (1993:11ff) gives an overview of the tradition. Ang's (1996, Part 1) is also an excellent summary and critique of the tradition.

leaves little room for criticism or advocating alteration of television viewing patterns, although many active audience researchers are of course
aware of the need for change.[7] Media ecologists such as Postman (1985,
1993) argue that television culture has had a major impact on society, an
impact which can be criticized. The impact is all bad. We know far more
than ever before about the world, about the private lives of public figures
and about behavior outside the home. What we do not do is examine the
televisual world critically. It is that critical process that is advocated here.

## DOES THE ACTIVE AUDIENCE THINK TELEVISION IS REAL?

Have people really made mistakes about what is real and what is not?
Is this a new phenomenon? The dividing line between truth and representation has always been porous. From earliest times, fiction and myth have
seemed to readers and listeners to be real. The assimilation accelerated
during the twentieth century, the century of the media. Half a century ago,
there were panic reactions to the radio broadcast of Orson Welles' *War of
the Worlds*. Thousands who had missed the initial announcement that the
broadcast was a play fled from their homes, believing that the science fiction scenario of an interplanetary invasion was real.

Less spectacular everyday examples confirm that media consumers
characteristically worry about what is real. In a longitudinal study of
memories of the media[8] conducted in 14 countries, we talked with focus

7    For instance David Buckingham, a noted defender of models of child-based audience
     research and of research which valorizes the understanding that viewers bring to the
     media, talks of the danger of "sentimentalizing" children's grasp of television and the
     need for critical views. He made these remarks in "Teaching the Media," a talk given
     at NYU (25 February 1997) subtitled "cultural literacy in the electronic age." He took
     "literacy [to be] a kind of guarantee of citizenship" and said "modern societies are
     based on the electronic media." The argument is developed more fully in Buckingham
     (2000b, chapter 9).

8    This study was conducted under the auspices of Radio Television Luxembourg, with a
     team led by Professor Ingrid Volkmer of Augsburg University. This 14-nation study
     compared data from a number of nations. Here I use my own Australian material and
     make reference to the Mexican material, the collection of which I also supervised. I am
     grateful to those who were interviewed for allowing me to use the material, as I am to
     Professor Volkmer for permission to quote from the study in this work, and Fiona Co-
     hon who prepared the transcripts.

groups of three cohorts about the media memories of their youth. One cohort was the first radio generation, now in their seventies; another was the
first television generation, now in their forties, and the final cohort was
that group of teenagers who are the first Internet generation. The Australian and Mexican studies are cited here.[9]

All groups had concerns about the verisimilitude of the mediated message. In a focus group of six 70– to 75-year-old Australians, for instance,
one woman was shocked to discover that the coverage of overseas cricket
matches between the wars was not the direct broadcast it had appeared to
be. In fact, announcers received telegrams of the progress of the match
from London, then relayed the information as a commentary and imitated
the noise of the cricket ball hitting the bat in the studio with a pencil.

> James: All the children from school would sit up until all hours, depending
> on the attitude of the parents. And I'm not sure whether we were really lis-
> tening to a direct broadcast or whether…
>
> Hilda: No, we weren't. We weren't. They used to knock a pencil on the table
> for the ball hitting the bat and they had cables coming through, I think.
>
> Interviewer: And they had to reconstruct it?
>
> Hilda: They reconstructed it and they really made it sound as if they were
> there. It was very cleverly done.
>
> Marjorie: That's cheating! (laughter)
>
> Georgie: Have you only just found out?
>
> Marjorie: Yes!
>
> Georgie *(inaudible, everyone talking at once)*:…the…the media lie! (Cohort 1,
> November 1998, Adelaide, Australia).

Other remarks from this cohort indicate that some members were well
aware of the reality gap of wartime news.

---

[9]   I was responsible for the Australian study and supervised the Mexican study. While
these two are only a subpart of the results, what I say here is consistent with reports of
the other studies.

Georgie: There was nothing like the graphic cover of the war that we have had the Vietnam War on the television. Nothing like—it was rather—it was—I don't mean censored, but it was sanitised, wasn't it, all that stuff?

Interviewer: Yes, mmm.

Hilda: Well, I think it probably was censored, because a lot of things we didn't know about. We didn't know about the bombing of Darwin!

*(General chorus of agreement)*

Marjorie: No, we didn't know about that for years. I think it was years afterwards, wasn't it?

Hilda: And bombs were dropped in north Queensland too and we didn't know about that.

Marjorie: We knew about the Jap submarines in Sydney harbour, //but nothing at all about...

Georgie: //nothing about the north.[10] (Cohort 1, November 1998, Adelaide, Australia)

This generation was, in effect, the first generation to have access to radio and film. They were well aware of the mediated nature of the news, yet they were equally convinced that the events they could see were real. The first newsreels of the prisoner of war camps, for instance, are recalled vividly and without any questioning as to whether or not they were real. Images in newspapers also have an automatic veracity, in the sense that there is no question that they were truly caused by real events.

Georgie: Oh, I can remember a picture on the front page of the *Advertiser* that I have never forgotten. It was a picture of an Australian airman with his hands tied behind his back, who was beheaded by the Japanese.

Marjorie: That was a picture we all saw, wasn't it?

Interviewer: So you remember it too, do you?

*(Chorus of agreement)* (Cohort 1, November 1998, Adelaide, Australia)

---

10   Double slashes // indicate overlapping talk.

Another example concerned advertisements.

> Georgie: I always thought it was the real actresses speaking, you know, saying, "Barbara Stanley uses Lux, 'I always use Lux'." And I thought, "That's Barbara Stanley." I took years before I realised that it was not her at all. (Cohort 1, November 1998, Adelaide, Australia)

In the subsequent focus group of people aged 40 to 45 years—the first television generation—we found a much greater sense of skepticism. This generation, who lived through the Vietnam War, is now far more suspicious of the media and, in fact, was more questioning at the time. Throughout the discussion, mention is made of press stereotypes:

> Roger: Well there has always been that type of stereotyping, if you look back on that, I mean the minute you have a Muslim, they're typically—you know, they're a freedom fighter, so we can say they are an extremist. (Cohort 2, December 1998, Canberra, Australia)

There is a constant attention to the fact of mediation; to the way the media present events.

> Morris: I suppose maybe television was still developing at that stage and still working out its news coverage, you know, and its use of images, its control of images...Newspapers had been at it a lot longer. (Cohort 2, December, 1998, Canberra, Australia)

The final focus group was a group of teenagers, between the ages of 15 and 20, the first Internet generation. We found that this generation has a wholesale cynicism about all media products. When they listen to the news, they take it very lightly. At the same time they question the reliability of the sources. However, their cynicism about the media has not led them to question or investigate any issues more deeply through other sources. One has the impression that the cynicism about the media is itself picked up from the media's self-criticism, rather than derived from any examination of different media sources, or from more direct forms of evidence.

It appears that skepticism about the media—the sense of the unreliability of the mediated events—has increased over the generations. Marjorie, in the older group, was clearly convinced by the pencil-tapping she heard during a direct broadcast of cricket, while Georgie believed she was listening to the actress, Barbara Stanley, advertising soap. For this generation the media had appeared transparent. The group discussed learning about the deceptions practiced by the media long after the event. For the younger generations, the assumption is that the media are not the real thing.

This is confirmed by studies of children's attitude towards television. Within the active audience tradition, there is a substantial body of work dealing with the ways children interpret the reality of television. As Hodge and Tripp (1986) note, being able to talk of fiction as if it were real is often a sign of sophistication. Adults use similar strategies in discussing fiction, talking of the events in a novel as if they were real. Hodge and Tripp introduce a notion of modality to mark the ways judgments about television register an awareness that it is mediated. The evidence, carefully collected by Buckingham (1993), of children's own reporting on the extent to which they see television as real, shows how complex the notions of reality may be. In his discussion (1993, chapter 9), Buckingham points out that almost all studies of television reality assume that the more a program is perceived to be realistic, the more likely it is to influence behavior. He argues that there is little evidence supporting the claim.

His views are clearly supported in our study of the younger cohort's memories of television. For instance, several of the younger cohort in Australia and Mexico talked of the terror they had felt when the Gulf War was reported in television news. They were sure that bombs were about to fall in their backyards. The fact that the report was real was indeed directly linked to the effect. Yet true reports about the Gulf War influenced behavior unrealistically at least in geographic terms. In the end the children's behavior was little altered by the reports of the War. The same groups talked with passion of their childhood fictional heroes, claiming that they had tried to dress and walk and behave as the heroes did. The fictional modelling, quite clearly perceived as fictional and unrealistic, had a clear impact on the way the children behaved.

What is evident from the research is that children, like adults, are highly sensitive to the generic conventions governing television programming and are far from gullible in the ways they identify and judge what is real on television. To use the Hawkins' (1977) phrase, they are aware of the artifice of the "magic window" of television. However, as Lembo (1997) puts it, there is an increasingly detached viewing style in which images are just images and the viewer does not ever treat the television as transparently real.

Children and adults are skeptical about televisual reality. Their skepticism is not justified, or so I will argue later in this chapter. However, their skeptical concerns cannot be legislated away. After all, television is not just a magic window; it is also the most commonly used window on the world outside the home and local area. Much of what we know about the world we learn from television. The problem of what is real is not a problem of television—it is a much worse philosophical problem than that. If children—and adults—are to come to terms with the complexity of the relationship between television and reality, they need a chance to talk about what reality is.

We can open up a space in which to talk, philosophically, about the content of advertisements, soap operas, cartoons and news, and whether they are real. Children watch and make sense of television in complex and generally uncharted ways. They use television, as we all do, both as a way of making sense of the world and as a mode of relaxing and of creating bonds. When a young child snuggles up on a bean bag by the set, or an older child surfs apparently randomly across the channels, only highly sophisticated viewers and researchers are able to interpret how they are engaged. But we can all talk about what is happening on television and about the issues that arise from it.

## TALKING ABOUT TELEVISION: THE *REACTIVE* AUDIENCE

Viewers of television and users of the Internet are not just passive recipients into which the media pour messages. They are active interpreters of the television product, making their own complex understandings of the messages. Furthermore, the audience is not just an active audience; it is also a *reactive* audience. The audience interprets what it sees; but it does more than that. It goes out and talks about the product, reinterprets it in the light of criticisms that others make, and reassesses the initial reaction. The television product is part of the common culture, and viewers react to it. The quality of the reactions may be questionable but they certainly exist. What is needed is not so much new television as new strategies for dealing with it and the ability to reason and be critical about it.

There are many ways of talking about television. We can gossip about the lives of soap opera characters, discuss the body language of Bill Clinton, ridicule the bald patch of a senior statesman, or share outrageous jokes from *The Simpsons*. All such talk is part of the reactive televisual culture; a consequence of the way televisual content has become part of everyday life. Children learn about the world from television and their moral universes, their friends; and their shared jokes are based on what they have seen on television. But there are other ways to talk about television. It is possible to talk rationally about the philosophical issues inherent in television.

It is a daunting prospect to delve into the philosophical issues that underpin television and, even more, our use of the Internet. Among the many endeavors that the burgeoning field of media literacy encompasses, the philosophical analysis of media at the level of content has been neglected. *A priori* theorizing on philosophical issues of the media always runs the risk of being outdated and outpaced by the technologies themselves. The strategy suggested here is to begin with content, generally televisual content, and move to the philosophical and argumentative levels on the basis of that content. In effect, the strategy is to draw on the philosophical tradition of densely argued issues to illuminate what is happening on television.

It would be a mistake to think that the skills of philosophical argumentation are innate. It was suggested previously that children and adults are inclined to talk philosophically about television content and that the philosophical issues involved are complex and worthy of debate. Indeed, it is difficult to see how a democratic society can survive without debating the issues of the day, and those issues are most widely disseminated on television. However, if discussion is to be valuable and productive, it will benefit from training in philosophical skills. To do this, it is useful to be aware of the philosophical traditions that have informed our everyday thinking. This does not mean subjecting everyone to a course in the history of philosophy. Reading potted Plato or Descartes is likely for many people to be an exercise in tedium that will kill for them the philosophical excitement of the media. What is important is to encourage rigorous philosophical debate.

Philosophical debate is characterized by the requirement of high standards of reasoning. The practice is not purely empirical but relies on extended passages of reasoning, at times drawing highly abstract conclusions. Talking philosophically about television thus has two distinct sets of outcomes. Not only does television viewing benefit from philosophical analysis but reasoning skills themselves can be developed through television.

The latter thought, one colleague told me, is one which makes most critics mock—"television and reasoning: an oxymoron." Television does not model rational behavior. In many television programs we see children behaving bravely and adults with sympathy. But we rarely see people interacting as self-conscious rational agents, making decisions on the basis of reasoning. Political debate has been reduced to a competition to discover who is more adroit with the one-liners. We do see deduction in a detective series, and complex argumentation and moral debate is assumed in much popular culture—cartoons, soap operas and advertisements. However, there is no rational evaluation of the arguments.

Nevertheless, television does involve reasoning at every level of production, interpretation and reception. We apply reasoning skills throughout the process of interpreting television, just as those who script and produce television expect us to. There would be no sense at all in television without the mutual expectation of producers and viewers that interpretation involves reason. Our television viewing is shot through with reasoning.

We should be wary of drawing too narrow an image of reasoning skills, seeing these as those skills which might be taught in a first-year critical thinking course. Traditionally such reasoning skills have been taught through written examples, some of which are highly anachronistic or artificial. That account of the reasoning skills does not encompass the skills used in philosophy, let alone those used to filter and interpret the rapidly changing circumstances of the world around us. All communication—visual, nonverbal and verbal—involves reasoning. Reasoning is far broader than the set of logical skills often caricatured by nonlogicians. It is rather those skills used in interpreting and evaluating arguments, with all due contextual sensitivity. What is more, reasoning is fundamentally linked to discourse. The most effective way to improve reasoning skills is by training children to reason together, to argue in a coherent and defensible way. Framing the rules of reasoned discourse is extraordinarily difficult, but children share an intuitive sense of what makes a good argument. It is that sense of what counts as a good argument we aim to refine.

We use television as a major source of information and basic understanding of the world: "our common culture is a product of what we watch rather than what we read." (Cheney quoted in Mitchell, 1994: 1) In developing philosophical debate about television and the media we can refine the reasoning skills so sadly lacking in the models offered by the media and at the same time put a philosophical filter on our reactions to television. Debate about the nature of reality and television is an obvious starting point for developing the reactive audience. Reality features large on television and in advertisements because it is a powerful and elusive philosophical concept. We need to allow this debate to go back to its philosophical beginnings; to the theories of truth and of reality which sustain lay talk about truth.

## THE REACTIVE AUDIENCE AND TELEVISION REALITY

Children are capable of philosophical debate about what they see on the television or interact with on the Internet. The experience in classrooms has been documented widely, with children raising philosophical questions (e.g., Lipman, 1991; Matthews, 1994; Slade, 1994). The example below is taken from a discussion page on the *Reason and Media* web site (Slade, 1998), a web site developed for students at university level and aiming to make them aware of the philosophical issues they confronted on television. In this case students had accessed a cartoon excerpt on the web and then asked about whether cartoon characters were real. They were then prompted with questions similar to those with which we began this chapter. One student reacted to questions about reality this way.

> I believe that objects that I consider to be real are more scientific in nature.
> Toys are not real, but actual photos and fossils are real, they come from a
> living being. The colour blue is real because it comes from a plant, yet the
> sea's blue colour isn't real because it is the depths of the sea and what lies on
> its bottom that creates the blue image we see. (first-year student, University
> of Canberra, 1998)

Here a student is grappling with the notion of reality with which we began. She is searching for a criterion to delimit what is real. She begins by saying that toys are not real, implicitly saying that they are not real animals. A toy elephant is certainly not a real elephant. She goes on to say that actual photos and fossils are real, and her criterion for the distinction is causal—she says they are real because "they come from a living being." Presumably the argument here is that whatever is caused by a real event is itself real. She then detours through the issue of color, looking for a distinction between the blue of a plant—real, because it is inherent in the plant—and of the sea—not real because it is caused by other objects, not the surface of the sea. Her argument here needs much development, but one can imagine refining it to give a coherent ontology, or theory of objects. She might decide that the toy, as a physical object, is real even if it is not a real elephant. She might suggest that to count as a real elephant an image—or fossil—must be caused by a member of the species. Defining the species might be difficult, but she could look to an account of natural kinds. Such a view would be consistent with some modern accounts that identify what is real, what is the ultimate furniture of the universe, in terms of physical properties. Color, species—all these will add complications. As the student notes, color is tricky, for it is a property not of the object itself, but of the perception of the object in certain light conditions and so on. The account, however, is waiting to be developed.

But what of younger children? Can they manage such philosophical debate? Yes, most emphatically. Over 10 years ago I was working with 6- to 7-year-olds in a philosophy for children class in an international school in Brussels. They were discussing whether ghosts are "real." This is the transcript of the videotaped class.

P: Remember one question: do ghosts exist?[11]

Derek: They exist in your mind.

P: So you think that when we talk about ghosts existing we mean they exist in your mind?

Sarah: It's not in my mind. Sally doesn't exist in my mind. 'Cause when you die your ghost comes up.

P: When you say ghosts exist what do you mean?

---

[11]  I conducted classes at the International School of Brussels from 1987 to 1989, with the permission of the headmistress and the parents of the children involved. I am P, the professor. The transcript is based on videotaped footage.

Aaron: It's on earth and if it's something on earth and if it doesn't exist then you don't know about it.

P: It's something we know about, that's in the mind, but it's on earth?

Aaron: Yeah, we know about it because it's on earth.

Matthew: Also it's kinda like on earth. And as you say you see this table in front of me. It means it's on earth because you see it.

P: OK, it's on earth because you see it.

Matthew: Like if it wasn't on earth you wouldn't see it. Like it's imaginary.

P: On earth that you can see?

Matthew: Yes.

P: Are there things that you can see that are not on earth?

Matthew: Yes. Like ghosts and things.

P: Do they exist?

Chorus: Yes, no.

Derek: Jupiter is not on earth and it exists.

P: Good point. Who was it who was using the "on the earth" criterion? Matthew and Aaron?

Matthew: But you don't see it. You look up in the sky.

Derek: You could see it at night.

Aaron: I can change that. Something that you know about.

P: But I read about ghosts in a book, so I know about them. Does that mean they exist?

Aaron: But if you know about it, it is true. (Grade 2, International School of Brussels, 1988)

The children are discussing a network of concepts—"real," "exists," and "truth"—which are all interwoven. The group of 6- to 7-year-olds is struggling to define what is meant by saying that an object exists. Derek suggests that apparently non-existent objects exist in your mind. Sarah objects that that is not what we mean by existence; her friend does not exist in her mind, she complains. Aaron offers another double-barreled and sophisticated criterion: that objects that exist are those that are on the earth and about which you know. Matthew suggests being visible as a criterion for existence. The discussion deals with a counterexample, of objects that you can see and which are not on earth. Derek raises the tricky case of a planet which is not visible and not on earth. Aaron comes back with a revised proposal: what exists is what we know about.

This is a sturdy philosophical discussion, even ignoring the age of the debaters. What happens during the discussion is an attempt to deal with questions of existence and, by extension, of what is real; not by proposing one or other physical criterion, but by moving the talk to questions of what we know—of epistemology and of truth. In a typically philosophical strategy, Aaron says we might not be able to decide by testing what counts as existing, but if I know something, then what I know must be about an object that exists. He can rest with that even when challenged by the teacher to explain that there are stories about ghosts in books. He relies on the implication that if I know something it must be true. If the ghosts don't exist, then even if I have read about them, and believe in them, I can't know about them. To know, properly speaking, is to know that it is true; and if a sentence about ghosts is true, then the ghosts do exist.

This strategy is in tune with the dominant mode of twentieth century philosophy in that it avoids trying to define a class of objects as real by physical or even causal criteria. Instead we translate the question of reality—what exists—into a question of which objects are identified in our language. When Aaron says the objects that exist are those that he knows about, because "if you know about it, it's true," it is just this intellectual step that he is preparing to take. He was 6 at the time. Children can be philosophically sensitive and adroit. Training children in reasoning is training them to refine that intuitive sense, and to judge their own and others' remarks by standards of good argument. I have found that children want to think about what is real; about whether the world of video games or television seems more real to them than the life of the family. They like to debate about what words mean, in a philosophical fashion. They often recapitulate arguments that are familiar from traditional philosophy. It is these arguments we will briefly revisit next.

## REALISM AND RELATIVISM

The philosophical issue of the nature of reality has generated two millennia of debate. The metaphysical debate is far from solved—what is reality; what are the ultimate components of the universe; which things are the real ones and do they exist independently of what we think? In the twentieth century, the philosophical search for an ontology or account of which objects are real was transformed from *ontological* or *epistemological* realism into a *semantic* form of realism. That is, questions about the evidence for the existence of objects or our ways of knowing about the world have been replaced by those about the way language represents the world.[12] The debate here is sketched from the broad viewpoint of analytical philosophy of language.

The students whose views we have looked at here all began by looking for the criterion for real objects, for deciding of any particular object whether it was real or not. Ghosts, numbers, love, and beauty then become intractable problems. Ghosts are illusions and are not real insofar as they do not correspond to what there is out there. Ghosts don't really cause anything. But they can frighten me, so they have a real causal role, we might say. Love and beauty or numbers are no more tangible than ghosts, yet we want to say they are real. What out there do they correspond to? Plato supposed a realm of ideas, the true reality; but the question then is what made those ideas real? For idealists, the objects perceived in the world were constructions of our minds; "ideas" rather than objects out there beyond the perceiver. Samuel Johnson is said to have refuted such idealism by kicking a chair, thus "proving" an object exists "out there." But this is no proof to the committed idealist who will reply that *of course* the object will *seem* to be out there—after all, that is how our minds construct the world. The issue between realist and idealist is intractable without some criterion for deciding what is indeed out there.

With the move to a linguistic or semantic focus in philosophy, the issue of realism becomes a question about how we use language to represent reality, rather than one about the ways that particular words refer to existent

---

12  Cf. Mautner (1996), entry on "Realism"; Quine (1953, 1960, 1974); Evans (1982); Dummett (1978, 1993); Rorty (1991). I here refer to the Anglo-Saxon philosophical tradition, but the semantic turn also characterises the European philosophical traditions of hermeneutics, poststructuralism and the postmodern sources of cultural studies from which much research on television derives. Foucault's *Les Mots et les Choses* (trans, 1973) is a fascinating account of how the European philosophical tradition came to language from Descartes to the twentieth century.

(or nonexistent) objects. The thought is that language relates to the world, not piecemeal with particular words referring to particular existent (or nonexistent) objects, but holistically. Language connects to the world at the level of sentences and of the entire language, not primarily at the level of words. The connection between language and reality is mediated by conventions, both at the level of language and at the level of interpreting others' behavior. Central to those conventions and what counts as real is the concept of truth. Crudely speaking, a realist conceives of the grounds of truth as possibly outrunning the evidence available to us. For realists, reality is at least in principle possibly beyond our grasp. The realist takes it that reality is not a human construct. The bland label 'anti-realism' is given to those who think that reality can only be what speakers can in principle recognize. For anti-realists, reality is limited by what human beings can conceive.

In terms of the debate about the reality of the television product, both realist and anti-realist assume that the role of language is to represent the world. Each allows that our language connects with the world in manifold ways. For the anti-realist, we can only understand sentences that could in principle be verified; whereas for the realist, we might understand in principle unverifiable sentences. Thus, for the realist, it is possible that there are bodies such as ghosts whose existence could never be verified. For the anti-realist, on the other hand, this is empty speculation. Yet for the realist, a claim that ghosts exist is a substantial claim about how the world is out there. When Derek said ghosts exist in the mind, Sarah, the determined realist, responded that that is not what we mean by existence. "Sally doesn't exist in my mind," she says crossly. For her, to exist is to be mind-independent. For the realist, numbers, like ghosts, exist independently of whether there are people. The number 7 and legal contracts and love and quasars exist. For the anti-realist, on the other hand, numbers, quasars, love and legal contracts exist only if we have clear and usable criteria for verifying or falsifying statements made about those objects.

The realist/anti-realist debate is only one of a number of active disputes about realism that characterized the twentieth century. Rorty (1991, introduction) offers an illuminating summary of the debates. Perhaps the most pervasive opposition to realism is variations of relativism. The relativist theses, derived from the German idealist philosophy of the nineteenth century and from sociologists of the twentieth, have become the homespun philosophy of the magazines. When children are asked what is real, what is true or what is good, the invariable response is: "It's all relative." Relativism, in this popular form, justifies any behavior while avoiding the need for justification: "What I do is right for me." However, it is generally forgotten that relativism entered the popular culture from a wave of post-Kantian philosophy. If we seek resources to debate the popular views, we can return to the philosophical tradition.

Linguistic relativism is the form of relativism most prevalent in philosophical debate and most generally applied to objects. For the linguistic relativist what we identify depends on the conceptual and linguistic resources of the language we use.[13] Take, for example, relativist views applied to the languages of Australian Aboriginal Peoples. Certain Aboriginal groups of Central Australia use a language of spatial reference very differently from that common to Indo-European language families (Levinson, 1992). Instead of referring to directions in the familiar way translated as "right of here," "left of here," they always use cardinal directions, translated as "to the north," "to the west-south-west," and so on. In describing an object in a store, they will not say, "It's to the left of the counter," but instead refer to its being, say, in the north-east corner of the store. For a learner of these languages, a complex calculation must be done each time they receive a direction—where is north, they wonder. For speakers of these tongues, on the other hand, there are different problems. They must first orient a map to their true north before they can understand it, for instance. For the linguistic relativist, this linguistic difference implies that the very idea of how the world is—how space is defined—is different for speakers of the Central Australian languages than it is for the Indo-European groups.

Relativist views of this type have been contested. The very fact that we have been able to explain the differences between the two conceptions of direction is *prima facie* evidence against stronger forms of relativism, for it

---

13   This claim has often been associated with Whorf (1956), and is expressed as the view that the understanding of the world implied by possession of a particular language is only accessible to speakers of that language. Linguistic relativism is one of the forms of relativism which has almost universal currency.

shows that the two different conceptions of direction can be grasped simultaneously by one person. Far more plausible is a weaker version of linguistic relativism, in which what we take to exist is relative to the language spoken. The weaker form of relativism accepts the argument that the world is infinitely various and that the objects we discern depend on the way our particular language divides up the world. English and Australian Aboriginal speakers all have conceptions of cardinal directions and of left and right directionality. However, for English speakers one way of putting things is preferred, whereas for Aborigines, cardinal directions are learnt first. Neither is prior. In principle, each group can with training understand the other.

On this view, there is no ultimate way to divide the universe and find out what is real. The objects we identify will depend on the best theory of what we and others think is real, as we talk and make sense of each other. So ghosts are "as real" as electrons, so long as there is some group for whom ghosts *are* real. However, we belong to a scientific community and our best explanation of the world uses electrons, not ghosts. But to attribute existence and reality to numbers, to the content of a legal contract (not just the document) or to concepts such as "love" is to say that those objects are needed to explain our own and others' behavior. Colors will count as existing if our best account, scientific and behavioral, requires them to exist. We will always want to admit that colors appear to exist, and that there is retinal activity, but how we describe colors will depend on our best general theory.

On this theory, television may well have an impact on our ontology. The things we take to exist depend on our general theories of the world. Television programs are important influences on our theories. Many of us only know about Kosovo from the television. "Chads," those elusive punched pieces of ballot papers that played such a peculiar role in the 2000 U.S. election, name objects that had, for must of us, never before had their own name. However, television's role in determining what objects we know of is not in itself a moral danger. Television is part of the way our world functions. It reflects events, at times even determines what happens. But television is merely part of the process whereby we come to our theory of the world.

This mild form of relativism is distasteful to the out-and-out realist.

The realist is in search of the one correct view of the world and of the one correct way to divide the world into objects. For many realists, direct personal experience is the best way to get it right and learn what objects there are. Television, by influencing the most direct forms of perceptions of objects, misleads us. The moral danger of television is that it creates objects which are mediated, which only exist because of television.

Many of the most stringent critics of television are, *au fond*, ardent realists. Plato was the archetypal realist and anti-relativist. For Plato, there is but one reality, even at the conceptual level. Poetic reality is simply a travesty of the real thing. Baudrillard too, in the final analysis, rejects television for its usurping of reality, implicitly assuming that reality is out there, waiting to be reflected more or less faithfully.[14] He is in a many ways a Platonic realist. Baudrillard fears that television's mimicry of reality may mislead, since television can distort our vision of the one true reality. But that assumes that there is a reality out there, an image of which can be distorted.

The difficulty with this version of the realist view is that the world cannot be reduced to one reality, let alone to those things of which we have direct personal experience. Even before television, the ways we discovered about the world were highly theorised and mediated. Television has accelerated the process of change, of course—our world and what we know of it *is* very different from that of our grandparents. But that is for the good. We could not function in our society using the knowledge and conceptual resources of our grandparents. The Internet, and television itself, are part of our reality. Reality is not undermined by television.

This is not to say that all television programs, being real, are therefore acceptable. Being real is not a moral guarantee; it is an ontological claim. It is important not to assimilate the sense in which real conveys approval

---

14   This is the fundamental error according to pragmatic theorists such as Rorty (1991) who reject any possibility of an external point of evaluation. Rorty argues that it is a mistake to think of language as serving to represent any reality at all. For Rorty there is no alternative but to see the world relative to the perspective of one's own culture, language, and ethical beliefs. However, such relativism is, he claims, harmless and inevitable. We cannot escape our own blinkers, but those blinkers are the ones we see through. We should not abstain from judging just because we know our vision is narrow. For Rorty, what is real is what we take to be real.

from the ontological sense. Corruption is real but it is not something of which we approve. Making a distinction between the ontological and the ethical force of real simplifies the debate about television.

Very often, there are good reasons to be concerned about television. Those reasons should be assessed piecemeal, case by case. For instance, television reports sometimes do, and sometimes do not, tell the truth. Untrue reports can mislead and hence can be dangerous. Sometimes programs are realistic, sometimes not. But the failings of television are not ontological failings.

Some reports are realistic, in the sense of telling the truth. Other programs, which are fictional, portray real aspects of the world. A cartoon series like *South Park* may make valid social criticisms, taking politicians to task for real iniquities. A fictional drama such as *Dawson's Creek* may describe the way things are at a West Coast U.S. high school more realistically than a documentary. When critics say that television is not real, they are using "real" as a term of moral evaluation. They suggest that television subverts real life. But that is nonsense. Television is *part* of real life.

Television's moral failings, if they exist, are not because television lays claim to be realistic when it should not. Any form of representation, whether of fiction or of reporting, lays claim to a degree of realism. Television does so too. The mere fact of representation is not likely to undermine social fabric, although, as Plato warned 2000 years ago, certain representations can mislead. Television may have dangers. Whatever those dangers are, they are not ontological.

CONCLUSION

New technologies raise complex philosophical issues, both at the level of content and at the metalevel at which we talk about those new technologies. What counts as "the real thing" is a paradigm example of the problem. The notion of the real thing is part and parcel of the content of television, of the Internet, and of the advertisements they contain. The Coke ads exploited the notion of the real things to its own end. Philosophical issues are the playthings of business, of television across all the newer technologies. Yet we rarely draw on the philosophical traditions in debate about television and new technology. By using the media for training in philosophical skills, we can draw on philosophical traditions while at the same time engaging children directly in the process of thinking rationally about their world.

We cannot simply assume the answer to the question "What is real?" and then demand of television that it be more realistic or that it be less transparently realistic. Reality is not to be captured by any set of rules or simple guidelines. When we call an object real, we are giving it a role within a particular framework; we are signaling approval. The framework that television supplies is interwoven with other nontelevisual frameworks. Television is part of our everyday reality, not separate from it. We react to television, talk about television, and use what we see and hear in multiple ways. Television does not have to prove that it is real.

Television and what we see on television are real. But that does not mean that we have resolved all there is to know about the concept of what it is to be real. That is a far larger task. The advertising history of Coke, "the Real Thing," provides a cautionary tale. The slogan has lasted nearly 30 years. As an example from a 1970s campaign in Mexico shows, however, reality is a two-edged sword.

> Coke had conducted extensive marketing studies in Mexico as it was intro-
> ducing the company's world-wide slogan "It's the real thing," which had
> worked wonders throughout the world, advertising industry sources recall.
> In line with Coca-Cola's international advertising campaign, it had trans-
> lated the slogan in Mexico almost literally to "Esta es la verdad" or "This is
> the truth." But it didn't work. Several focus groups assembled in Mexico
> City reacted coldly to it.
>
> "We found that the word *truth* had a negative connotation in Mexico," I was
> told by Jorge Matte Langlois, the Chilean-born psychologist, sociologist and
> theologian who had...conducted the focus groups for Coca-Cola years ear-
> lier. "People's reaction was, if it's the truth, it must be bad."
>
> Coca-Cola's Mexico division soon changed its slogan to "La chispa de la
> vida"—"The spark of life." (Oppenheimer, 1996: 269–270)

The morally positive overtones of "the real thing" did not translate to the Mexico of the 1960s. A relativist could suggest that the entire Mexican culture had a notion of reality different from that of the United States, where the slogan originated. What counts as appropriate and desirable changes with the cultural norms and over time. What is real also changes.

In 1996, McCann-Erikson[15] again proposed a Coke campaign for Mexico, based on the notion of reality. This time the campaign ideas concentrated on authenticity for the younger generation. For instance, a young girl goes on her first date and is disappointed by her unprepossessing escort. Nevertheless, she boasts of the evening she had dreamt of. Then along comes her escort, tidied up. He offers her a Coke and invites her out again. Reality can come up to scratch, it seems, if Coke is there to help. The logo now reads: "Real things are for ever. Always Coke."[16]

These Coke ads were designed to play on the fear that dreams, like television and advertising, could alter reality. The ad works precisely because we can see the absurdity of the claim, yet we are at the same time nervous about the effects of advertising. In the same way, television and virtual reality make us ontologically uneasy. However, that uneasiness is misplaced. There may be much else to fear of the newer media, of course. Television, and to an even greater extent the Internet, may mislead. But the failings of television are not ontological.

---

[15] I am grateful to Felix Stravens for alerting me to this campaign proposal.

[16] "Las cosas reales son para siempre. Siempre Coca-Cola."

# 2

N E W S   A S   S O A P   O P E R A

Truth and News

We begin with a Washington story that resounded around the world as Washington stories tend to but with a peculiar flavor. It is the tale of the State of the Union address vs O.J. The State of the Union was to begin at 9 p.m. in Washington on Tuesday February 4, 1997. It had already been moved once to avoid conflicting with the finals of Miss America. It was a tense moment for the networks when they discovered, on Tuesday afternoon, that the State of the Union was now scheduled at exactly the same time as the 6 p.m. Los Angeles announcement of the verdict of the O.J. Simpson case, the notorious case of a sports and media hero accused of murdering his wife.

Martin Walker, the *Guardian* correspondent in Washington, claims that the White House press office called in the news chiefs and said:

> Of course we don't and won't tell you what to do. But the President is fulfilling his constitutional obligation to tell the people of the State of the Union.[1]

As it was, the networks hedged their bets. NBC ran the State of the Union. Their corresponding cable company, CNBC, covered O.J. CNN Headline news had O.J., CNN itself stuck with the President. ABC and CBC took the subtitle route—the O.J. verdict was run on a title line all through the last 10 minutes of Clinton's declamation.

---

[1]  Walker was talking at the Brookings Institute in Washington to Harkness scholars, 7 February 1997.

In 1998 and 1999, the State of the Union was again overshadowed;
this time by the even less salubrious events of the Monica Lewinsky case.[2]
In 1999 it was the curiously modern event of the Internet release of the
documents put forward as evidence in the case to impeach the President.
Materials had been released which had the potential of unprecedented
public importance, yet had an unprecedentedly private flavor. By 2000, in
fact, the State of the Union had become a sideshow: the last quack of the
so-called "lame duck presidency." The good economic news and worthy
programs announced by Clinton were rarely mentioned in the press coverage; the focus was on the forthcoming presidential election.

The issue here is not that the media is failing to tell the truth. For the
reports on Monica, O.J. and the State of the Nation are *true*. Few claims
made on the television news are made without evidence. What O.J.'s
judge, Monica, and Starr said are accurately reported, with all the objectivity which has become the hallmark of contemporary journalism. Yet the
feel is at best insalubrious; the overall impression is of news that is not
true.

There is an increasing tendency for news to adopt the generic conventions of the soap opera.[3] Soap opera's repertoire of plots, from romance to
violence, are domestic in focus and designed so that the story goes on for
ever. The characters are also from a limited repertoire, with good looks
and sporting prowess pitted against evil and the terrors of female sexual
aggression. O.J. fits the mold, whereas the State of the Union, dealing
with the large public issues of the economy, education, and health does
not. And competition it is—as the commentators the next day made clear.
Networks and cable channels are out for consumers' blood. Television sells
consumers to advertisers, not news to citizens, and consumers prefer O.J.[4]
In the event, there was a twist to the final score. For an unprecedented

---

2   Carlos Fuentes (1998) actually called the Monica Lewinsky case "a global telenovela."

3   John Ellis's *Visible Fictions* (1982) is a notable precursor to the argument I propound
here, but with a different focus. Catherine Lumby's *Gotcha* (1999) contains an excellent recent exposition similar to the views about news I develop here.

4   Ralph Begleiter of CNN claimed at a Media Studies Forum, New York (20 February
1997) that CNN 's ratings quintupled as a result of their choice to run the first O.J.
trial. The public taste for the trial proved utterly insatiable.

number of viewers saw the State of the Union simply because they were already tuned in, waiting for the O.J. result. Happily, the result was delayed, and the President was nearly finished when he lost the limelight.

This chapter begins with the views expressed by strident media critics condemning the degeneration of the news. In the United States, the change from the television news style of the fifties to the "tabloid television" of today is an example of the historical process of stereotyping the news. We then turn to the notions of truth and objectivity that are at the heart of news coverage.

## "ILLITERATE BOOBS SITTING DUMBLY AROUND THE TV SET"

The most common reaction to the perceived degradation of the news is outrage. William Shirer, in the final volume of his autobiography, charts the decline of news in caustic terms:

> For news I have to turn to my local paper, and since I live in the north east, to the *New York Times*...I gather there is not much general reading, at least of books, in our country anymore. Gazing at the tube has replaced it as it has replaced social conversation. Are the consequences not predictable: a country of illiterate boobs sitting dumbly around the TV set, like ancient cavemen around a fire, unable to communicate or articulate, stupefied by inanities? (Shirer, 1990: 288)

Klite *et al.* talk derisively of tabloid journalism, applying the phrase to televised news:

> the empty calories of tabloid journalism [which] have become the standard fare on newscasts...the very idea of news has been perverted into a steady diet of titillating, terrifying, and manipulative entertainment (Klite, 1997: 102)

They go on

> A constellation of excess—mayhem, fluff, filler, ads, and racial and gender stereotyping—characterises local TV newscasts across the United States. (Klite *et al.*, 1997: 108)

In a sense both Shirer and Klite underrate the danger, for it is not just the US—"our country"—that is under threat, but the global viewing public. The global news presentation style is heavily influenced by that of the United States; global news content throughout the world is dominated by

U.S. stories. Both in format and content, the soap opera style of the news
has spread throughout the world. In some senses the consequences are
worse outside the United States. Australian students, for instance, with a
diet of *LA Law* and O.J., are confused to find that the Australian legal system is not like that of the United States. The information about the world
distributed by global television is skewed in ways that young Australians
have not learned to recognize.

At another level, the pessimism of critics is unwarranted. Critics of the
media of all flavors assume that viewers simply absorb uncritically—to use
Shirer's words, viewers are "illiterate boobs sitting dumbly around the TV
set, like ancient cavemen around a fire." In conceptualizing viewers as passive receivers, uncritically soaking up what is thrown at them, he fails to
recognize that the audience actively interprets television. Critics of television rarely do the hard philosophical and historical legwork necessary to
explain just why the tabloid news story is likely to undermine the character of a nation. Between the viewing of television and any claim that viewing television hurts a nation lies an intermediate step. Just what sense are
viewers making of what they see? Should we be worried at the sense viewers are making of the world as they watch television?

Sartori (1998) makes explicit one fundamental reason for concern: the
connection between people's ability to interpret the news and their democratic participation in a society. If all we get for news is O.J. and Monica,
how are we, the voters, in a position to make informed judgments? Sartori's account is a well-argued and compelling critique of the manner in
which news in the televisual world of today is denatured and loses its effectiveness as a tool for citizens. All too often, however, critics fail to identify the complexities of the connection between the role of television and
the decay in the social fabric. There are too many intervening factors—social change, globalization, and the broadening of the political base of
democratic societies—to make facile assumptions.

Equally fundamental is the connection between the news and morality.
Frequently, presenters of news programs adopt the role of moral arbiter.
In one Australian "exposé" in 1994, for instance, the Australian *Sixty Minutes* program went to an auction of "antique" furniture and "revealed" to
the allegedly gullible bidders that the furniture was reproduction work im-

ported from Indonesia.[5] The intrusive interviewing style of the *Sixty Min-utes* team was emphasized in the production, with vivid images of the auc-tioneers pushing the camera away. One bidder even thanked the team for revealing the fraud. Yet the presenter's assumption of the moral high ground failed to bring out many aspects of the issue, especially the fact that there is very little true antique furniture in Australia and that bidders were almost certainly in the market for reproduction furniture. The fundamental objection is not that the furniture was reproduction. It was, rather, that the furniture was not European but Asian. Yet Indonesian-made reproduc-tions are of at least the quality of European versions; Indonesia has ex-tremely fine timber and craftsmen, many of whom earn little. The implicit racism of the "revelations" of the *Sixty Minutes* team was accompanied by the characteristic self-righteousness of the investigators. Those who report the news self-consciously take on the role of the high priests of the televi-sion generation.

The high priests range from the serious news anchor to the morning talk-back radio host. The network news programs, the BBC World News and CNN International give their consumers news that has been checked, that has good vision, and that comes in short segments. The *Time Magazine* formula is used for presenting difficult items: journalists take one point of view and then the opposing view, finishing with a synthesis. The assump-tion is that there can only be two views and that each can be summarized in a sound bite. Thus presented, each item of the news may be true, but the overall impression is misleading. The consequences of the sound bite view of the world have been criticized forcefully by Chomsky and Herman (1994).

But if CNN and the BBC World Service deserve criticism, how much more do sensationalist news programs, often put together under the label of "tabloid TV"? Tabloid news also pretends to balance, just as network news does, using devices such as interviews with those of opposing views. But the story is more likely to be a financial or sexual scandal than a event of greater import. At the same time as news has become more tabloid in style and oversimplified, cynicism has become widespread. Readers and viewers have grown suspicious of the elegantly edited report from a war

---

5    I am grateful to Joelle van der Mensbrugghe for bringing this episode to my attention.

zone; they suspect the too-fluent speaker. In a sense the news has undermined its own credibility in its apparently overwhelmingly realistic presentations.

Reality television, in which real criminals are apprehended, plays on the disquiet of the viewer about misleading television. Reality television purposely eschews the elegant presentation style of the evening news. It trumpets its own reality through its lack of polish. By being literally on the spot, unedited, reality television claims truth and moral superiority. The same holds of the new wave of reality movies. When the plot of the movie is that a video made by youth is found after their disappearance, as in *The Blair Witch Project*, the wobbling camera movements of the handheld video camera are to be expected. It is the lack of professionalism that suggests that the story is true.

Tabloid television and morning talk-back programs exploit the preference for the spontaneous and unprofessional presentation. Tabloid news uses the conventions of serious anchors to develop a form of news which is very close to gossip. There is no pretence of objectivity and very little of the elegant editing found in high-budget news. The morning programs give an added sense of reality by inserting "real" participants who are far from fluent.

One response to the flood of tabloid-style news is to call for a change in the ways television presents news, by regulation. The sterner critics advocate public pressure to alter what can be seen on television and to censor what can be accessed on the Internet. There are lobbies to reduce violence on television, and others to promote religion in the hope that by altering what is seen on television and reached on the Internet, society might improve. This is a vain hope. In the global world of the media, anything legally prevented from entering the home by broadcast or cable will come through the phone lines and modem. Regulation has been playing a hopeless game of tag with the media since the beginning and, with the massive financial clout of the media now, it is unlikely ever to catch up.

The alternative strategy to regulating the media is understanding how and why it has changed. Is it really all for the worse? What do we mean by the notions of truth and objectivity and why do we value them? Do we really want to return to the days of being told what is true by a middle-aged white man in a suit? Are we really "illiterate boobs sitting dumbly around the TV set," or we are viewers who make sense of television in a complex social structure where we evaluate what is true in many ways? Television news may mislead us in dangerous ways. If there are reasons for concern in the way that television presents the news, we should identify those reasons precisely.

## THE DEVELOPMENT OF TABLOID TV NEWS :
### THE CASE OF THE UNITED STATES

Tabloid TV news is now a global phenomenon. It began in the United States, and its history there serves to illuminate the process that led from the old-fashioned news report to "infotainment." In the early days of commercial television, brief newscasts were scattered among quiz shows, situation comedies, and soaps. However, by the early 1960s, networks were attempting to produce a broadsheet journalistic style. Hallin (1994: 97) significantly comments that the news gave the networks "a claim to be something more than a high-tech way of selling detergent." News and entertainment divisions became entirely separate. Indeed, the networks made the news the flagships of their channels, giving them pride of place as "responsible television"—television that performed a vital social role. Unlike the entertainment programs, newsrooms were not held to ratings. Newsrooms at NBC were never even told their ratings until the mid-1980s.[6] The news borrowed its generic style from the print media, with broadsheet print-based values providing the stylistic structure of television news. In particular, the print-based discursive analytic style was taken over in the highly formalized tones of anchors. In this way the values of the print media dominated the model of the television news.

News and soap opera are traditionally seen as disjoint sets, utterly distinct in their focus and methodology. News, on the one hand, is information about real public events. Soaps, on the other, are entertainment about imagined private events. The newsroom is engaged in finding out what has happened that day—and verifying stories. The soap production team is

---

6    According to Carl Stern, professor of journalism at the School of Media and Public Affairs at George Washington University and former law correspondent for NBC news, in a meeting at George Washington University (4 March 1997) and in subsequent telephone conversations (17 April 1997).

creating myths that are purportedly timeless. The move to the hybrid genre of "infotainment" offends practitioners and viewers precisely because they conceive that there is, or should be, a gulf between the two types. Morning programs, even in the early days, displayed a tendency to emphasize personalities and images over content. This was regarded as a failing and was firmly resisted by the evening network news, which maintained its broadsheet tones.

By the end of the 1960s, however, the divide between news and entertainment was under pressure. *Sixty Minutes,* which premiered on CBS in 1968, showed that news and current affairs could do well on the ratings. Once it became clear the kind of role of news and current affairs played in determining what channel was watched for an entire evening, the evening news shows began competing for audiences. The growth of cable and regional networks accelerated the process until in the late 1980s there were four commercial networks and more than 100 regional and cable networks.

The major change came with Murdoch's introduction of a new style of news reporting on the Fox network: tabloid television.[7] He introduced *A Current Affair,* which was followed by *Inside Edition* in 1988 and *Hard Copy* in 1989. Their style was quite distinct from the conservative authoritative voice of traditional news shows. While they still used the settings of a news show such as a desk, reporters, and interviews, the solemnity of the news reader had gone. No topic was taboo, however personal or sexual. The anchors became flirtatious, engaged personally with their interviewees and the audience. Finally with *America's Most Wanted* and *Cops*—the first reality show, using real police chasing real suspects—the blurring of fact and fiction, soap, and news had set in.

The traditional news stories defined a sphere of appropriate comment. Their role was to inform the populace about events of public concern, such as the economy and the weather. The tabloid news shows have no such constraints. They emphasize personal stories and demand personal identification of the viewer with the characters in the story. The viewer is no longer positioned as the impassive and judgmental observer but as a family member, intimately involved in the issues and able to identify with the

---

7    Lumby (1999, chapter 2) gives a racy introduction to the tale on which I have drawn here.

plight—or good fortune—of all those portrayed. The stories are highly personalized and emphasize subjective reactions. Close-ups of interviewees addressed by their first names show their emotional reactions. Viewers are located so that they can identify with the anchor, in whatever moral pose chosen. In special reports, reporters, while using traditional models of voiceovers, make highly subjective comments.

It would be simplistic to accuse the tabloid news alone of possessing such characteristics. Traditional news presentations increasingly use many of the techniques and formats of soap opera and share the tendency to personalize and simplify issues. The lead-in gives the range of the news, to tie in viewers. The anchors use teasers to guarantee that the audience will stay on for the commercial break, as in "After this break…." Reporters are placed "on the scene" and report their reactions; even in the most "objective" of reports, voice-overs give the impression of "really being there."

The increasingly soapy style of news is a global phenomenon. There *are* cultural variations in the television product and the large corporations, for instance in India, have learned at a price that a diet of straight U.S. product is not what everyone wants. Regional patterns of television news and soap opera are not so much either global or national as communal. For instance, the Chinese diaspora across Southeast and East Asia creates a global Chinese culture with components produced in Taiwan, Hong Kong, Singapore, and the Mainland that are also viewed in Thailand, Malaysia, and Indonesia (cf, e.g., Sinclair *et al.*, 1995). Even so, there is still a recognizable continuity between news formats and between the soap genre and news.

An interesting recent version of the development of soap operas and news in Eastern Europe is reported by Eugene Secunda of the United States based Central European Media Enterprises Group. This group set out to buy private channels in the emerging markets of the Czech Republic and Slovakia. Secunda explained the strategy as "start a local soap and get in the audience, then bring the newsroom staff to New York and give them a crash course in exciting news at NY1" (a flagship New York news program).[8]

---

8   Eugene Secunda, Central European Media Enterprises Group (NYU, 26 February 1997) went on to explain that the CME group stations have an astonishingly high viewership—80% ratings in several markets.

The link between soaps and NY1-style news bulletins is not a coincidence. There is a seamless web of television content that merges soaps, commercials, and news into a nightly diet based on the U.S. model. It is a diet with a great deal of verve and excitement; high, or at least costly, production values; and an immensely subtle approach by the advertisers. It has produced a televisually literate generation, whose skills include the ability to deconstruct the medium itself. As the media guru Rushkoff puts it:

> Most kids are doing media deconstruction while watching television....Their favorite shows come "pre-deconstructed" that is with built in distancing devices...such shows earn the ultimate youthful phrase "cool." By cool, I mean seeing things from a distance. (Gabriel, 1996)

Rushkoff goes on to talk of the sort of deconstruction that children seek in watching television:

> What screenagers seek from television, multi media and other entertainment is the "aha" experience of making connections across their storehouse of media images. (Gabriel, 1996)

The sophistication of the audience has been part of the complex situation in which news and soap opera interpenetrate. News is deconstructed by children, but it is also interpreted through the understandings of the media they have gained through soap opera. A form of highly sophisticated intertextuality has served to superimpose genres across the converging technologies, so that the soap format has bled into the news.

At one level then, the news became soapy because of the assimilation of two formerly distinct genres under pressure from the style of that new medium—television. The explanation of the rise of infotainment at another level is economic. In the mid–1980s the heads of newsrooms in the networks, most of whom had been reporters, were replaced by managers. The change came in the wake of a recognition by the networks that news could rate, and hence make—instead of lose—money. At the same time, network ownership moved from family hands into those of corporations, who insisted on profits. When Turner's CNN showed massive profits, in part because they used nonunion labor, the networks followed. NBC cut their 105 correspondents worldwide to 33 and at the same time stopped hiring union labor. The structure of the news was popularized and streamlined, so that news slots were determined well in advance of the stories coming in. By the late 1980s, not a single producer in the NBC newsroom came from a background in journalism; all were managers. News was seen purely as a profit center. [9]

The economic story is a major factor in the changing of attitudes to news. News is no longer a product of a culture trained in determining and presenting the truth, but of a culture aimed at producing high ratings. The impression of the network having privileged access and the ability to make firsthand "objective" comment is a manufactured one. A striking example concerns a report about gun control in Britain on ABC, NBC, and CBS on 16 October 1996.[10] Although all three networks have offices in London, they not only used the footage supplied by the British reports but also ran the footage in the same order with virtually identical commentary and reflecting the British edit, although with their own voiceovers.[11] The networks implicitly lay claim to a personal journalistic view that was in fact plagiarized.

Katz (1997) argues that new technology will remedy the problem. Cable, and now the Internet, he argues, have so altered viewing habits that consumption of network television news will soon be only a minor factor in how the world is perceived. Thirty years ago, most people in the United States—over 60%—watched the networks. A major report could be seen by huge numbers and have a major political impact. That is no longer so in the United States, for the television audience has fragmented, with cable networks and the Internet coming into direct competition. This means that the networks share less than 50% of the audience. Nielsen's ratings showed that viewers of television were down by 1 million in February 1997,[12] a "precipitous drop." Others contest these results at least as they

---

[9]   Carl Stern claimed that until the mid-1980s news at NBC was losing money, yet the newsroom never even saw the ratings (17 April 1997).

[10]  Given by Bill McLaughlin, Media Studies Center seminar (20 February 1997).

[11]  The global correlate of this process of reusing footage and the accompanying voiceovers has been traced by Peter Putnis in Australia—often the very same comments survive transpositions from U.S., British, Australian, and even Singaporean commentaries.

[12]  Carter (1997), D1.

apply to news. Surveys in the late 1990s by the Newseum Roper Centre[13] suggest that more than half—54%—of Americans report that they watch the local news every day, that local TV anchors were seen as reliable, and that the news is trusted.

Neverthless, it is apparent that the Internet has invaded the domain of the television news. Katz claims[14] that the young no longer acquire their news from the network evening news or the newspapers. Rather, they download from wire agencies, surf the radio, and pick and choose. Katz claims that the Internet offers tailored news and the user group sites that have reclaimed interactivity for the media. Many are scornful of the abusive and often unscholarly dialect of the Internet. Others defend it. Katz points out that the press, in the times of Thomas Paine, was originally partisan, abusive and highly interactive. Katz is broadly optimistic about the prospects of a highly literate and informed readership emerging from the Internet. His view is that Shirer's "illiterate boobs" will become a highly argumentative public as they learn the highways of cyberspace.

Others are more skeptical, for the Internet is already turning into as much a global information tip as a resource. Lacking the gatekeepers and traditions of journalism, the Internet is even less reliable than the media. Moreoever, as a supplier of news, the Internet is not yet truly revolutionary. It simply cobbles together news sources and interest groups in a novel fashion. The pattern of Internet use is likely to reflect the model of information found in more familiar media, at least in the short term.

We should be wary of technological utopianism. When satellites beam 500 channels into the house and Internet news groups proliferate, there may, it is true, be a niche for specialized news, but that is little consolation to those concerned about the news as it is now viewed.

### NEWS EVENTS ARE AND ALWAYS HAVE BEEN SOAPY

Much news just *is* soapy. News and soap opera do have common ground. News stories tend to continue as soap operas do. News reports

---

[13]   Reported in the Freedom Forum seminar, "If It Leads, It Bleeds" (New York, 1 May 1997).

[14]   At a seminar, Centre for Communication Inc. (19 November 1996). See also his (1997) for the argument in full.

have a fairly constant cast of celebrities and politicians, who reappear from time to time, and these characters edge each subplot along, just as in a soap opera. However, the similarities between the genres of news and soap opera cut even deeper than the fact that both news and soap opera are narratives without a *dénouement*. Both news and soap opera provide a template for understanding the society in which we move. Both do so primarily in narrative format. News thus often fits the soap mold and stereotypes with its generic beautiful heroines; its wealthy, sporty heroes; and its ill-fated romance—seen not only in O.J. but also Princess Diana, J.F.K., Jr., and a raft of others.

This should not be surprising: news with elements of romantic fiction has always been popular. Homeric tales were also news reports; sagas of the French Revolution were no doubt consumed in England with the gusto that the French now show for stories about British royals. Over fifty years ago, when King Edward VIII abdicated the British throne for "the woman I love," the whole world hung on the details of the story. An informant from the 70–75-year-old cohort of Australians, talking of the media memories of her youth put it thus:

> Georgie: Oh yeah, and then of course, after that, we had all the crisis of the abdication of the Prince of Wales, and don't you remember that speech on the radio, I don't know how we heard, how we came to hear that, and he ends up. "I'm prepared to give everything up for the woman I love," and I thought, "Ahhh." *(laughter)* (Cohort 1, November 1998, Adelaide, Australia)

This, of course, is soap opera with a vengeance. What has changed, with the new methods for delivery of news, is the rapidity with which news is broadcast and the way television can saturate a story with visual effects. In consequence, both the expectations of viewers and the content of news have come to concentrate increasingly on the soapy end of the spectrum. It is no longer the case that the soap operatic elements of news attract attention; news has to be soap opera in format to be seen as newsworthy.

The life of the Princess of Wales was already planned as a serial, well before her dramatic death. Death is, of course, unwelcome in a soap and does not fit the generic pattern. Perhaps this is why, just a year after her death caused an international outpouring of grief, the event was simply put aside. It is a harsh judgment on those who produce and consume news that events whose importance was so immensely exaggerated are so quickly forgotten. Possibly some element of self-dramatization was involved in the car chase—that the driver was seeing himself as a hero. The accident, indeed, might be causally connected to the very genre of soap opera itself. The death destroyed the possibility of a long-running serial; death ended the soap opera tale of the Princess too early.

Within hours of the death of young John Kennedy, critics were complaining of the media hype—critics who were themselves writing within the media. So, for instance, we find Cal Thomas declaring that "J.F.K., Jr.'s death marked the end of broadcast journalism":

> A once-proud profession has become all tabloid, all the time. A profession once respected in the past, which once informed, now titillates. The most outrageous untruths and inaccuracies are tolerated, even promoted, so long as they ratify the favored myth. (Thomas, 1999)

The life of John F. Kennedy as President had been cast in the mythic terms of Camelot well before his death. John and his wife Caroline had also been cast in fairy-tale mode before their death: the rich, young, diffident but brave and risk-taking hero and his beautiful, intelligent wife. It is in this context that we must see the inflated reaction to their death. That the death of a famous but scarcely globally important young man and his wife engulfed the world in morbid speculation and grief *is* disproportionate, but it can be traced in part to the continuing fairy story. The importance of such figures as news is surely not as much of a moral problem as Thomas suggests. After all, it was the romantic fairy story behind the abdication in 1936 of Edward VIII that made it newsworthy (if not actually news in the United Kingdom and the Empire until after it occurred, for reasons of *lèse-majesté*). If there is a moral issue here it is that the image of himself as heroic may have influenced the decisions made by J.F.K., Jr., when flying his plane, and hence marred his judgment. But even were this true, it could not be sheeted home direct to the media. From Icarus on, there are precedents of those who destroy themselves to maintain an inflated image.

For many of those who reacted to J.F.K., Jr.'s death, there was a mythic pattern in the story. Their first media memory may have been the assassination of J.F.K. and his young son saluting the flag-draped casket at the state funeral. With the son's accidental death, the story of J.F.K., Jr. finally played out in reality the full pattern of a tragic soap opera. Just as if in a movie, or a long-running soap, the story came full circle. There is nothing wrong with interpreting a life as a dramatic story, of making sense of events in soap-opera terms. The moral issues are pressing only when the soap opera or mythic structures are left unexamined and come to distort the processes of justice and participation in society.

A good example of the dangers of the interweaving of soap opera and news comes from Mexico. The world of the Mexican *telenovela* is, if different from the daytime soap, very similar in generic format. The rich young male hero and the poor young beauty are generally united after a series of often violent tests. On 7 June 1999, the bloody assassination of a popular Mexico City television talk show host, Francisco (Paco) Stanley, brought all these elements into play. He was shot thirty times as he emerged, on the busy peripheral road of Mexico City, from a popular restaurant, *El Charco de Los Ranas* (charmingly named the "Frog Pond") and got into his car with his entourage. The event was replayed all afternoon in the shops, and there was a sudden slowing of the normally frantic traffic of the city. People in drugstores were in tears. A personality they all knew had been brutally murdered.

After a period of initial shock, the whole city blamed the security forces for what was taken to be a political killing, since Stanley had been involved in a TV Azteca antidrug campaign. Then information slowly leaked out. Stanley was carrying cocaine on him. Was this a drug death for a debt? Next, Stanley's offsider on the talk show, Mario Bezares, who had providentially been in the bathroom when Stanley was shot, was taken into custody with his pretty young wife, Brenda. They were held in a form of house arrest in a cheap downtown hotel, "generally used for assignations," and the plot thickened. Brenda had worked for Stanley, who was fair-haired and blue-eyed, and had a fair-haired child, though both she and her husband were dark. Bezares was also the butt of many of Stanley's jokes on the talk show. He, too, had connections to the drug trade. Just as the limit of time for house arrest expired, a bald and tattooed giant was arrested as the leader of the gangsters, and another television personality was accused of orchestrating the crime with Bezares.

The story remained frontpage news in Mexico for the next 18 months. The flagship broadsheet newpaper *Reforma* developed a special logo for events associated with the case. The story unfolded at roughly soap opera pace, with a major incident or accusation each month, and a series of sub-plots interweaving over the period. For instance, through the year 2000 corruption claims about leading political figures formed a *leitmotiv* to the story. Zamarippa (2000) reported that in the process of attempting to establish guilt for the Stanley murder, TV Azteca had been implicated in a series of coverups. The first magistrate for the case, Del Villar, suggested that TV Azteca was set up as a money-laundering operation for the notoriously corrupt brother of a former president, Salinas. In the runup to a major election campaign, the attribution of guilt became blatantly political.

With the election of Vicente Fox in Mexico roughly a year after the murder and his inauguration in December 2000, the investigating magistrate was replaced. Finally, on 25 January 2001, Bezares and others accused in the case were released on the grounds that the evidence against them was not conclusive. TV Azteca spent the entire day televising the events at the prison with tearful close-up scenes of the reunion of Bezares with his wife and fair son. Bezares immediately returned as a talk show host to TV Azteca (de León, 2001a, 2001b; *Reforma*, 2001). In the meantime, the legal process is being appealed. Each player in the drama and each political party continue to make accusations of corruption (Guerrero, 2001). Bezares' popularity rating on TV Azteca is higher than ever. Soap opera with a vengeance.

In a society with drug smuggling, violence, and little security, life may well resemble a gangster movie. Indeed, gangster movies as a genre are based on events such as this. There is no philosophical problem in the story, we might say, although there is obviously a moral problem. But this is not all. The Mexico City papers and television news reports followed the story, as the U.S. papers did the death of J.F.K., Jr., with very little regard for the processes of establishing truth or for independent investigation or fresh judgment. Each story repeated the ever-more salacious details of the domestic lives of the personalities. The front-page coverage and evening news bulletins became more and more tabloid and personalized: interviews with Bezares' mother, emotional tear-filled scenes with his wife, photographs of Bezares' fair-haired great uncle, and then of Bezares hugging his son. The quality or pretense of objective reporting was utterly lost. In the interplay of gossip, there is almost too much irony in the Mexico City news show advertising itself for "La Fuerza de la Verdad," the strength of truth.

When a nation becomes emotional after the death of J.F.K., Jr., conservative news critics may shudder, but in no real sense is justice perverted. In the Stanley murder case it is difficult to see any possibility of justice emerging from the newspaper blitz. The lack of justice is not new—there have been unfair lynchings and horrifying murders for centuries. What is questionable is the responsibility of the press and the apparent inability not merely of the press but also of those who read or view the news events on television to react critically to the events that occur. The press and the readers, it would seem, are so taken with the narrative pattern of a generic style that they appear to forget the need for a critical process of debate and searching for facts.

## WHAT IS WRONG?

The increasing juxtaposition of the fictional soap opera format and the news bulletin has serious consequences. It is not a trivial matter if the viewer of the evening news bulletin is geared to expect soap opera themes. Soaps, intended though they may be to help us understand the world, are not intended to be about the "public" world of the news, nor are they intended to be true. As the evening news assimilates the conventions of soap opera, we are no longer asked to judge what is the appropriate behavior for a president or a secretary of state in the public domain. Instead we hear of their private lives. However, viewers of television and those who surf the Net are not just consumers of private tidbits; they are also citizens, voters, and members of a society. They are called to choose the leaders of the state and need reliable information about matters of public concern in order to do so.

The solution is not to return to all the traditional broadsheet values. The style of the old-fashioned news was far from perfect. Buckingham (2000a, 2000b) discusses his studies of children in the United States and Britain and argues that the traditional news shows are often perceived as boring and condescending by kids. The forms of language used in broadsheet press and in traditional television news draw on what Bernstein (1977) calls "the elaborated code": the language of the formal, adult, public domain, using complex syntactic structures, impersonal forms, and distancing devices to imply objectivity. Yet, as Bernstein and others have pointed out, those devices are superficial features of the code, which are neither necessary nor sufficient for either truth or lack of bias. It is quite possible to mislead using the most elaborate of codes.

It is not only children who are alienated by the language of the formal traditional newsroom. The public modes of talk of the traditional news were, and still are, gendered and ethnically marked in tone. Kress (1986) discusses the print media and the details of the contrast between the public objective tone of the broadsheet and the personalized tone of the tabloid press report of the same story, concerning a court decision on the actions of the Builder's Labourer's Federation, an Australian union. He draws attention to implicit class categorizations in the manner of constructing the audience by broadsheet and tabloid press. The public domain of government and the law is reserved for those who are educated while less educated groups are restricted to a more personal private space. For instance, the quality press headline reads "Full Bench announces decision on BLF today," and goes on to describe the case using the passive and impersonal forms of verbs and abbreviations to exclude readers whose language is not elaborated and who are unfamiliar with the conventions of the court. The tabloid reads: "Too busy for court, says Norm." It concentrates on personalities, quoting the leader of the BLF and structuring the story around his direct—in both senses—speech. Kress's point is that the conventions of the broadsheet privilege middle-class attitudes.

The first and simplest reaction to the issue of what should count as news is to say that news should deal with the *public* domain, not with the *private* domain. There is much to recommend this way of making the distinction, and I will revert to it in the final chapter.[15] However, Kress's example points up a difficulty. We are accustomed to identify the public domain with the particular style of presentation of the traditional broadsheet press and of the serious newsreader. The syntactic ploys of the

15  There are many excellent discussions of the notion of the public and private in the press and the ways in which the recent tabloidization of news has led to a collapse of once strict divisions between what is public and what private. I refer to chapter 7, in which the public/ private divide is the focus. However, I should note the seminal work of Meyrowitz (1985) where the public/private divide is applied to reception of news, and for an Australian perspective, Lumby (1997, 1999).

broadsheet press and the serious newsreader, such as the use of the passive voice and the assumption of objectivity, are neither necessary nor sufficient to delimit what we mean by the appropriate domain of public news. We need to distinguish news from soap while still incorporating voices and argument styles and the language of a range of classes into the public voice. Yet we cannot dismiss the concerns of those who have criticized the tabloidization of news too quickly. While many critics of the media have explicitly called for a return to the broadsheet style, and most have implicitly assumed it to be desirable, their concerns often go beyond a distaste for the modern linguistic style of news.

The most prescient of the commentators on this aspect of the media was Habermas. In *The Structural Transformation of the Public Sphere*, written in 1962, he said:

> In comparison with printed communication the programs sent by the new media curtail the reactions of the recipients in a peculiar way. They draw the eyes and the ears of the public under their spell but at the same time, by taking away its distance, place it under "tutelage," which is to say they deprive it of the opportunity to say something and to disagree. The critical discussion of a reading public tends to give way to "exchanges about tastes and preferences" between consumers. (Habermas, 1989: 171-172)

Here Habermas is criticizing a feature of the media common to the more pompous forms of traditional television news broadcasts and the worst of tabloid TV. Habermas argues that the fault of the new media is that it places the audience under tutelage. That was certainly the style of the network news broadcasts. Characteristically the news bulletins of the 1960s and the 1970s were delivered by middle-aged, middle-class men, who became the voices of authority of the nation. That was true of the U.S. networks, of the BBC news in Britain, of the ABC in Australia, and indeed, of the dominant Mexican channel, Televisa, whose newsreader, Jacobo Zabludovsky, was known as the friend of presidents. Zabludovsky was notorious for never criticizing a president or government official, for allowing government figures news time to argue their case, and for leading the government election campaigns (Fernández & Paxman, 2000). Zabludovsky, like the moral arbiters of *Sixty Minutes* criticized earlier, told the audience what to think. It is this tutelage which, according to Habermas, is the danger of the new media. He claims that viewers of the media should be encouraged to "say something and disagree" rather than make "exchanges about tastes and preferences." In effect, he is calling for a critical audience.

Deborah Tannen in *The Argument Culture* (1998), labeled on the cover "The book that will transform our notions of truth and debate," disagrees. For Tannen, the weakness of the modern media culture is not the lack but the excess of critical thought. She argues that it is a consequence of the highly gendered "aggression culture" of news reporters that the news is always presented as a fight between views. She is certainly correct to identify as fallacious the style of presenting news in terms of a choice between two opposed alternatives. It simply does not follow that, because we are shown two alternatives, we are closer to the truth than if we knew only one. Two alternatives, even opposed alternatives, can be as far wrong as one. However, she sets herself against what she sees as the "male" style of critical debate as a method for evaluating news. Again, she is right to suggest that aggressive disagreement can be counterproductive. However, as she admits, there are cooperative ways of challenging views, debating, and being "critical." Being critical tends to receive a bad press, to be associated with nitpicking nastiness, aggression, and lack of creativity. It should not be for being critical can be creative and generous. *Pace* Tannen, it is not the critical tone of the news that is at fault in modern news culture. It is the audience's lack of involvement in the critical process. If Habermas is correct, we need more, not less argument. The suggestion here is that the argument need not be aggressive or destructive but aimed at uncovering truths of public importance.

News should be opened to the possibility of disagreement and challenge. Indeed, it will be argued that the fact that challenges are appropriate for a serious news report distinguishes news from soap.

## THE NEWS SHOULD BE TRUE

The function of the news is not only to empower, or to entertain, but also to inform and to convey truths. But what do we mean by saying that news should be true? Will truth serve as a criterion to delimit what is newsworthy? The difficulty is that even soapy news is *true*. The strategy here is to attempt to distinguish newsworthy news from soap opera by means of a double-barreled criterion: news should be true and open to critical questioning. This section deals with the notion of truth.

What do we mean by saying that a news report is true? How can we tell it is? Firstly, we must note that truth is primarily a property of utterances, statements, or propositions. The sorts of things that can be true or false are things that someone says or conveys at a time or things that are believed. In a secondary sense, we can also say of an image that is a true picture if the image purports to represent actual events. To say of something that it is true is to assume that could *fail* to be true. There is no conception of truth without a conception of falsity. Moreover, only utterances, or propositions, or images which can be used meaningfully can be true or false. Objects are not true, at least in this primary sense of true. When we say that she is a true friend, we use the term to mean by extension "good."

To say that truth is a property of things which can convey meaning is not to say anything controversial. It is merely to reflect on our practice in using the predicate, "is true." When we say that that some item of a news report is true, we are saying that we understand under what conditions it would be true, and that we have evidence that those conditions obtain. It is true that Fox was elected president of Mexico in 2000. The conditions that would make that true are *inter alia* that the Mexican people voted for him and that the Mexican electoral body, the Instituto Federal Electoral (IFE), confirmed the vote. The evidence for showing the truth of the statement is normally indirect. For most of us the evidence derives from a news report on the television or in the press. That evidence in turn depends on reporters who received the information from reliable sources. The most reliable sources in Mexico are those from the IFE. Those sources in turn gather evidence, indirectly, from the computer readouts of those counting the votes. In the final analysis, the canonical evidence is the actual votes of the citizens, weighted and distributed as the constitution decrees.

When we say that the original statement is true we are gesturing at an entire network of interlinked chains of evidence. How we check any particular link will depend on the sort of evidence appropriate at that stage. There may be a canonical test for of what is true, on which other tests depend. In the case of an election result, as we know from the 2000 U.S. election, the canonical test based on how people voted can itself be challenged. The voting process is a complex one, embedded in social practices.

Feelings ran high as the world watched the parties debate about what should be the canonical method for establishing the truth of a statement that Bush was elected president of the United States in 2000. How we establish what is true can be very important.

This approach to the notion of truth is intentionally deflationary. The suggestion is that we can rescue what is useful in the traditional notion that news should be true by requiring that news should be backed by evidence of a particular sort, depending on what type of news it is. This will not be news to reporters. It is, however, unfashionable among theorists. Those concerned with the slipperiness of the abstract conception of truth have too often rejected truth wholesale. Rather than reject the notion of truth in the abstract, the strategy here is begin with the clearer and more basic concept of how we show an utterance, a statement, a proposition, or an image to be true. That is already difficult, and can lead to disagreement. There are many different ways of establishing whether an utterance or an image is true. What are the methods we use to establish that news reports are true? Let us consider an example.

When asked what she remembered about first hearing of the death of the Princess Diana, Sarah (age 16) said she heard about the accident on the radio:

> Sarah: Yeah, oh, I didn't believe it. I just thought it was a joke. But, yeah.
>
> Interviewer: You were with the rest of your family?
>
> Sarah: I'm not sure, I can't remember. I remember I was in the car and I just thought it was a joke and then they just kept repeating it every like five minutes or something. So I decided it must have been true after about an hour. (Cohort 3, December 1998, Adelaide, Australia)

In effect, Sarah is offering a pretheoretic account of what she takes as a guarantee of truth: an event being mentioned often on the radio. It is not a sophisticated response, but it is one with a certain currency among the suspicious young. She says that truth is what is offered by a source many times—even if that source is not in itself reliable. Given that Sarah was not in a position to travel to Paris to see the accident, her reaction is rational. Several news sources are more reliable than one.

Most students are more skeptical about the possibility of the media reporting truthfully:

It is virtually impossible to be assured of a balanced view on news and current affairs, especially with international reports. So many people have vested interests in ensuring that we believe what they want that it is impossible that we receive unadulterated news. I'm not saying that we don't receive accurate reports, just that if someone wants to distort a story they can and do. With that being the case how can we trust any story? Whole truth, partial truth, no truth…who really knows? (first-year student, University of Canberra, 1999).

Many professional theorists agree and simply deny that any news report can be true. News is always biased, written from one point of view or another. They decry the appeal to truth as some Platonic ideal that exists independently of human apprehension, in a God's-eye view of the world. They argue that fiction and nonfiction are far more deeply intertwined than a simplistic division suggests. The very possibilities of what can be said truly or falsely are themselves set by the fictional discourse.

Miller (1993) gives a sophisticated version of this style of argument. He suggests that the influence is mutual; from fiction to nonfiction and back again:

> meaning is fixed at the level of the structures of the text, but compromised by shifting relations between particular discourses of the human sciences and the representational text—for instance, the state of popular medical knowledge and its intersection with an account of science fiction medicine in a short story…. It is in tracing the deployment of these protocols of mapping, the actual cartography of superimposing nonfictive knowledge onto fictive that we may find the meaning, the referentiality, the political effect/affect of texts. (Miller, 1993 : 65)

Applied to our problem, Miller's argument is that there is a symbiotic relationship between soap opera and news, with each influencing the other. His point is well taken: our very conception of what is true is largely determined by fiction. But a relationship is quite consistent with the need to draw a distinction between the fictional and nonfictional. As Miller argues, the fictional sets the parameters of citizenship, so that actual political action is circumscribed by the possibilities of action in fiction. Even if soap opera delimits what it is possible to believe, however, we can still distinguish truth and fiction. We had better continue to do so if we hope to act effectively.

Granted there is a difficulty with a conception of universal, nonperspectival truth—the truth, the whole truth and nothing but the truth—in that it assumes a unique way of assessing the truth that applies to all cultures and all languages. The case of the election results shows just how elusive such a unique method of establishing the truth may be, even within one culture. The considerations of the last chapter suggest that, at the very least, we should take into account the fact that different languages have different conceptual resources and refer to different objects. It is not always possible to say the same thing in different languages, so the best notion of truth cannot be supralinguistic. We must content ourselves with truth within a language.

This does not mean that we should abandon the notion of truth. Let us distinguish a notion of being TRUE, universally, from the question of whether the particular statements in particular languages can be true. We establish whether a particular statement in a particular language is true by checking the world, using familiar methods. We can tell if it is raining here and now, or not, at least if we are outside and suitably sentient. The methods of establishing justification for statements are, and must be, part of the repertoire of competent speakers of a language—they are part of the way we learn language. To be true in this sense is not a metaphysical problem.

There may be no TRUTH about Kosovo, but there may still be many true statements, statements about what happened, statements from victims. It is natural to think of these statements as true in so far as they *correspond* to how things are in the world. The idea of a correspondence theory of truth is particularly seductive when it comes to television news because television news has a relatively uncomplicated relationship to fact.[16] We tend to think of television news as reflecting the world, just as television images reflect the world like photographs. That view is too simple because of the way language, unlike photography, divides up the world conceptually. But it also has a core of truth.

---

[16] A version of the picture theory of meaning, such as that proposed by the early Wittgenstein of the *Tractatus*, seems tailor-made for television news. Wittgenstein himself, in the *Philosophical Investigations*, grew skeptical of the approach of the *Tractatus*, in particular of the search for a relation of correspondence and of assumptions about the way language is constructed and related to the world. Others such as Davidson (1967) have been more sanguine about the possibility of using a Tarski-style truth definition, in a suitably relativized way, to spell out the way the structure of the language is related to the truth predicate.

Skepticism about the possibility of locating a way of showing corre-spondence has led to varieties of relativism, the doctrine described with re-spect to language in chapter 1. Many have come to advocate relativism about truth—the claim that what is truth is relative in some way to a fur-ther category of truths. There are mild forms of relativism implicit in Da-vidson's (1984) holism, in which judgments of truth are relative to an understanding of the entire culture (and language). Postmodernism can be read as global skepticism about truth. In the case of television news, rela-tivism manifests itself in the claim that viewers understand the world vari-ously, and the particular models of truth that are assumed by the nightly news are just one among a variety of routes for understanding the world.

Relativism is the most common theory adopted by students discussing truth and the media. Comments like the following show how pervasive relativism is:

> Just as the world is viewed differently by every person so is the meaning of truth. Truth is a person's belief that an event happened the way they saw it. This person is influenced by different schemas so one person's truth may vary from another person's truth. Truth can also be stretched or can just be a word used to give credibility to a story. etc. The problem with the word truth, is that it is only a person's word and carries absolutely no physical evidence. (first-year student, University of Canberra, 1999)

> It is quite interesting considering the way different people from different cultures view current affairs in diverse ways. Truth can be a very tricky concept as different people can have extremely opposing views toward what is true and what is false. What each person views as true or false can be shaped by one's own culture, moral values and beliefs. It is even shaped by the people who surround you, family and friends. In this sense it seems im-possible that there be a universal way of establishing truth, does this matter? WE don't know. (first-year student, University of Canberra, 1999)

The students' remarks also show the dangers of relativism. The rela-tivist must allow different notions of truth yet at the same time accept that it is possible to communicate. So for instance, some students argue for global subjectivism:

> It doesn't matter what race you are or where you are when it comes to es-tablishing truth; ideas and beliefs are affected by culture. We believe there is no universal way of establishing truth, it is subjective and depends on the individual person. (first-year students, University of Canberra, 1999)

Others point out the necessity for a shared concept of truth:

> It is not as important what the objective truth is—it is the perception of that
> objective truth which we communicate which matters most. This is the truth
> we share with others (first-year student, University of Canberra, 1999).

If, in fact, we had no shared notion of "true" (as opposed to THE
TRUTH), then it would not be possible to communicate. The pervasive
relativism of the young comes up against the problem of how we communicate without a "shared" truth or language.

The slide into relativism can be prevented, however, without returning
to the elusive one whole TRUTH. Let us think again of reports about the
world, in particular news reports, as something that can be challenged.
Soap opera is fiction, so it would be pointless to ask for evidence that, for
instance, a character in *Neighbours* had really died. That is not so when it
comes to the news. News reports should always be open to the challenge
from any viewer who asks, "What is your evidence?"

Television news is not interactive, so there can be no response. However, as interactivity develops, challenging news for evidence should begin.
It is this interactivity that we aimed to foster with the news clips and questions used in the the *Reason and Media* web site. This was designed to raise
philosophical questions relating to a range of television products and consisted of a combination of snippets of television linked to questions about
their philosophical content. There are also logical exercises and a public
space for commentary and development of new examples. Each news clip
can be downloaded. Associated with it are what are called "Big Ideas":
philosophical questions and some logic exercises. Students are asked to
comment on the questions in a familiar style of chatroom called "Have
your say." In regard to news, each item comes with a set of particular
questions, while other questions are generic. So, for instance, one set of
questions relates to the issue "Is the news true?"

> Is the news true? The notion of truth is complex. We have grown suspicious
> of the idea that news can be objective, because we think that there is no one
> truth. What is true from one perspective may not be true from another. Can
> we rescue the idea of being true, in terms of the ways we establish truth?
>
> 1)   If you say it is raining, how would you check if it were true?
>
> 2)   If your friend said it was raining, how could you check if it were true?

3) If a friend in London phones and tells you it is raining, how could you check if it were true?

4) If a television report said that it was raining in London, how could you check if it were true?

5) If you were trying to check if it were true that it is raining, does it make a difference what your race is?

6) If you were trying to check if it were true that it is raining, does it make a difference where you are?

7) If you were trying to check if it were true that $2 + 2 = 4$, does it make a difference what your race is or where you are?

8) If you say you feel sick, how could you check if it were true?

9) If you were trying to check if it were true that you felt sick, does it make a difference who you are?

10) Is there a universal way of establishing truth? Does it matter?

The responses to the questions ask students to consider how to establish truth. One pragmatic student replied to the final question:

> The truth is the truth, whoever you are. If there are conflicting stories about the same event, at least one, if not both or all parties are not telling the truth—even if they are not lying. Whether they believe what they saw or witnessed or whatever, or not, there is a truthful story if the event actually happened. (first-year student, University of Canberra, 1999)

These remarks are made by first-year students with no training in philosophy. They are planning to become journalists or public relations experts or advertising executives. Yet they are both concerned with and determined to tease out a notion of truth for their everyday discourse. They generally begin as out-and-out relativists, committed to the notion that truth on television is not "true" but just a version of the truth. They are skeptical and self-confident at the same time. The function of the somewhat simplistic questions on the web site is to raise questions that will force students to be critical of their pretheoretic ideas. These questions, typical of the style of the Philosophy for Children Program, urge students to come down from their metaphysical high horses and engage with concrete examples. With that grounding they are led to the broader philosophical issues.

The style of questioning is characteristic of the tradition of linguistic philosophy, beginning with examples and leaving theory to the last. From the perspective of postmodern theorists it may seem a grossly undertheorized approach. But there is a proud philosophical tradition on which it draws. The philosophical groundings can be traced on the one hand to the view of Dewey that education needs to be based on the concrete. On the other hand, the approach draws on the work of the later Wittgenstein (1953). He argued that many philosophical debates are literally meaningless, deriving from false analogies and misuse of language. For Wittgenstein, philosophy has a deflationary role. We should, he says, "let the fly out of the fly bottle"—a much-debated phrase but one that suggests that at least some philosophical debate is mere buzzing. The idea of these questions for students is to unravel their philosophical prejudices before seeking their own views.

In this pragmatic fashion, we can come to some answer to the problem of truth. There is a strong and accessible notion of being true that enables us to distinguish truth from fiction, news from soap opera. The strategy is to distinguish "strict and literal" truths, associated with canonical means of establishing veracity, from truths in fiction, where veracity does not depend in the same way on the world. News is open for verification, soap operas are not. When we accuse a politician of lying, we appeal to those modes of determining truth in the broadest sense. The practices of establishing truth are deeply established in the culture. We can accept that fiction is a route to understanding the world but that assertions made in fiction are not strictly and literally true. News is intended to be strictly and literally true.

## NEWS CAN BE CRITICIZED

We have not yet drawn a distinction between soapy and nonsoapy news. O.J.'s verdict is strictly and literally true, but its importance is exaggerated. How do we provide a finer-grained notion of truth—truth that is both relevant and useful to society and is important for the well-being of those who watch television, among them citizens who vote for governments?

The daily paper of the southern Mexican state of Yucatan (Local, 2000) reported on 26 December 2000 that over 82% of households in the state had television, although only 28% had telephones, 23% cars, and 18% hot water systems. Even in one of the poorer states of Mexico, most children have access to television. They learn about the world from television. News may be only a very small proportion of what they watch, but it is through television news that they primarily learn of the society they live in. It is from television news that they will learn much of the information that determines how they vote and how they will behave in a society. In early 2001, the state of Yucatan pushed Mexico to the edge of a constitutional crisis when the sitting governor refused to accept the federal appointment of independent electoral commissioners. Thousands of Yucatecos marched on the capital of the state, Merida, in support of the sitting governor, whose television interviews and publicity campaigns drew the populace behind him. As one reporter explained, the Yucatecos were accustomed to following their leader. They were accustomed to "tutelage," in terms Habermas uses: of being told what to do. If Habermas is correct, the style of television news may have fostered the traditional obedience of the Yucatec *campesinos*.

Television news is ubiquitous. The case of Yucatan is one of many. In richer nations the television set is in virtually every household. The style of reporting of television news has immense potential impact. If television news is seen simply as entertainment, rather than as providing citizens with information, then citizens are likely to receive less information. Without appropriate information, decisions are less likely to be well based. The danger then is that, by transforming news into soap opera, the public will be ill served.

Again Habermas has an interesting perspective on the phenomenon:

> The integration of the once separate domains of journalism and literature, that is to say of information and rational-critical argument on the one side and *belles lettres* on the other, brings about a peculiar shifting of reality—even a conflation of different levels of reality. Under the common denominator of so-called human interest emerges the *mixtum compositum* of a pleasant and at the same time convenient subject for entertainment that, instead of doing justice to reality, has a tendency to present a substitute more palatable for consumption and more likely to give rise to an impersonal indulgence in stimulating relaxation than to the public use of reason. (Habermas, 1989: 170)

There are several elements in this complaint. Habermas suggests that what is lost with the decay of news values is "justice to reality" and the

"public use of reason." We take the two notions in turn. The notion of doing justice to reality is difficult to unpack because it assumes we are capable of *judging* reality. How can we judge reality, other than distinguishing
between what is true and what is not? It is not just that news must do justice to reality in so far as it should be true for, as we pointed out, soapy —
and often unjust — news can be true. Nor does it help to say that justice to
reality implies a balanced objective presentation. The notion of objectivity
itself has fallen into disrepute and that of balance is scarcely more helpful.

Objectivity is also a complex notion, all too easy to deride. In one
sense it means independence of opinion; in another it refers to impartiality
of judgment; and in yet another to be objective is not to be dependent on
being perceived.[17] In media studies, objectivity is often summed up as balance and as independence from personal bias. But balance, in itself, is not
a criterion. Balance implies balance between opposing views and, as we
have already remarked, the mere fact of opposing views does not guarantee that the news is either appropriate or true. There were opposing views
on Bill Clinton's sex life that were no doubt well balanced in some news
reports, but the news, objective though it might be, was pure soap. Moreover, objectivity cannot be reduced to a simple formula of avoiding personal
bias. There were those who thought that the epitome of lack of personal
bias could be captured on a television news broadcast with a BBC style.
Yet there was a very strong class bias in BBC news, just as there is a different yet no less pervasive bias in the CNN style.

The second notion, of the importance of the "public use of reason" is
more promising. But who is to decide what counts as the appropriate public use of reason? Traditional nightly news bulletins implicitly defined
categories of news suitable for broadcast, drawing on the categories earlier
established in the broadsheet press. Those categories, however, should not
be taken for granted. As Chomsky (e.g., 1994) has so often argued, those
who determine what is news are often influenced by the military and in-
dustrial establishment. It is far too easy to declare what is appropriate for
the public use of reason and set limits on debate about issues which are in
some sense not public. Yet the distinction between what is or should be
public and what is or should be private is at the heart of the distinction we

---

[17] This gloss derives from Mautner (1996).

are seeking to define.

One approach is to turn to the Habermasian "ideal public sphere" as a model. For Habermas, there is one style of interaction that defines what is appropriate in the public, as opposed to the private, domain. This is the model of reasoned debate that reached its apogee in the debates in the coffee shops of the emerging European democracies. When he talks of the public use of reason, he has this public debate in mind. The public use of reason differs in one crucial respect from the model of television news. It involves debate, criticism and interaction between the provider of the news and the recipient. It is debate of a particular limited form, of course, more common in parliaments of the world than in living rooms in front of television. But the idea is clear, when it comes to television news. Television news should not just entertain, it should also be debated using the modes of talk of the "public use of reason." Television news should be open to rational criticism, criticism at the level of argument as well as fact.

This criterion draws a very rough and ready line between two categories of news. On the one hand there is news which, while of human interest, is not a matter to be debated using reasoned modes of talk. There is and was very little mileage in reasoning about Clinton's sex life. On the other hand, some news calls for reasoned debate. Electoral policies should be debated, for there are substantial questions about how elections should be run.

This is a very rough criterion. There will be those who suggest that Clinton's sex life is the appropriate domain of debate, and electoral policy is boring or irrelevant to their lives. Clinton's sex life is, after all, far more relevant to the personal dilemmas of the lives many. Why should women or ethnic minorities accept the topics and style of talk of the Habermasian "public use of reason" if that public effectively disenfranchises them? It is easy to criticize the assumption that the reasoned modes of talk in the traditional male coffee shop are universal. Not all are capable of talking in public debate. It requires a style of talk, a vocabulary, and an aggressive identification of the weaknesses of others' arguments that is alien to some cultural groups and many women. Feminists such as Nancy Fraser (1993) and Iris Marion Young (1990) are rightly suspicious of the Habermasian prescription.

What is essential to Habermas's notion is the necessity for public criticism. The public sphere in Habermas' own definition is gendered and eurocentric. However, it is possible to define the practices of what Habermas calls "information and rational-critical argument" broadly. It is not necessary to define reasoning in terms of particular logical styles. Criticism should be redefined to capture what is genuinely central to the notion. Careful criticism need not be aggressive. A question like: "I wonder if you have thought of this view?" can be as effective a criticism as a sharp counter example. The ways of presenting "rational-critical argument" are various. The same questions and arguments can come in variety of styles, some feminine, some domestic, some peculiar to one or other ethnic groups. That does not mean that reason itself differs between different groups. It means that there are different ways to voice reasons.

Being reasonable and being critical need not and should not involve blind adherence to rules of logic or a sniping and carping insistence on narrowly defined terms. It may require imagination and a suspension of disbelief to understand another's point of view, to enter into their way of conceiving the world. It might require encouragement to extract the presuppositions and justify them, to analyze apparent fallacies and find they are acceptable. It may take time and persistence.

We need to conceive of the news as open to criticism in this broad sense. However, not just any criticism is acceptable. The weight or lisp of a public figure should not be criticized while their misuse of public funds should be. Nor should news be criticized because it, or its conclusions, disagree with the views of the viewer. How do we establish which type of criticism is appropriate? One strategy is to suggest that news should be open to a critical response in such a way that it might lead to action. There is no critical response appropriate for much television news, precisely because, to refer again to the earlier quotation from Habermas, it has become "'exchanges about tastes and preferences' between consumers." (Habermas, 1989: 172) There is no room for reasoned debate about a taste for chocolate or a preference for blue.

Subjecting an issue to critical questioning is allowing it, in principle, to be challenged. There are many ways we challenge others' utterances as untrue, inappropriate, boring, irrelevant, funny, absurd, incomprehensible, vague, distasteful, inelegant, or trite. The process of challenging advocated here as the hallmark of news worthy of the name relies on criteria of rationality, very broadly conceived. It is most apparent in debate of a particular form. The news as we receive it through the television is never subjected to real debate from those it is supposed to inform. The viewers are not asked directly what they take to be reliable or interesting or valuable as news. Instead, an indirect measure, namely the ratings, is taken as evidence that viewers like particular kinds of news. Ratings never give us a chance to answer back. While viewers at times make it clear that they are skeptical of the news they receive, the producers of TV news until recently had never opened news to debate.

To some extent, the process is already beginning. Internet sites for television news channels and the press allow individuals to challenge those who provide the news. But contributions to the sites are often disappointing, as they are in talk back radio or television. Viewers are not trained to respond critically to television, to look for weaknesses of evidence or argument. Viewers can voice their own opinions or lay down the law about moral issues, but they are less capable of listening carefully and criticising content. Training in those fundamental skills was part of the aim in producing the *Reason and Media* web site. There are questions about news reports and about the ways in which they are constructed. For instance, we asked about the fact that there is rarely a news report when there is no vision or image to accompany the item and also about the fact that much news is supplied by public relations agencies. A preliminary set of questions ran:

**"Is the news new?"**

We are interested in news which matters to us, which is relevant to our lives. But we also prefer news which we understand, that deals with story lines we are familiar with. Often those story lines are very like soap operas. In April 1998, the *New York Times* had a front page story about a broken elevator.

1) Would it be a news story if it happened in your town?

2) Would it be a news story if it happened in a town where nearly everyone lived and worked in buildings with elevators?

3) Would it be a news story if it happened in a town where no one lived and worked in buildings with elevators?

4) Would it be a news story if it happened in a town in Africa?

5)  Would it be a news story if it happened every day?

6)  Would it be a news story if it happened to a film star?

7)  Would it be a news story if someone was killed?

8)  Would it be a news story if twenty people were killed?

9)  Would it be a news story if it happened just when someone took a video?

10) Would it be a news story if the story had been supplied by a repair company?

The exercises are intended to alert students to strategies for challenging the news. In this case relevance is the criterion. Each news report should, at least in principle, be challenged. We *can* develop a habit of challenging news stories. If every news report were challenged in terms of the criteria of truth it was using, in terms of the evidence adduced, and in terms of the consequences to the society of revealing the news, then there would be a good reason to reject the most tabloid of stories. Gossip is sometimes important in terms of consequences; if so, it is news. When it is not, it should be reserved for the private sphere.

News which is entertaining is interesting. News, however, is not just about entertainment. News should be true and should be open to criticism. Soap opera is open for discussion of its artistic merits and, as we shall find in the next chapter, as the basis of debate about morality. Soap opera and news are however separate genres and should remain so.

## CONCLUSION

The assimilation of the two separate categories of news and entertainment has brought in its wake an unreality to news and a realism to fiction. The assimilation of genres is not in itself destructive. What is of real concern is the effect on the ability of viewers to criticize the news. That has consequences for their ability to act as citizens. Televised and now Internet news treats viewers as consumers, as passive receivers who should be told what to believe and what to do. However, viewers are also voters. They should be given the chance to debate and inquire into the news. Far more than media critics realize, viewers are capable of reacting to and being critical about television itself and about the ways in which television news is presented.

Accepting that the aim of news is to be true and open to criticism does not simplify the debate about how we assess or deal with the truth claims made on the news. The methods for establishing truth differ depending on the issues. There is not a unique and special way of guaranteeing that news is true. Nor is there a unique and special way to debate and challenge the news. There is no one way to define the public use of reason. But the public should reason.

A 1997 advertisement for the *New York Times*/CNN evening news bulletin, NY1, claimed that it was "The voice of reason." Unfortunately, reason and truth are what is conspicuously lacking in the tabloid television and, indeed, in NY1's racy and highly parochial news reports. Yet the audience is not fooled or at least not all of the time. Reasoning is what we do for ourselves when we challenge the news. No one else can do our reasoning for us: the voices of reason are our own voices.

# 3

# WHY NOT LIE?

## Discourse Ethics

PARTY OF FIVE

Claudia: No, uh, ah, no way.

Charlie: Claudia…

Claudia: No, forget it. That's, that is a terrible thing to do.

Julia: Yeah, it is. It is, but how else, Claude, I mean, how else are we going to get him here?

Claudia: I don't know, but that? No, you can't tell him that. You can't have him get in his car and drive all the way over here thinking that. You don't think this is the cruelest thing you could do to a person; I mean you're actually OK with this?

Sarah: I know it'll get him here Claudia, so yeah I am.

Claudia: Well, I don't care. I won't. I don't care, you know, if you think it is such a great idea, you call him!

Julia: It won't make any sense coming from Sarah or me or Charlie.

Charlie: If it's you, Claude, if you call him and say that you need his help and don't know what to do, then he'll believe you and he'll come.

Julia: He's in trouble, Claudia; I mean aren't you willing to do whatever it takes to help him? I am.

Claudia: *(dials)* Bai, Bai, um, it's Owen, he, I wasn't looking and he and he, he fell down the stairs and he, he hit his head, hard…I don't know, I don't know, he's breathing, but he, he's not moving, Bailey, and I don't know what to do. You just, you, you gotta, you gotta…OK, OK, but hurry.

*(Turns to group)* Shame on you.

*Party of Five* episode, "Intervention"

This brief transcript is taken from a popular evening soap opera, *Party of Five*, which deals with a family of five orphaned children ranging in age from the eldest boy, Charlie, in his twenties, to a preschooler, Owen. Their struggles to survive, work, and pass through youth and adolescence provide the structure of the soap's episodes. In this episode the focus is the drinking problem of the teenage boy, Bailey. The family had decided to confront him but, when he failed to come to the meeting, Claudia, the youngest girl who is his special ally, was asked by the others to phone him and pretend that Owen has been hurt. The excerpt is, at one level, a piece of effective television; at another it is a classic exposition of the debate between those who believe in crude consequentialism, the view that what is moral is what has the best consequences, and those who doubt that consequences can ever justify a morally distasteful action.

When this segment was shown to a group of fifth-grade children in New Jersey in early 1997, the classroom exploded in discussion.[1] Some talked of their own experiences of having family members confront difficulty. One boy talked of his uncle who is a crack addict, and the need to get him to talk. Others focused on just when it is right to lie. They struggled with the notion that a lie is for another's good and the question of who is to be the judge of what is good for others. But, with some subtle leadership from the philosopher running the group, they finally focused on the issue of whether consequences can ever justify actions that otherwise would be reprehensible.

Later in the same year, the segment was shown to a group of graduates and graduate students of the Media Ecology Program from New York University.[2] Their discussion, while conducted in more sophisticated

---

1    I am grateful to Professor Matthew Lipman, the Institute for the Advancement of Philosophy for Children, and Montclair State University for allowing me to teach a course in their program. The article reports on the work of a student in the Masters program at the International Association for Philosophy for Children (IAPC), Darryl di Marzio, at a local school. The session mentioned here occurred on 11 March 1997, with grades 5 and 6.

2    Media Ecology Conference, Department of Communication and Culture, New York

terms, covered much the same ground as the fifth graders. There was some concern about the way the young Claudia was manipulated by her peers but, in general, the issues were similar. When is it right to lie? How do we judge the higher good?

Both of these examples show that television can engender moral debate. We should harness television more effectively for such purposes. But why use soap operas rather than carefully crafted pieces with appropriate moral messages? The previous chapter undervalued the content of soap opera and suggested the assimilation of features of the genre had undermined the quality of the news. There is, indeed, little to commend the impact of the soap opera on the genre of news. The argument of the previous chapter was that the assimilation of news and soap opera had made it more difficult for viewers of the news to be critical about what they learnt, at least with respect to the truth and public interest of the news. This is not however to denigrate the content of soap opera. Soap operas may be excellent or may be trite, but in a variety of forms they have had an immense impact on society. Soap operas are not, and do not claim to be factual, or to address public issues directly. Nevertheless, in their own fictional terms, they often address the ethical issues which confront society. In this chapter, I argue that soap operas, and more broadly television drama, provide an important space of ethical[3] debate in modern society.

## WHY SOAPS? PROBLEMS OF DEFINITION

Soap operas originally sandwiched soap-powder ads. Indeed, soaps were, and still are, produced by the soap-powder firms — Proctor & Gamble, for example, produced three soap operas in 1997, including *Another*

---

University, 7 November 1997. I am grateful to Professor Neil Postman for the opportunity to address the group.

[3] Mautner (1996) in the entries on "ethics" and that on "morals" explains that the Latin term *moralis* was originally used by Cicero as a translation of the Greek *ëthikos*. Authors do use the words in different senses, but given the complexity of the uses of both terms (cf. Mautner), I prefer not to draw a sharp distinction. I am concerned here with what might be called normative ethics, sometimes known as moral philosophy, namely, debates about right conduct. In later sections I also deal with metaethical questions.

*World* (Canedy, 1997). The format was driven by advertising needs. The aim was to keep the attention of the audience through the ads and bring them back for another ad-filled episode. Since the ads were for household goods, the focus of the stories had to appeal to those engaged in domestic settings. Long-running family dramas proved most successful.

There is an extensive literature on the soap opera format. Researchers describe how soaps are structured, how new proposals are tested, how ratings are determined, and how sensitively—or insensitively—they are viewed.[4] I am using the term more broadly than some critics, who reserve the term for daytime shows and label continuing similar evening programs as "drama."[5] I do this advisedly. With the advent of cable and the use of video, once-rigid distinctions between daytime and evening television genres have disappeared, making the evening soap a common phenomenon.

What defines the notion of soap opera are the characteristics mentioned in the previous chapter. Soap operas have a range of generic features: domestic settings, low production costs, and romantic themes are frequent though not universal. In production, there is an emphasis on the close-up shot of the face—of the emotional suspense of watching a face—but again this is not universal. What is common is the narrative structure of the genre. Soaps interweave several plot lines. Closure of the subplots is rare. Events, and particularly love affairs, tend to reshuffle and begin again on soaps as they do in real life.

Soaps *are* in some senses lifelike. The regular daily appearance of soaps and the unpretentious domestic settings give the impression that they are realistic. Yet even the most cursory viewing shows how unrealistic the genre is. Convenient relations appear from nowhere, and others disappear to fit the timetables of actors. One example of the phenomenon can be seen in the Australian soap, *Echo Point*. Just in time for the 1995 Christmas break and the suspension of the series, the long-lost mother of a 14-year-old boy turns up, announces that the supposed father and care-giver was unrelated ("But he's not your son") and goes on to admit she had killed the

---

4    Allen (1985); Ang (1985), Berger (1992), Cantor (1983), Geraghty (1992), Nightingale (1990), to mention but a few.

5    This definition is close to that of Geraghty (1992: 2-3) with whose remarks on the value of definition I concur.

real father. Such extraordinary coincidences are part of the fabric of soaps, which are still registered as realistic by viewers.

Soap operas have become perhaps the most generally successful and universal entertainment style in the world. The spread of the soap genre is one of the most remarkable features of modern global cultures. In some cases, soaps themselves travel. The success of Mexican "*telenovelas*" in Russia and China or of Australian soap operas such as *Neighbours* in Europe is a remarkable feature of modern culture. In other cases, the genre is adapted to local customs, as in Japan, India and Taiwan, so that the format and story lines are taken over and adapted to local circumstance. Moreover, soaps now constitute the common culture, much as a century ago the Bible and the received literary canon served as common culture. Our culture is one in which the lives of soap opera characters play a role, and the conventions of life in soaps are what we expect of our political figures. This does not necessarily mean we take soap opera stars as models (although at times we could do worse), but that soap operas and other television products are essential to the shared global culture of a generation. Children all over the world know *The Nanny*, just as they know *The Simpsons*, *Seinfeld*, and details of Bill Clinton's sex life.

There is a range of different models for the production of soap operas. British, Australian and U.S-based soap operas, once successful, go on for ever. Mexican *telenovelas* last nine months. In the Anglo-Saxon industry, plot lines are often defined months or years in advance, particularly with successful series. In Mexico, scripts are developed week by week. In Australia and the United Kingdom, themes frequently touch on what is controversial within the home culture—drug use, sexual ambiguity, and the like. In Mexico, until recently, controversial issues were avoided.

Differences in the structure of the industry lead to superficial differences in style. The economics of soap opera production in the West also determines plot lines and the paucity of new themes. When successful, a soap or evening serial breeds spin-offs—as Todd Gitlin put it in his book, *Inside Prime Time* (1983) new soaps are normally "copies," "spin offs" (*Mad Max II*) or "recombinants." Some recombinants may be merely mechanical. However recombinants may be genuinely creative. As Gitlin says, in defense of the recombinant:

> …recombinant thinking is rooted deeply in all modern culture and thought.

> [T]he strategy of collage, of juxtaposition, is both recognition of and roman-
> tic protest against the idea that the world is finished, worn out. (1983: 77)

He goes on to talk of the role of the recombinant in the network board-
room:

> Recombinant talk is splendidly practical, too, providing signposts for rapid
> recognition, streamlining discussion that might otherwise seem unwieldy.
> (1983: 77)

The Brazilian and Mexican producers of *telenovelas* also use the strategy of recombination, but here the production parameters are different.
The companies that produced the soap operas are mainly profitable monopolies. In Mexico, until quite recently, all *telenovelas* were produced by
the Azcárraga family company, Televisa. They typically produce a *telenovela* on a particular theme daily for a 9-month period. Actors and actresses do not even learn their lines—they wear earphones and are
prompted as they are filming, a factor that has accustomed viewers to the
long significant glance between utterances. Generally there is a 2-hour
summary of the week's episodes on the weekend for successful *telenovelas*.
The themes then must wind up before the summer. The plot lines were
extremely limited—poor girl meets rich boy—and there was never any
mention of the political and economic problems of the nation. These for-
mulaic *telenovelas* are extremely successful not merely in Latin America but
in Spain, Eastern Europe, and Asia.

Successful English-language soaps, such as the *East Enders* from Britain, *Dallas* from the United States, or *Neighbours* from Australia, were developed in an atmosphere of intense competition. Until the early eighties,
there was no competition to speak of in the Latin American market. The
*telenovela* discussed in this chapter, *Mirada de Mujer*, is a product of an
emerging competitive market in Mexico. Produced by a production company rather than by Televisa or the alternative commercial network, TV
Azteca, it draws on the more confrontational models of anglophone soap
operas. It became a landmark of Mexican television.

## THE SOCIAL ROLE OF SOAP OPERA

Since their inception, soaps have had a central role in the social fabric.
When talking of their media memories, members of the 70- to 75-year-old

Australian cohort spoke with passion about the soaps of their youth. One, talking of the rituals of boarding school during the years of the World War II, said:

> Georgie: Some of the younger ones used to watch the radio *(laughter)*. We **did**. We sat and watched it. We weren't allowed to speak. When I was a child we weren't allowed to speak. And um at boarding school, we went to the Physics lab and we had a hot water bottle and a rug and we wrapped ourselves up with this and we listened to the Lux radio play in the physics lab. And that was great, that was you know, every Sat—every Sunday night and that is where soap word came from of course. (Cohort 1, December 1998, Adelaide, Australia)

Remarkably similar observations are made by members of the older Mexican cohort.

> Raul: We used to listen to the *radionovelas*. I remember *Anita de Monte Mar, Ave sin Nido, Chucho el Roto, Rafles*...We liked them very much because everyone sat around the radio after dinner and listened to the radionovela.

> Laura: Sundays there used to be some very good one on the radio. I remember that we sat around the radio to listen. (Cohort 1, March 1999, Mexico City)[6]

The crucial issue for the cohort was access and permission to listen to the soaps

> Hilda: Oh I was allowed to listen to *Dad and Dave*. That came on at quarter past six and I was allowed to listen to that. I wasn't allowed to listen to *Fred and Maggie. Fred and Maggie* preceded *Dad and Dave*.

> Interviewer: What was wrong with *Fred and Maggie*?

> Hilda: Well, I think my father thought that it was a stupid little soapie thing and he didn't care for it at all. He didn't mind *Dad and Dave*. I think that was because he was a country boy and *Dad and Dave* was all about the country. It was sort of Hill Billy Country—

> Marjorie: Wasn't *Fred and Maggie* called *Fred and Maggie Everybody*?

> Hilda: Well, I wasn't allowed to listen to that, but I **could** because we hap-

---

6    Thanks to Margarita Maass for permission to use this data.

pened to have a radio in the car, and in those days you didn't ever lock your motorcars, and this was a particular radio that was not integrated. It had been added afterwards, so you could just turn the knob without having to turn the key in the ignition and I used to sneak out and hide under the dashboard and turn on the radio and listen to *Fred and Maggie (laughter)*. (Cohort 1, December 1998 , Adelaide, Australia)

Most touching is the saga of one family in which the grandparents owned the radio, which then had a feeder line into the house.

Don: Well, I was brought up at Hectorville and my grandfather had a radio in his house, and we had a set of wires going across through the orchard to our house so we could only have the radio on whenever Grandfather — *(laughter)*

Georgie: So you had a speaker/ the speaker in your house or a separate — ?

Don: Yes. A separate speaker and a switch. We could switch it on and off and

Georgie: But only if he had it on?

Don: Well probably my grandmother.

(Cohort 1, December 1998, Adelaide, Australia)

These attitudes are very similar to those reported by the cohort who were teenagers during the 1960s. In their case radio had become unexceptional, so it was television viewing that was strictly regulated.

Roger: I recall going to Sydney once when my great uncle owned a television set. This was you know real gadgetry and we begged all day could we watch it. We turned it on for *Robin Hood* and then turned it off immediately it was over saying he didn't want to run the set too low or run it out. (Cohort 2, December 1998, Canberra, Australia)

The cohort had strong memories of various programs, which they talked about with great emotion.

Morris: *The White Coolies*! There was a wonderful show on and it was about the female prisoners of war in Singapore and it was called *White Coolies*. And it was just a wonderful program. But very sad. (Cohort 2, December 1998, Canberra, Australia)

In general the programs that any member of the cohort mentioned were known to all, whether they were soap operas, music shows, or adver-tisements. Only one of the people interviewed was excluded:

> Anna: I was born in Newcastle. Moved around a bit. Moved to Tamworth when I was about three, moved back to Newcastle when I was about seven, moved to Young when I was about twelve. That was horrible. We had a television, when we moved back to Newcastle when I was about seven we got a television, but it broke down fairly quickly and my parents refused to get another one. So, I had terribly deprived childhood actually. I was ex-cluded at school because I couldn't talk about, you know, television shows. Listened to the radio a lot yeah. Played the piano. (Cohort 2, December 1998, Canberra, Australia)

The resentment and sense of exclusion from the social scene is palpable.

The shared culture of soap operas is also apparent in the equivalent Mexican cohort. While Mexican television at the time was very limited, and poorer members could only watch television by paying by the hour at the local shop or with richer neighbors, the cohort knew the same figures, shared the same songs, and had a common history of soap opera. One of the most remarkable incidents of the Mexican material was the discovery that one of the members of the group had been in a television series as a child. Another talked of the control of the television:

> Teodoro: In Holy Week they turned off the TV.

> Elena: In my house, on Good Friday…television and radio were prohibited. (Cohort 2, April 1999, Mexico City)[7]

The cohort of 15- to 20-year-olds in 1999 was conversant with a huge range of soap operas and possessed a very strong sense of involvement in the currently trendy episodes. In both the Mexican and Australian data, U.S.-based soap operas are a common culture. Kids from both countries mentioned the same characters, and could cite events from the same epi-sodes. The attitudes to characters within the soaps are also startlingly uni-form. Mexicans and Australians, whether they love or hate the Nanny, can explain just what is wrong with her New Jersey accent. There is also evi-dence of a culture of debate about the soap operas. As one 15-year old said during the first week back at school after the antipodean summer:

---

[7]  I am grateful to Andrés Hoffman for permission to cite these incidents.

Everybody at school was talking about *Dawson's Creek*. It just started after
school went back and like everyone is watching...We finally caught up with
the episodes from the States (Edward, February 2000, Canberra, Australia).

The soap operas of a cohort become the mark of the "in" group, and
talk about soaps plays an important social role. Recent studies (e.g., Steele
& Brown, 1995)[8] fill out the anecdotal evidence of the role of soap opera in
adolescent lives. Another 15-year-old, Chelsea, says of the soap *Growing
Pains*:

> it has a teenager in it and there are typical problems that you would have
> every day. It kinda helps you look at it and say, "oh yeah, that's a different
> way to solve that problem." (Steele & Brown, 1995: 566)

It would be simple to label the tendency to talk of fictional rather than
real-life events as escapism. Yet moral dilemmas have long been a training
technique in the classroom, both at school and at college level. All too often
such exercises tend to degenerate into a dry rehearsal of options. Television, on the other hand, draws on the visual experience and the ability to
identify with characters to make such moral dilemmas vivid. As one Mexican informant said referring to a television soap opera, *El fugitivo*.

> Gustavo: My first moral lesson was when a man was chased for a crime he
> hadn't committed.... (Cohort 2, April 1999, Mexico City)

The fictional life of soaps is easier to discuss than fragmented private
personal lives. When it is too painful to discuss our own moral problems,
we can instead turn to similar moral dilemmas presented in fiction and discuss the issues indirectly. The moral testing ground of the soap opera provides a reflection of the moral issues in our own life, with one difference:
we can discuss the soap without the intense emotional involvement we
have in our own dilemmas. Radio soap operas had this role, just in the way
television soaps do. One case is described in Sandra Benitez' novel *Bitter
Grounds*, which charts the role of a radio soap in San Salvadorean society
between the wars. The novel tells of wealthy and interrelated family
groups and their servants—of the births out of wedlock, of the family ri-

---

8    I am grateful to Fisherkeller for this reference.

valries, of infidelities, and of violent death. The soap opera reflects, in scarcely less garish tones, the dilemmas faced by the household. The moral questions that arise in the soap opera are actually discussed by the household, even though none of them dare mention the violence and inequity of their own lives. The discussion of who was right in the soap serves as a counterpoint to the lack of discussion about the personal difficulties of the household. When the soap is interrupted by the announcement of the dropping of the atomic bomb on Hiroshima, the reaction is one of irritation—would they ever know what had happened in the soap?

Fiction and myth have always had a moral role to play.[9] Homer's *Odyssey*, George Eliot's *Mill on the Floss*, even Tom Wolfe's *Bonfire of the Vanities*, are not only social commentary but also blueprints for making moral sense of the world. The fictional presentation of human behavior inevitably uncovers moral attitudes and gives rise to issues about right and wrong. In this sense, television fiction plays the role of the great novel of the nineteenth century. It is not easy to discuss a personal decision about abortion publicly. It is far less difficult to discuss whether a girl who had been raped in a *telenovela* should have an abortion, as many Mexicans did while watching *Mirada de Mujer*. The fictional soap operas give us an impersonal way to begin debate about moral issues.

There is a solid literature on the role of the *telenovela* in Latin culture (e.g., Mazziotti, 1996) and a dauntingly voluminous literature on the role of soap operas and popular romance in the anglophone world. From studies of the role of romantic fiction, such as Janice Radway's (1984) study of the impact of forms of identification in women reading romance novels, through Ang's (1985) detailed study of *Dallas*, and Geraghty's (1991) contrast between the role of women in British and U.S.-based soaps, this literature engages with the importance of popular romance in the modern world. Numerous studies deconstruct the attitudes and stereotypes of those watching soap operas with increasing sympathy and sophistication.[10]

---

9  The tradition of using tales for a moral message is of course notably exemplified in the Bible. Robert Coles (1997, chapter 2) gives examples of children's moral debate on historical topics. The Philosophy for Children tradition (cf. Splitter & Sharp, 1995 chapters 6 & 7) is a rich source of sophisticated ethical debate among school children.

10  For instance, Buckingham's (1987) account of *East Enders*.

The focus here, however, is specifically the moral debate engendered by soap opera. I suggest that when we gossip about soap opera figures and treat them as part of our families, we are drawing out the moral implications of actions. We learn lessons from soap operas and read moral fables into them. It is this process, illustrated below with a Mexican example, that is spelled out in more detail in the following section.

## MIRADA DE MUJER

In the latter part of 1997, for the first time since the end of the Revolution (1910-1920), the Mexican state was confronted by a genuine political opposition. Huge shifts in the economic and political life of the country were underway. The PRI (the Institutional Revolutionary Party) and its allies, including the television conglomerate Televisa, were under pressure.

Televisa belongs to the Azcárraga family. From 1951, when the radio company of Emilo Azcárraga Vidaurreta began television broadcasting with a baseball match, the company had been allied to the government. The family of Miguel Alemán, the then President, had significant interests in the channel. In 1955 the competing channels merged on the grounds that the independent channels were losing money. This process was repeated whenever a competitor entered the market. For instance, Grupo Alfa bought Canal 8 in 1968 but combined with the Azcárraga group to form Televisa 1972. By 1982, the son of the family, Emilio Azcárraga Milmo, had bought out Grupo Alfa, and Televisa was the biggest Spanish network in the world (Mejía, 1998). It had significant U.S. holdings (240 channels by 1983), and major share in Megavisión in Chile (49%) and Galavisión in Europe. In 1986, Azcárraga was forced to divest himself of his U.S. holdings after a long-running case concentrating on the fact that he had control yet was not a U.S. citizen (Mejía, 1998).

Throughout this period, Televisa was the largest producer of Spanish-language programming, and more specifically *telenovelas*, in the world. Azcárraga Milmo set the style of the *telenovelas*. One formula became known as the "María" *telenovelas*. Predominantly fair heroines, maids in the houses of the rich, played out Cinderella stories by marrying the son of the house. Another formula was first used by the *telenovela* writer, Fernanda Villeli, in the 1960 *telenovela, Senda Prohibida*. It was a reverse fairy tale. The younger mistress of an older man, typically a young woman who has come to the city from the pueblo, is finally rejected in favor of the wife (Fernández & Paxman, 2000: 77).

The conventions governing the *telenovela* were very strict: no smoking, no poverty, no abortion, no politicians, noone of Indian descent, except as maids or laborers. Azcárraga Milmo himself kept a close watch on the themes as well as the budding actresses (Fernández & Paxman, 2000: 211-212), as did the government censors who sat in the background during filming (Quiñones, 1998; 41). Azcárraga Milmo is quoted as saying

> Mexico is a country with a large class of people who are screwed. Television's responsibility is to bring these people entertainment and distract them from their sad reality and difficult future. (Quiñones, 1998; 42)

From the actresses and crew, to the studios and the production houses, Televisa had complete control. They owned each stage of the process of producing and distributing *telenovelas*. And it was an enormously profitable business. Televisa claimed its sales of *telenovelas* were Mexico's largest export, with markets in 125 countries outside Latin America, including Eastern Europe, Vietnam, China and now France. With a monopoly in Mexico, cheap labor costs, and an industry that was both horizontally and vertically integrated, Televisa's *telenovelas* were a cash cow. Televisa kept close to the PRI, and Azcárrago Milmo was friend to virtually every president.

This was to change with the deregulatory policies of the government of Carlos Salinas Gortari (1988-1994). The commercial television sector was opened to competition. In 1993, the Government sold two of its stations to Televisión Azteca, commonly known as TV Azteca. In the meantime, the political tone of the country was changing, and the PRI domination faltering. When Azcárraga Milmo died in 1997, his son Azcárraga Jean took over. In the meantime, TV Azteca made a real attempt to challenge the ratings of Televisa. It began producing soap operas of startling relevance in co-production with smaller companies. No longer reverential about government and politicians, the new *telenovelas* literally described what was happening in the country. Days after political events occurred they appeared in a fictionalized form in *telenovelas* such as *Nada Personal*. Drugs, AIDS, teenage pregnancy, and political assassination proliferated in plots.

It was in this context that *Mirada de Mujer* appeared midway through

1997. It took TV Azteca ahead in the ratings war and shook the *telenovela* industry to the core. It was written by Bernado Romero and Mónica Agudelo and was produced under Epigmenio Ibarra in a co-production between the company Argos and TV Azteca. It is the tale of the separation of a wealthy Mexico City couple, their children and their younger lovers, the mistress of the man, and the younger lover taken by his wife after they had separated. *Mirada de Mujer*, roughly, "a woman's glance," was shown every night at 9:00 p.m. It was at the higher end of the quality *telenovela*s and dealt with a woman *d'un certain age*, María Inés, whose wealthy husband abandoned her for a younger professional woman. María Inés' entire life had revolved around her husband and children, and in the process of reconstructing her life she took a younger lover, helped her children through unwanted pregnancy and other disasters, and supported her best friend as she died of AIDS.

In terms of the impact of television, *Mirada de Mujer* was an extraordinary phenomenon. The events of each episode provided a constant topic of conversation among the multitudinous middle classes of Mexico City. In fact, the crises of María Inés' life provoked almost as much debate in the quality Mexican press as the political changes occurring over the same period. She was denounced as immoral. The very direction of the plot was sometimes influenced by the fury of the public reaction. For example, when María Inés' elder daughter was pregnant, she decided to have an abortion, although this was still illegal in Mexico. The public reaction proved to be so violent during the week this was screening that the producers chose to let the daughter have a miscarriage instead.

*Mirada de Mujer*, in spite of its concessions to public opinion, was one of a group that had produced a breakthrough in Mexican *telenovela*s. The earlier TV Azteca series *Nada Personal* ("Nothing Personal") dealt with political issues and quite explicitly drew on current events to suggest the corruption in government and PRI circles. Yet *Mirada de Mujer* was exceptional: never before and rarely since have the Mexican bourgeois stereotypes been so blatantly confronted in a *telenovela*. There is a moving moment early in the series when María Inés' husband Ignacio, a wealthy lawyer, rejects her advances and says:

Ignacio: María Inés, don't say you still have desires at your age?

She replies

María Inés: Of course, don't you feel anything, Ignacio?

The assumption that a man will take a younger mistress because he "needs" to—an assumption still current among the Mexican middle class—is challenged directly here. Within this *telenovela* the figure of Paulina, a divorced contemporary of María Inés, is the stereotype of an elegant but ruthless female sexual predator familiar from Televisa *telenovelas*. It is Paulina who dies of AIDS. María Inés, however, is a quite different character and is portrayed as the ideal mother, loving, warm and devoted to her children, who learns to work and create her own life and loves. Her taking a younger lover simply cannot be shrugged off as the act of an immoral woman like Paulina.

Angélica Aragón, the actress who played María Inés, has an immense following among the Mexican people and her behavior, even within the *telenovela*, has become synonymous with probity. The characteristic close-ups of the *telenovela* genre allowed her to use a wide range of subtle facial expressions to convey views utterly at odds with the dominant style of the Mexican middle class. She became the focus of the *telenovela*, with her affair with the much younger journalist, Alejandro, becoming the emotional center of the plot to an unusual degree. In fact, the unraveling of the subplots became even more marginal than is usual in such *telenovela*s. The romantic central plot was atypical, too, in that it could not, or did not, end well—the journalist took a job in Italy, urged on by the selfless María Inés, and the relationship ended. It was an ending that neither audience nor actors found satisfactory.

*Mirada de Mujer* dealt with issues that provoked a storm of controversy in Mexico City. The *telenovela* opened a space for discussion in quite a new way, concerning itself with the morality of the characters' behavior. The heroine was a Mexican—devoted to her family, her mother, her children and her domestic activities. As such, she was clearly a role model for Mexican women. While Mexican audiences are saturated with U.S. soaps, they do not take the ethical issues seriously. In the United States, they think, anything goes. A *telenovela* about Mexicans is different. The relentless pace of the plot confronted the middle-class populace with issues they had thought of as belonging to others. The questions were, as in most soap operas, mainly domestic issues, but they were presented in a tone of a larger debate: in the language of a larger world.

This was clearly intentional. Among the crucial elements in the impact of *Mirada de Mujer* is the self-consciousness of those involved in producing and acting in the *telenovela*. The actors and producers knew what they were doing and were well aware of the impact the story would have. In a seminar broadcast direct to students across Central America from the Technological University of Monterrey (*Reforma*, 1997), the producer, Epigmenio Ibarra, made it clear that the *telenovela* was intended to have the effect of encouraging debate. He denied, however, that it would in any way undermine values.

> [It] was envisaged as a 'mirror of society'...to talk of the disintegration of
> the family is not to foster disintegration, but to encourage discussion of the
> causes of disintegration. We hoped to initiate debate with the soap opera, to
> provoke polemic, reflections. *(Reforma*, 1997: 9E)

Ibarra's view of the role of the *telenovela* is that it should portray social issues confronting a society but which, for one reason or another, are being ignored by that society. Angélica Aragón, the actress who portrayed María Inés, put the point clearly when she said, "The *telenovela* treats themes that society conceals, and it does so in an honest, realistic and ultimately valuable way." *(Reforma*, 1997: 9E) The *telenovela*, that is, provides a testing ground for ethical attitudes and a starting point for debate. Professor José Carlos Lozano put it thus:

> In many countries of the world, soap operas or their equivalents are de-
> signed to generate controversy, precisely because they focus on social and
> personal problems. In Quebec, the *téléroman* is a barometer of public opin-
> ion... In Brazil too... It is a positive and healthy thing that a soap opera cre-
> ates a forum of discussion. *Mirada de Mujer* does so with characters that are
> not one dimensional, they are neither obviously good, nor obviously bad...
> And perhaps this is what has generated the controversy: when a soap tells us
> what is good or bad, the problem is clear, whereas in the case of this soap,
> the responsibility of defining good and bad is left to the audience... (*Reforma*,
> 1997: 9E)

The soap opera, like the novel of the nineteenth century, gives the imaginative space in which moral debate can take place. Some are better than others at engendering debate — at outlining the moral possibilities. The impact of *Mirada de Mujer* was a function of its relevance and its success in personalizing the social issues that are so often ignored in Mexico. Those reactions were various, at times criticizing and others approving the morality implicit in the *telenovela*. They used *Mirada de Mujer* as a starting point not the end point of ethical questioning. As one leading columnist in Mexico, Germán Dehesa says in an introduction to the novelistic version of the *telenovela*:

> Truly there were many successes, discoveries and novelties that *Mirada de Mujer* brought to Mexican television. One of them was the fluidity and naturalism of the dialogue…[Yet] The morality implicit in the illness of Paulina, who was the most liberated woman of the drama, implies a somewhat reactionary morality. (Romero & Agudelo, 1998: 7-8)

It is not so much television show itself, but the debate about television, that is important. The framing of the social debate in Mexico was significantly altered by the discussion of *Mirada de Mujer*. However, the debate does not end with viewing. A divorce in a soap is not an argument for divorce, but the basis for further questioning. The difficulty is establishing with what criteria the debate should be conducted. What is lacking is the framework of argumentation in which, even if it is impossible to answer the questions, an approach can be made. It is at this point that philosophical traditions, and the sorts of questions philosophers raise, provide a structure for developing talk about television.

## ETHICAL DISPUTES

Talking about ethical questions happens at two interrelated levels. When the dinner parties of Mexico city discussed whether María Inés' behavior was or was not appropriate, the debate generally stayed at the level of searching for justifications of, or good reasons for condemning, her behavior. It rarely moved to the level of a search for ethical principles underlying the judgments. The process of evaluating the ethical reasoning itself is at the heart of the philosophical understanding of moral debate.

This is not to say that moral chat at the dinner table is without value. To raise the issue of the asymmetry that exists between what counts as acceptable behavior for middle aged men and women in Mexico prompts questions which are fundamentally important in the society—questions which concern not only the middle class but also the lower middle class in which a startlingly high proportion of children are raised in female-headed single-parent households with absolutely no access to any form of social security. Raising the question of such behavioral asymmetry is crucial to any recognition of the need for social change.

Implicit in any discussion of such issues, however, is an appeal to notions like "fairness" or justice. "Why shouldn't María Inés take a lover? — Ignacio did," is an implicit appeal to justice—versions of a principle that Hare (1952) labels "universalizability." Universalizability states that moral judgment appropriate for one person in particular circumstances should equally apply to a similar person in the same circumstances. As an ethical principle, this does seem to encapsulate one important element of fairness: treat like cases likewise, so long as they are similar in the relevant respects.

Thus, the principle itself leaves open the issue of whether men and women are similar in the relevant respect when it comes to sexual liberation. The response of the traditional *macho* men is that men have a right to sexual freedom but women do not. From the perspective of most people today, that is absurd. Certainly there have been principles restricting women's sexual freedom in many societies: principles that were presumably derived from the need to protect men from supporting another man's children. Those principles are now no longer generally accepted. However, there are still those committed to the principle that there is a gender-based difference in what counts as appropriate sexual behavior. How should the debate proceed?

If we remain at the level of what each thinks is right, then indeed there can be nothing to debate. Mired in ethical relativism, the debate stops. What is right for the *machos* is right for them, but not for those who disagree. The debate, however, can go forward, by searching for the underlying principles that inform the judgments and attempting to evaluate those principles. We could look at the justification for using gender as the basis of discrimination between sexual behavior. There are, after all, good reasons for accepting that age is a basis for discrimination with respect to sexual behavior. Children who are different in no other respect except age are treated differently by the law and by most moral principles in respect to sexual behavior. That seems right—age is a salient difference when it comes to sexual behavior because we accept that those who are immature need protection. Can we find a similar difference, however, with respect to gender? There is no obvious reason linking gender and sexual behavior. Gender is not a relevant basis of discrimination in the same way as age.

However confidently we assert that there is no relevant difference, the committed *macho* man may persist in his beliefs. The strategies for challenging the view are various. We could ask this person to try the thought experiment of the Rawlsian (1972) "veil of ignorance." A just society is one in which, even were you not to know your role in the society, you would accept the principles in force. Would the *macho* man accept the veil of ignorance test for a society that treated men and women differently in this regard? What if he were a woman in that society? Surely then he would not argue so strongly for the asymmetry? After all, being unable to choose how to behave is what is at issue. If the *macho* man really believes that a just society is asymmetrical with respect to sexual behavior, then everyone should accept the asymmetry, women as well as men.

Another strategy would be to ask the *macho* to agree that if an action is good it should lead to the best outcome. The utilitarian will hope to maximize the happiness of all. Consider two societies, one in which the attitudes toward the sexual behavior of men and women were similar and one in which they were not. Surely the society with the asymmetry would be less happy than the symmetric, given that it would be possible for all, not just half of the population, to choose how to act sexually.[11]

This very crude sketch of the ethical debate shows only how the debate might go. The assumption is that it is worth debating ethical issues. However this assumption is not acceptable to an out-and-out ethical relativist. The ethical relativist does not occupy a comfortable philosophical position. It is essential to our notion of good that we think of it as applying to actions in general. If we are content to allow each person their own view of what is "good," "good" simply becomes a matter of taste. There are many forms of ethical relativism, claiming that what is right is relative to the person judging (subjectivism) or the culture in which they live (cultural relativism). The force of "this is right" and other ethical statements is thus dependent either on who is speaking, or from what culture they come. The consequences of adopting such relativist claims are potentially para-

---

11  This is far too rapid. However the argument is not of course that sexual liberation makes for happiness, just that the freedom of choice is important to happiness.

doxical. From what cultural perspective, for instance, is it true to say that what is right is relative to a culture?

What is important for encouraging philosophical debate about such issues is that there is a constant interplay between the level of application and that of principle. A moral dilemma of this sort is a dilemma precisely because there is no one easy solution. Were we to accept the ruling of the church on an issue, there would be nothing ethical about the decision; it would just be rule-following. The possibility of a tension in views, the possibility of a real, not trivial, disagreement is at the heart of ethics. The example of the question of gender-based discrimination about sexual behavior is not a hot ethical debate in Western societies—there is almost general agreement that discrimination is wrong. However, it serves as an example of the process of refinement that debate about ethical issues requires.

Soap opera is well suited to develop issues that are genuinely divisive within a society, since soap operas are successful only if they grab the audience's attention. Effective soap operas cut to the underlying angst of a society. *Neighbours* was very successful in part because it coexisted with the loss of the neighborhood. As more and more families in the First World consisted of two working parents and children, all of whom rushed from the suburbs early in the day, the networks of community have been lost. The notion of supportive, or even gossiping neighbors, became a space that needed to be revisited and thought about. *Party of Five*, likewise, raises the fear of the disintegrating family insofar as the children are orphans, supporting each other against the community. *Mirada de Mujer* was remarkable for the light it threw on Mexican social practices.

### DISCOURSE ETHICS

Ethical disputes often do arise from soap operas, even those less provocative than *Mirada de Mujer*. Pertinent though soap operas may be, however, they cannot alone embody the ethical debate that needs to be conducted. To develop a perspective on ethical debate and to avoid the stalemate of raw ethical difference, it is necessary to talk about the process of ethical debate itself. We look for principles to guide ethical decision-making—principles in the light of which difficult decisions can be made. Such metaethical debate is at the heart of the philosophical traditions of ethics.

There is a metaethical theory, again due to Habermas (1987), that suggests that it is debate that defines the ethical sphere. It is this theory that is called "discourse ethics," the theory that ethics consists of a well-governed debate on the issue of what is right. Discourse ethics emphasizes the importance of justification and argument in ethical judgment. When we argue about ethical issues, we might on the one hand call on a moral authority, such as the Bible or the Koran, or appeal to an overarching ethical principle such as that inherent in utilitarianism, to maximise happiness. On the other hand, we might seek to justify particular moral positions by drawing out their consequences or by seeking the assumptions of adopting those views. For one who espouses discourse ethics, the practices of justification characterize a position as ethical, rather than the claims of moral authorities. The theory can be contrasted with the utilitarian view that the ultimate judgment of what is right depends on the consequences of an action. For the utilitarian, the subtle process of evaluating outcomes of actions is at the heart of ethics. For those who believe in discourse ethics, it is the process of examining issues in terms of criteria of good argumentation that is at the heart of ethical judgment.

The relativist will not accept either the utilitarian or discourse-based views about ethics. For the relativist, what is right is relative to a society. Even to talk of the consequences of actions is, for a relativist, to prejudge what each society values. Moreover, to talk of ethical debate conducted according to criteria is also to prejudge what counts as criteria of good debate. Can we expect that those with profound differences in values will be able to resolve the differences in a well-conducted debate? Is it not possible that the debate may never be resolved? There may be a profound disagreement about what counts as the criteria for conducting the debate.

Habermas is optimistic that there can be a universal procedure for rational debate about ethical issues. Others are less certain. Thompson (1998)[12] discusses a range of positions that might be defended by those who suggest that ethics should best be defined in terms of practices of ethical debate. One version of this position is that in which the procedures

---

[12] My arguments relating to ethical disagreement were based on an earlier paper by Janna Thompson, which has since been revised in her *Discourse and Knowledge* (1998).

of justification are universal—one aspires to the sort of justification that would sway any interlocutor of any ethnic, cultural, or linguistic background. Such a view of discourse ethics differs at most in detail from traditional consequentialist accounts. The justification of an action would, in this version, have to be such that it would sway anyone to agreement given relevantly similar circumstances. This is in effect a return to the principle of universalizability.

It is important to note that this version does not allow genuine ethical disagreement. If one is in a position to hear the arguments, one should be in a position to arrive at the same conclusion. Paradoxically, this view of the process of justifying ethical decisions yields the same result as ethical relativism—there can be no substantial disagreement about ethical issues.

However, Thompson points out that there is an alternative version of discourse ethics, a version that allows that the process of justifying ethical views cannot be guaranteed to yield a unique outcome. Precisely because participants in the debate may come from varied backgrounds, it might be that—even after the most extensive and rigorous examination of views— no single course of action would fulfil the ethical imperatives. The existence of different backgrounds may prevent agents from agreeing to the relevant universal principle.[13] Universalizability simply does not apply once one admits that certain aspects of difference may be relevant to ethical decisions. Particular social relations, for instance, may be relevant to a judgment of what is right for me that could not be relevant to others— those who are not women, for instance.

Thompson suggests that we should not see the failure of universalizability as a flaw, but rather as the virtue of this second version of discourse ethics. The model of ethics as based on a process of judgment and argument is one that gives difference a role. If, in the long run, everyone should come to agreement on what is right, then the model of discourse

---

[13]  Pettit (1992) argues that the consequentialist can accommodate certain of the apparently special ethical imperatives, such as the imperative to save the life of one's own child, but not—at least with equal force—that of another's child. The point being made here is that such personal ethical obligations are just a subset of a larger set of perspectival ethical principles. Peter Singer also argues for special duties within a utilitarian framework (August, 2000) during the Jack Smart Lecture, Australian National University.

ethics is merely a heuristic device. If, on the other hand, we take ethical
difference seriously, then difference might survive the process of ethical
debate. We should not take ethical disagreement lightly, for it is a serious
matter worthy of attention and reasoned argument. But we cannot assume
it is eliminable. Indeed, by allowing for difference we build into the procedures of discourse ethics the respect for persons and for difference that
underpins many of our relativistic leanings.

Clearly it is possible for intransigent differences to emerge or to remain. Advocating a process of ethical debate about soap opera, however,
requires only the belief that debate about the ethical issues being raised is
important. This is central to the move towards making sense of television.

## *PARTY OF FIVE*: DEVELOPING A WEB SITE OF ETHICAL QUESTIONS

How can we encourage higher-level ethical debate about television
products? One way is to use it as the beginning of a process of philosophical inquiry. In principle, a Socratic dialogue about the soap opera or an
episode of *The Simpsons* would be the ideal. One could imagine questions
such as:

> What do you think were the moral issues underlying the episode when Mel
> Gibson joined Bart Simpson to revise his movie, and made it even more vio-
> lent? Do you think violent television makes us violent?

In practice, with my own and others' children, the Socratic dialogue
while the television program is on has proved a disaster. Kids do not want
to be interrupted when they are laughing at *The Simpsons*, although they
will happily talk about it later. What is needed is a structured space in
which to talk about ethical issues, in particular on television—a space
where there is time to rethink just what is happening in a certain program.

This was the aim behind the design of the *Reason and Media* web site.
The strategy was to make a short excerpt of television product available
online, together with the possibility of discussion about it. The aim, of
course, was to encourage a particular sort of debate, based on television
but different from the familiar style of prurient speculation or questions of
"who won"—a debate, instead, about the philosophical and logical moves
made in television product. It is here that soap operas can offer fertile
ground. The *Party of Five* episode, discussed at the beginning of the chap-

ter, is particularly suitable for ethical debate for just the same reason as it is successful television — it makes vivid a disturbing moral dilemma. However, moral dilemmas take us nowhere, unless we examine the reasoning involved to see how the lesson applies in other cases. It was obvious in the New Jersey classroom (mentioned earlier in this chapter) that children wanted to engage in reasoning about the episode. After all, it is part of their culture.

On the web site, unfortunately, the discussion group cannot be as vivid as that engendered by a face-to-face debate. However, I found that students do participate. Each video clip came with a transcript and animated *gif* for those with slower machines. Following from this there was a page of "Big Ideas." In this case I wrote a series of relatively simple questions:

> While looking at this excerpt from *Party of Five* (or reading the transcript if you wish), think about these questions.
>
> 1) What is a lie? Is it ever right to lie?
> 2) Claudia says "You can't have him get in his car and drive all the way over here thinking that. You don't think this is the cruelest thing you could do to a person?" What does it mean to say that some things you shouldn't do to a person?
> 3) Is Julia fair to ask Claudia whether she is willing to do anything to get Bai over? When do the ends justify the means?
> 4) Who has responsibility for Bailey? Does the family?
> 5) Charlie says: "If it's you, Claude, if you call him and say that you need his help and don't know what to do, then he'll believe you and he'll come." If this is true what follows? Does it follow that no one else could get Bailey to come?
> 6) When Claudia says "That's a terrible thing to do", is it because of the consequences and context of the action, or just because lying is always wrong?
> 7) Look again at the excerpt. Does it make you feel how Claudia feels? How?

The questions relate to each of the Big Ideas. So, for instance, questions relating to lying are:

> **What is a lie?**
> 1) What is the difference between a lie and a mistake?
> 2) Could you tell a lie and still be telling the truth?
> 3) Could you tell a lie without saying anything?
> 4) Can a dog tell a lie?

5) Could you tell a lie if you had never learned a language?
6) If you told a lie and it turned out to be true, would you have done something wrong?
7) If you thought you were telling the truth and it turned out to be wrong, would you have done something wrong?

Notice that these questions are by no means trivial. The first group is an attempt to clarify the concept of a lie. The questions invite readers to think about how a lie works and the connection between intention and meaning. A well-motivated error is not a lie. Then the questioning turns to the relationship between having a language and the possibility of lying. Again this is a very complex issue: those who believe that only language use allows a concept of truth will be obliged to say that animals cannot lie. Lies that turn out to be true are also strange: such as when I intend to mislead you saying that there was an earthquake, but one did indeed occur. Is this a lie? Is it culpable?

The second group of questions takes us directly to the moral issue of when it is right to tell a lie. Rather than begin with a debate about the nature of ethical behavior, these questions invite readers to provide their own judgements, with each question carefully graded to suggest counter examples to possible answers to previous questions. So for instance, the list reads:

**When is it right to tell a lie?**
1) If by telling a lie that hurt no one you could make one person very happy, should you tell that lie?
2) If telling the truth would make someone very unhappy and would not benefit anyone else, should you tell a lie?
3) Should you tell a lie to save someone's life?
4) If by telling a lie you could save 100,000 lives, should you tell the lie?
5) Is it better to lie to save 100,000 lives than to tell a lie to save one life?
6) Are there some lies you should never tell?
7) Should Claudia have lied to Bailey?

The question-and-answer page allows those using the page to make their own responses and comment on those made by others. So for instance, one student in response to the question "Is it ever right to lie?" answered:

This is a really hard question. The easy answer is just to say that lying is always wrong but we live in the real world. So when does the end justify the means? I borrow from the Shaolin monks in their saying: Avoid rather than check/ check rather than hurt/ hurt rather than maim/ maim rather than kill. What does this mean? In my humble opinion if it takes a small infraction to prevent a larger one, then it's okay. (first-year student, University of Canberra, 2000)

The mixture of consequentialism and Eastern tags leaves room for much debate, but there is a genuine sense of engagement in the response and the beginning of an argument. The question-and-answer page allows the issue to be debated between students.

Another set of questions deals with the nature of persons and the fact that Claudia is concerned that her siblings are not treating Bailey as a person. The questions are again carefully graded. Here the pattern of questions begins with a discussion plan, based on one from the Philosophy for Children Program.

**Discussion plan: Putting oneself in another's place.**
1) Can you describe what it feels like to be you?
2) Can you describe your best friend as he or she appears to you?
3) Can you tell how it feels to be that other person? How can you tell?

**Exercise: What makes you you?**
1) What is there about you that makes you you?
2) If you had a different name, would you still be you?
3) If you had a different face, would you still be you?
4) If, for some reason, you couldn't use your arm, would you still be you?
5) If, for some reason, you couldn't use your mind, would you still be you?
6) Are you the same person you were yesterday?
7) Are you the same person you were last year at this time?
8) Are you the same person you were ten years ago?
9) Are you the same person you were when you were born?
10) If you had a twin, would you still be you?
11) Would you still be you if you had an operation to change your fingerprints?
12) If you and your best friend could change minds, so that you would think all his thoughts and he'd think all yours, would you still be you?

These questions, again based on the Philosophy for Children Program, open a Pandora's box of issues about personal identity, change, and development. Question 10 asks about genetic identity as a criterion of personal identity and raises the questions related to whether identity is a matter of nature or environment. Question 12 raises the question of whether bodily continuity or mental continuity should count as the basis of personal identity. With young children the issue can be made vivid by asking:

> If you changed your body with your best friend, so your mind was in another body, whose home would you go to, the body's or the mind's?

We would not expect television viewers to come up with responses that would contribute to a sophisticated philosophical debate, just as we would not expect untrained historians or mathematicians to contribute to current debates in the forefront of the field, but we can introduce philosophical questions as they arise. For philosophical questions can be formulated in terms familiar to the television viewer. Indeed, they arise out of the practice of television viewing. For this reason, even if the level of debate may not be sophisticated, it is a debate that is worth having. Plato thought philosophy too dangerous to be taught to any but the most gifted and then not until maturity. Not teaching philosophy might be even worse.

## CONCLUSION

Television is an important part of the lives of children. Children talk about television in the school yard, on the bus, with their friends. They are willing to talk about television with teachers too, as long they can talk about the episodes they have seen and their own views of television.[14] Children do not want to be told that they are being manipulated by media conglomerates, advertising firms or the government. They want to talk about the content of television: the programs they watch and dream about; the people who, as much as their real life friends, inhabit their worlds. All too often media education programs repeat the stale messages of those for whom television is a trivial medium.

I am suggesting that we have failed to listen to what kids are talking about. They are longing to find ways of talking about what they see. Our experience, in the New Jersey classroom, as elsewhere, is that children leap at the chance to add rigor to their discussions of television. At times, of course, particularly in mid-flow of the plot, they will not want to stop

---

14   The evidence for this claim comes from many hours of discussing television with children, but for further evidence see e.g. Buckingham *passim*. My point is that children do not want to be told about television, they want to talk about it.

and talk: they will prefer to think and wait to talk after a program has finished. This is only to be expected: readers feel the same about literature.

The debates generated by television are at the heart of social debate. Moral and ethical issues abound. Soap operas, in particular, are uniquely well endowed with the outlines of moral decisions taken in domestic settings. They provide, in fact, the bones on which the flesh of ethical argumentation can be—and should be—fruitfully developed.

## MEDIA EFFECTS

*South Park,* created by the youthful Trey Parker and Matt Stone from animated images drawn on brown paper, was first seen in 1996 on the Internet in a bootleg episode called "The Spirit of Christmas." This, the first of the cartoon series, describes a kung fu match between Santa Claus and Jesus over who owns Christmas. They are watched by two of the four 10-year-old boys, Kyle, Stan, Cartman and Kenny, who live in South Park, Colorado, and who form the core of the program.

Stan:Here we are Jesus, South Park Mall. Who are you looking for?

Jesus: Him.

Santa: Hoh, hoh hoh, we meet again, Jesus.

Jesus: You have blemished the meaning of Christmas. For the last time, Kringle.

Santa: I bring happiness and love to children all over the world.

Jesus: Christmas is for celebrating my birth.

Santa: Christmas is for giving.

Jesus: I am here to put an end to your blasphemy.

Santa: This time we finish it. There can be only one.

Stan & Kyle: this is pretty fucked up right here…

Santa: Jesus: ah…YAH! *(kung fu kick)*

Stan & Kyle: Go Santa! *(pause. Jesus looks over angrily)*

Stan & Kyle: uhhhhh, Go Jesus!

The Christmas episode gets its humor from the juxtaposition of Jesus and Santa Claus, the central figures of the Christmas myth who are purportedly figures of "good will towards men" fighting it out. Santa leaps up to confront Jesus, unceremoniously unseating a small child and tipping her from his lap onto the ground. Then Santa and Jesus stand off in classic *kung fu* poses. The violence is absurd and amusing and serves as a device to trigger a sense of the hypocrisy of much of the Christmas cant. Neither Jesus nor Santa is hurt, and the violence, like most cartoon violence, is purely for show.

The real South Park is near Denver, and the characters are an agglomeration of the children of the two creators' childhoods. The Jewish Kyle is based on Stone, Stan on Trey, and the others on friends or, better, acquaintances. As Trey Parker puts it:

> The bus stop sort of dictated who your friends were. It wasn't like you
> picked your friends. It was who was at your bus stop. (*Aerial*, 1998: 7)

Kenny, the almost incomprehensible and most sophisticated of the children, is killed in the first cartoon—as he is in every subsequent episode, in increasingly baroque ways. "The Spirit of Christmas" was an immediate cult success.

Despite the profanity of the cartoon, it was picked up in August 1997 by Comedy Central, where it was aired on Wednesday nights at 10 p.m. and received cable's highest-ever rating points.[1] In the U.S. in June 1998 the audience was reported at 4.5 million viewers, of which most were in the 18–24 age group.[2] SBS carried the program in Australia.[3] The outrage the program generated was defused by moving it from its 7:30 p.m. time-

---

[1]   It has had an average of 3 to 5 points since its debut in August of 1997.

[2]   More specifically, 50.1% are men aged 18 to 24 and 35.9% are women aged 18 to 24. However, cable TV figures, however high, still do not compete with the network figures. As Robert Allen, professor of communications, University of North Carolina puts it: "Remember this is on Comedy Central, it's definitely a minority viewing option for most Americans." (ABC Media Report, 1998)

[3]   No Mexican figures or comments on *South Park* are cited, because it has not been available on free-to-air or Mexican cable TV. Illegal cable TV operators have been tapping into US cable TV. Some wealthy individuals in Mexico City know the program.

slot to the later time of 9:30 p.m. on Mondays. Nevertheless, it remained the highest-rating show on SBS.[4] The show has spawned a huge number of Internet sites, including the official site owned by the U.S. cable network and a "Rights for Kenny" page.

The program continues to generate controversy. The press has run hot with articles analysing, decrying, or deifying *South Park* as immoral, postmodern, crude, or just childish. The fictional location is just next door to Columbine High School, in Littleton, Colorado, where two students went on a violent rampage on April 20, 1999, killing fifteen. The random violence, the vulgarity, and the skewed values evident in *South Park* were, it was suggested, related to the Columbine High School disaster.

That reaction is excessive. In this chapter we begin with the controversy over the impact of vulgar and violent television, such as is seen in *South Park*, then turn to the impact cartoon images have on youth, and the ways cartoons function on television. Finally, we turn to the possibilities of moral debate inherent in some episodes of *South Park*. This chapter looks closely at the argumentation of one of the programs dealing with genetic engineering. Entitled "An Elephant Makes Love to a Pig," the episode begins with the elephant being presented to the school bus driver as "the new disabled kid at school." The program opens a debate on the virtues of genetic engineering with the teacher's hand puppet, Mr. Hat, saying, "We could have avoided terrible mistakes, like German people." The show both offends and ridicules received moral values and does so with an astonishingly excessive use of violence. However, analysis of "An Elephant Makes Love to a Pig" shows how superficially absurd situations conceal sophisticated argumentation strategies. The violence of *South Park* is unlikely to lead children to violence. It is a trick for garnering attention and can serve to persuade children to focus on issues of some importance.

## IS *SOUTH PARK* PROSOCIAL?

When Stan's homosexual dog runs away to learn about gay rights, or when Jesus is cut off by a commercial break just as he is about to reveal

---

[4]    The viewership on SBS, the multicultural government network in Australia, is normally negligible. With *South Park*, viewership rose to 1.3 million, with about 45% of viewers in the 13- to 24- year old age group. (ABC Media Report, 1998:.8)

how he feels about homosexuality, humor and crudeness are being used on complex issues, with some sensitivity. Doug Stewart, the censor at SBS, says:

> Paradoxically, it's a quite prosocial series, I mean it's satirising things like racism and sexism and homophobia, it's satirising gun culture, fast food advertising on television, mindless television. (ABC Media Report, 1998: 8)

The "prosocial" view is taken to the extreme in *Spin* magazine's March 1998 issue, in which the cartoon is given a disembodied life as a course in moral education, or as a series of moral fables, by eliminating the vulgarity and sexism and reducing each episode to brief synopsis, media references, and moral values (Norris, 1998). In a similar vein, Fox executive Brian Graden is quoted as saying:

> If you pay attention, they tell good stories about issues, but people think they're watching some naughty cartoon…There are some things that are kind of wholesome about *South Park*. The bottom line is that as insane as it gets, right always sort of wins. (McDonald, 1998)

In fact, the moral force of *South Park* has become a matter of constant media debate. Robert Bolton, Professor of Communications at the University of North Carolina takes a more balanced view, arguing that:

> I don't think that *South Park* has a particular political agenda, and I think it shares this kind of very profound political ambivalence with an awful lot of popular culture in America…. What it does do is open up as a source of humor an awful lot of things that could either be read as being left or right. (ABC Media Report, 1998:4)

Writing in *The Australian*, Helen Musa, on the other hand, is scornful of such suggestions.

> If you have not yet indulged…you should know that this cartoon…has spurned a truckload of pretentious talk…. Really *South Park* says as much about contemporary theories of representation as the Nescafé ad did about the shifting nature of gender relations. Nothing. (1998:15)

Interestingly, the diametrically opposed views of the critics share a fundamental assumption: that the moral impact of the program is the responsibility of the program producers and writers. Even those who understand the vagaries of audiences tend to treat the audience as monolithic when discussing shows like *South Park*. For those who advocate *South Park*, the program deals with moral issues, so it is prosocial. For those with the opposite view, *South Park* ignores the basic human values, and glorifies random violence, so it is dangerous. Neither view takes account of the importance of audience reaction. *South Park* itself is a funny and somewhat simplistic parody of a range of views, some of which are worthy of criticism. However, children are watching *South Park* and laughing at the jokes days after they first saw the program. The issues are hot and kids talk about them. Indeed, those who are not allowed to watch feel left out of many social circles.

But that does not mean we should take *South Park* as it comes. The issues raised can and should be discussed not just in the style of playground reminiscence but critically, with an eye to making children aware of the philosophical angst that grounds much of the humor with its objectionable racism, sexism, and sheer crudity.

The varying attitudes about *South Park* follow a trajectory familiar to that great cult cartoon program of the 1990s, *The Simpsons*. When it was first introduced in 1990, Mrs. Bush is claimed to have said that it was "the dumbest program" she had ever seen (Sutel, 2000). Now, ten years later, with *The Simpsons* occupying the position of the longest-running American prime-time program still showing, and with an audience that is truly global, intellectuals have added their imprimateur. Stephen Jay Gould and Stephen Hawking have made guest (voice) appearances, and critics talk of the fundamental values of the program: "At the end of the day, though, the positive message of familiar love pushes through all the cultural satire." (Sutel, 2000)

*South Park*, like *The Simpsons*, turns an ironic eye on the questions of the day. Self-righteousness and bombast of all sorts are taken up as ripe ground for ridicule. Moral issues breed the attitudes that cartoonists can send up. Politically correct views tend to be intolerant, lacking in openness to critical views. It is easy, and at the same time shocking, to ridicule such views. Humor in these cases derives from the unexpected conjunction of events or attitudes: an element of shock or surprise is essential. Bart Simpson and his father, Homer, are the paradigms of cartoon incongruity. They espouse, with all the bigotry of the self-righteous, attitudes that are utterly unacceptable to everyday middle-class morality. They are funny because they are inappropriate. When Homer absent-mindedly dips a finger into a

100 SPEAKING OF *SOUTH PARK*

tube of radioactive substance to taste it or fails to remember his baby's name, he is doing the unthinkable. That opens up the space for both adults and children to think about why we hold the views that we do, for instance about remembering the names of our children.

Humor is a powerful weapon. Humor juxtaposes unexpected elements and takes us outside our familiar paradigms of viewing the world, allowing us to look afresh. The role of humor in cartoons is worth discussing, especially with those who are amused by cartoons. This set of questions from the *Reason and Media* web site were designed to begin the debate about the role of humor.

**Why is it funny?**

There are many theories about what makes people laugh. Some people think we laugh when we are almost afraid. Other people think that we laugh when we hear or see something unexpected—or ridiculous. Ridiculous, of course, just means likely to make you laugh, so we cannot define what is funny by saying it is ridiculous.

Try to think about what is funny. Did you laugh in the episode in *South Park*? When? Now think about these general questions about humor.

1) Can you imagine laughing when someone falls over, or talks about toilets, or farts? When? Describe the circumstances.
2) Can you imagine laughing when someone shocks you? When? Describe the circumstances.
3) Can you imagine laughing when someone ridicules people who are important? When? Describe the circumstances.
4) Do you like laughing? Why?
5) Do you sometimes laugh even when you don't want to?
6) Do you ever laugh just remembering something funny? Why?
7) Can the same joke be funny twice? If it is, is it funny in the same way twice?

Answers to these questions, debatable although they might be, should suggest some of the appeal of *South Park*. The program is funny because it turns what is accepted as normal into absurd situations; it questions and refigures the framework of accepted behavior. By perceiving the incongruity of "inappropriate" actions, we become aware that being "appropriate" is very restrictive. The humor of *South Park* is not the slapstick humor of people falling over, of pies, and simple misunderstanding. It is the humor of social criticism, the sort of humor that can be remembered as funny. It does not depend on simple feature of an absurd situation, as slap-

but instead relies on the social context of events, ridiculing social norms and pretension. Of course, humor in *South Park* does depend at times on crudity, at times on toilet humor, and at others on blasphemy and inappropriate violence. But then social criticism that uses humor often makes use of such blunt weapons—think, for example, of *Gulliver's Travels*. Cartoons like *South Park* make audiences laugh time after time. The sheer force of the humor has given the cartoon series the status of a cult classic.

*South Park*, in itself, is not prosocial. It raises social issues in a peculiarly direct and catchy way. It is for those who watch the program to discern and debate the moral issues. The cool of the program and its ability to tap into the concerns of youth make it an obvious site for beginning debate. Of course cartoons and caricatures have always been a vehicle for social criticism.

MEDIA MEMORIES: CARTOONS AND CROSS-REFERENCING

Cartoons are not a new phenomenon. They, like earlier forms of caricature, have served as social criticism since the earliest days of images. We find exaggerated and ridiculous human forms at Pompeii, in the Maya cultures of Bonampak and Chichen Itza, and in the Valley of the Dead in Luxor, Egypt. Caricatures have simplified and placed excessive emphasis on peculiar features to ridicule pomposity or to make a joke. Cartoon strips use a simplified design vocabulary to amuse readers or tell a story vividly. Television cartoons carry that process of simplification and excess even further, using voice and motion as well as images. What is remarkable about the cartoons of the twentieth century, both in strip and in televised form, is the immense emotional impact they appear to have had on generations of people.

In talk of childhood media memories, cartoons loom large for the three generations of the twentieth century that we interviewed. Comic strips and cartoons stand out as prominent in the common culture of children. What is more, cartoons were highly globalized and Americanized from the beginning. Those in the group we interviewed who were aged 70 to 75 years old talked of cartoons much as the young now talk of *South Park*. All in the Australian group were familiar with the national cartoon *Ginger Meggs* and could cite endlessly from the cartoon strips. The early comic strips such as

*Phantom* and *Batman*, which had just entered the market, were forbidden as too "American" by most conservative parents but were accordingly desirable to the members of the group. This result was equally true of the equivalent Mexican cohort. They had, of course, their own cartoon strips, as the Australians did, but cartoons from the United States were familiar to those of the middle classes.

In the next cohort of those aged 40 to 45, the common cartoon culture still included comic strips. The ubiquitous *Charlie Brown* was known by all in the group; others mentioned the boys' comics:

Int: We were talking about your brother. He was allowed to have comics?

Anna: They were allowed to have those war comics with you know…. Swine hund *(laughter)* //Combat comics.

Roger: //*Superman* of course, and the *Phantom.*

Anna: It was the *Phantom* once a year for me and no girlie magazines or anything. Nothing like that. (Cohort 2, December 1998, Canberra, Australia)

Disney is ubiquitous as a maker of cartoons.

Beth: I can relate to a lot of the shows we're talking about. Um…I had *Mickey Mouse.* I can remember *Mickey Mouse.*

Sue: So did I. (Cohort 2, December 1998, Canberra, Australia)

The cartoon experiences remembered by the Mexican cohort overlapped significantly with those the Australian group recalled. This is striking given that, in general, American cartoons in Mexico were shown in English and not dubbed. Even so, the members could still, 20 years later, sing the title song of *Felix the Cat* and knew and were passionately involved in cartoons in English. Although they quote such programs as *Huckleberry Hound* and *The Adams Family*, they are also aware of local cartoon characters such as *Rolando Rabios* and *Los Supersabios* and so on.[5]

In the Internet generation, Japanese cartoons, Game Boy, and Nin-

---

5    Mexico City, March 1999. Thanks to Andrés Hoffman for permission to use this information.

tendo figures were universally known among children of the middle class. Cartoons are these days always dubbed. They are in fact easy to dub, since animated verbalization is not language specific. In the Australian cohort, there was a long list of familiar cartoon series, of both U.S. and Japanese origin. *Inspector Gadget, She-Ra, Roger Ramjet, Sesame Street*, and the Japanese *Astro Boy* were mentioned, as well as the Australian cartoon, *Blinky Bill* and the successful children's program, *Playschool*. This was a pattern very closely reflected in the Mexican cohort. *The Flintstones, The Jetsons*, and toys based on cartoons such as G.I. Joes and Maskmen were mentioned by the Mexican cohort. There were, of course, local variations. The Mexican cartoon *Cascarrabias* was mentioned, as were Mexican characters such as *Rosita Fresita*. However, the overwhelming impression of cartoon culture is that of a global culture. Barbie dolls and supersonic toys related the young to a larger world. One Mexican of this younger group made the point explicitly when talking of watching the *The Jetsons*:

> Mario: I don't know how to say it, I tell you that I went in for supersonics because I had always had this idea of travelling, for instance, and you know that if you go to France you will see things that don't exist in your country, and if you go to India you'll see things you have never seen in your life, and if you go to South Africa, you see, it's like we said the other day about kangaroos: for me Australia is super distant. (Cohort 3, March 1999, Mexico City)[6]

The spin-off toys are international products, generally raising more money than the cartoon series themselves. The carefully orchestrated rise of the transformers, of G.I. Joes, of Ninja Turtles and of Pokemons have been all enveloping global events. The computer games of the new generation are played with icons that children can manipulate on the screen often before they can talk, certainly before they can read.

What has changed with the younger generation is the longevity of the iconic characters. Postmodern uncertainty about identity has entered with a flourish. *Charlie Brown* kept the same blanket and woeful expression for 40 years; transformers alter all the time. The figures that haunt the computer games and characters from comic strips now invade each other's

---

6   Mexico City, March 1999. Thanks to Daniela Rivera, for permission to use this quotation.

spaces: Pokemons come on to *South Park*, and the new genre of crossover cartoons mix characters like Superman with the Fantastic Four. This interweaving of formerly distinct cartoon stories is both shocking and amusing—it reminds us that the cartoon characters are not real, but constructs, and that their worlds can interpenetrate.

Televised cartoon characters are also flexible in this way. *The Simpsons* is a postmodern artefact insofar as it makes constant reflexive reference to itself as television product (cf e.g., Wark, 1992). From the moment the show begins, with the family rushing to turn on the television, the show revels in self-reference. *South Park* takes *The Simpsons* even further. While drawing to an even greater extent than *The Simpsons* on the televisual world, *South Park* is even more vulgar and shocking. Like *The Simpsons*, it tends to end with a moral lesson, but the moral lesson is itself a send-up—a postmodern twist to the moral tales of the school-room. It plays on the interweaving of texts that is typical of postmodern culture. So, for instance, events are drawn in from the news and from the pop culture of an era, then played out in a televisual space. Just weeks after TV personality Ellen DeGeneris came out as gay in a much-touted television program which received unprecedented media coverage, "Miss Ellen" came as a substitute teacher to South Park Elementary, causing heartbreak among the boys and flirting with the jealous girls.

The use of media cross-references is an important part of the *South Park* style. Children are well aware of the phenomenon. The web site explores the issues of how we make sense of television genres.

**What do links to the media do?**

South Park, like much modern media, constantly sends up other television programs. The cartoon characters look like Japanese cartoons, and the battle between Father Christmas and Jesus is kung fu. In the second episode, the substitute teacher is Miss Ellen, is based on a television personality.

1) Do you prefer to watch programs you are familiar with, or a brand new show? Why?
2) Do you talk about programs with your friends? With your family?
3) If your friends are all watching a new show, will you try to watch it too?
4) When you recognize that a new show uses characters you already know, do you appreciate it? Why?
5) When you recognize that a new show uses the style of other programs,

do you enjoy it? Why?

6)  Could there be a completely new style of program, unrelated to what came before? If there were, would you understand it?

7)  Would a program which used only old elements, but put together differently, be new?

These questions were designed to focus on the ways we make sense of television. We all appreciate the familiar being recast in new ways. The questions ask students to reflect on their attitudes towards television and the ways that television exploits cross-referencing.

One student wrote:

> The crossover phenomenon in TV shows today has become quite common. I think the reason for this is it adds realism to the program. It is like they are living in your world and are watching the same shows you are. This helps you believe that the people in the show actually exist in your world. (first-year student, University of Canberra, March 1999)

This is a significant response. The student, aware of the importance of the crossover between genres, argues that the cross-referencing adds to the realism of the cartoons. This is a curious response in the context of this set of questions based on *South Park*, since cartoons are anything but realistic portrayals of people. It shows just how philosophically complex kids' ideas of televisual reality can be. She goes on:

> It is like they are living in your world and are watching the same shows you are. This helps you believe that the people in the show actually exist in your world. (first-year student, University of Canberra, March 1999)

It is important to this student that the televisual characters share a televisual world. Television characters, even cartoon characters, are as much part of our culture now as the biblical figures were until recently in Christian cultures or as the Royal family was in the British Empire. The common culture is the world of television. Cartoons give a version of our reality, and modern cartoons inevitably include the television experience itself. *South Park* works because it does get to the heart of children's experiences.

## CARTOONS AS ICONS

Watching television cartoons is not a simple process. Children take years to acquire the skills to grasp the meaning of cartoons. They begin with the simple story lines of *Sesame Street* and advance to the complexities of the *Bugs Bunny* style in which temporal and spatial unities are utterly broken. As any adult newcomer to the genre of cartoons can explain, cartoons are hard to understand. Children grow quickly bored when watching television and are quick to flick the remote to another channel. Only a diet of constant surprise, of unpredictable story lines, sharp jokes, and absurdity can be successful. MTV videos, with their rapid changes of pace and scene, are paradigmatic in the new television-viewing era. So are the new wave of cartoons such as the rapid and unpredictable world of *South Park*. Does this mean that children are no longer able to think straight as, say, Postman (1985) would suggest?

Douglas Rushkoff, in *Children of Chaos> [Surviving the End of the World as We Know It]*, talks of the expectations of young viewers and argues that the turbulent viewing behavior of the young is a new paradigm:

> The "well-behaved" viewer, who never listens quietly, never talks back to the screen, and never changes channels, is learning *what* to think and losing his own grasp on *how* to think...the viewing style of our children is actually more adult. (1997: 49)

For Rushkoff, what is characteristic of the younger generation of viewers is its ability to understand multiply-layered "non-linear" story lines. We will return to this point in chapter 6, but for now we note his argument that young viewers view differently from the middle-aged. In particular they have very different views of cartoons. Rushkoff suggests that the cartoon format itself is a highly significant form for conveying meaning.

He talks at first of the comic strip, then transfers his observations to televised cartoons. He claims that cartoons, by providing icons of human figures rather than full realistic detail, gave access to a streamlined representation which "free[s] the comic medium from the constraints of linear storytelling, and thus trains comic book readers to see the world in new ways." (1997:57) He goes on to argue that comics also free the reader from the constraints of linear thinking because the images are laid out on the screen and spatial conventions can take the place of temporal sequence.

Rushkoff is right about *South Park*. It is certainly not linear or realistic in the sense of, say, the early Disney cartoons. The story lines are more rapid-fire and unpredictable than that. Kenny dies in each episode and comes back for the next one; catastrophic events have unexpected out-comes. Nevertheless, it is important to be clear about the force of the claim that cartoons are nonlinear. Icons of human figures still act in ways that are fundamentally linear. Cause-effect relations are not normally reversed. Characters have the familiar dilemmas of children everywhere—dilemmas that are always linear, at least in the sense that they are ordered in time. In the Miss Ellen episode, when the schoolgirl Wendy becomes jealous of the substitute, the reactions are linear. Wendy is angry; her friend gives her a makeover, and Miss Ellen outdoes her. The story is as linear as it could be: it might have come from directly from a magazine column. The dialogue is predictably amusing:

Wendy: Thanks for coming over, Bebe.

Bebe: That's OK, Wendy. I brought my makeup kit, like you asked me. What are we doing anyway?

Wendy: That mean old substitute isn't going to stop until she takes every-thing from me, Bebe.

Bebe: Really?

Wendy: Yeah. What I'd really like to do is to load her into a rocket and have her shot into the center of the sun. But instead I'll just get Stan to notice me again. Bebe, I need a makeover.

Bebe: Oh, Cool.

*(Cut to school next day. Enter Wendy in black leather)*

Wendy: Hey guys, what's up?

Cartman: Wow, Wendy looks like that chick from *Grease*, Elton John.

Stan: Hi, Wendy.

Wendy: Hi, Stan. *(To Bebe)* I think it worked, Bebe.

*(Enter Miss Ellen in black leather)*

Miss Ellen: Good morning, children.

Boys: Wow yeah…

Miss Ellen: Oh Wendy, you wore black leather too! We're like sisters.

Wendy: DIE!

(South Park episode, "Miss Ellen")

Television is an inherently linear medium since it displays actions over time. Even in drawn comic strips, the lack of linearity is only superficial. We make sense of events by attributing cause-effect sequencing, even if the temporal dimension is, in comic strips, represented in progression of drawings across the page.

What is correct in Rushkoff's view is his account of the role of the iconic cartoon figures. Cartoons free the imagination and allow us to see aspects of people that are only marginally observable in human characters. Physical features can be exaggerated. Marge Simpson's hairdo, a blue beehive half her height, would unbalance any woman who chose to imitate it. Peculiar tendencies can be recognized and parodied in a way that may be intolerable if it were happening to real people. Events can be taken to ludicrous extremes. The dense cloud of nits flying around Bart Simpson's head when he has head lice reproduces not the look but the feeling of being infested.

The relation between reality and cartoons is an issue on which there were the most and most lengthy responses on the *Reason and Media* web site. The questions ran:

1) Are cartoons realistic?
2) Cartoons rarely look realistic. Do they make comments about how people really are?
3) Are cartoons of people better when they look like real people?
4) Are cartoons necessarily more lifelike when they look like real events?
5) Could a cartoon, like *South Park*, have characters more like real children than a cartoon with much more exact animation?
6) In *South Park* Kenny dies in every episode and comes back in the next one. This could not happen in the real world. In many cartoons, characters are blown up and survive. Does this mean the cartoons are just not real in any way?

Among the responses was:

Q3. Cartoons are no better when they look like real people than when they look abstract. It is what they say that makes them funny. Q.4 Yes, cartoons are more life like when they look like real events; viewers can identify with the cartoon more and then find it more funny. Q.5 *South Park* can have more character reality than a cartoon that has more real-looking animation. Again, it is what is said that matters, not necessarily the animation. I also believe that the dodgyness of *South Park* animation contributes to its being funny. (first-year student, University of Canberra, 1998)

This is clearly inconsistent. In answer to question 1 we are told that it is the words that makes cartoons funny. The student adds that the more realistic the cartoon the funnier, then recants at question 5 and says that it is the "dodgyness of *South Park* animation" that makes it funny. The answers to questions 3 and 5 cannot both be true.

Another student was slightly more coherent in his views, arguing that the nonrealism of the cartoon characters is essential to the genre.

…no, cartoon characters are better when they don't actually look exactly like humans—the *South Park* episode where Cartman took the "Beefcake" (Beefcake!!) product to "bulk up" for his television appearance wouldn't have looked quite as good if he didn't turn out as big as he did—and no normal human would ever be that big. (first-year student, University of Canberra, 1998)

Cartoonists use the iconic force of the animation to their own ends. The minimal animation of *South Park* is effective in drawing children's attention and disarming criticism. Television humor in cartoons is essentially iconic, not representational. The aim is to develop the aspects of characters that could not be emphasized were the characters real actors. The same holds true of *South Park*. Jonathan Swift's devastating critiques of British society in *Gulliver's Travels* used a similar technique to abstract from the confusing detail of the real world and get to the elements he wished to criticize. The Big Enders and Little Enders of Lilliput were fighting to the death over the issue of which end to cut their hard-boiled eggs. Swift uses this absurd debate to ridicule the political disputes of his time. His point survives the unreality of Lilliput.

One student paradoxically remarked:

Q.4: I don't think that cartoons could be made to say they are not real in ANY way because characters die and come back to life. (first-year student, University of Canberra, 1998)

Dying and coming back to life is not real. The student must mean that the allegorical force of the cartoon is not undermined by nonrealistic events.

However absurd the events on the cartoon, we make perfectly good sense of them as allegories and iconic representations of our lives.

### "AN ELEPHANT MAKES LOVE TO A PIG"

In "An elephant makes love to a pig,"[7] the boys learn about genetic engineering from the primary school teacher, Mr. Garrison. To research the possibilities of splicing a potbelly pig with an elephant as a school science fair project, the boys decide to visit a genetic engineering ranch. Here, they meet a scientist who experiments with genetic engineering by creating animals with 4 asses. The scientist tells them he cannot clone a potbelly pig and an elephant, but that he would happily produce a potbelly pig with 4 asses. As they leave, the scientist takes a sample of Stan's blood, planning to create a clone of Stan. The children then go to the school cafeteria and tell their friend chef (the school cook) the sorry story of their failure to produce potbelly elephants by genetic engineering. After giving it some thought, he suggests that the children combine the pig and the elephant DNA the old-fashioned-way, "by making sweet love." His idea is that the female pig could give birth and that he and the children could make money from the sale of potbelly elephants. He fills the elephant and the pig with alcohol and leaves them to it, with Elton John singing to create an appropriate ambience.

In the morning, the genetic engineer tells them Stan's clone is destroying South Park. Stan takes the clone back home to meet his abusive older sister. Stan asks the clone to beat up his sister. However, the clone misunderstands and destroys Stan's house while Stan's sister ultimately knocks the clone unconscious. At this point, the genetic engineer claims that he had no right to interfere and pretend to be God, that he will put an end to this horrible creature. He then shoots the clone in the head.

The arguments here are limited, and familiar. We have the case for genetic engineering, presented first by the schoolteacher's accomplice, his hand puppet, Mr. Hat, then by the genetic engineer:

Mr. Hat: That's right, Mr. Garrison, genetic engineering is an exciting new science. You can splice the DNA from some animals and make them better.

---

7    I was introduced to this episode by a student at NYU, Janine Michael.

Yes Mr. Garrison, genetic engineering lets us correct God's horrible mistakes, like German people....

and later

> Genetic Engineer: It's thanks to the wonders of genetic engineering that soon there will be an end to hunger, disease, pollution, even war. I've created things that will make the world better. For instance, here's a monkey with 4 asses.

In each case, the argument that genetic engineering might help people is immediately countered with the argument, amusingly put but cogent, that genetic engineering might be misused. The first argument is that genetic engineers might undervalue people and implicitly refers back to a busload of disabled children presented in the introductory segment—presumably these children would be what Mr. Hat would call "God's horrible mistakes." The second argument is based on the ludicrous conjunction of the genetic engineer's claim to have created things to make the world better by developing his 4-assed animals. As Stan says: "Why does a monkey with 4 asses make the world better?"

As the action moves on to the deviant clone, we call upon another form of argument. If there are dangers in genetic engineering, the program seems to suggest, then we should avoid any form of it. Again, humor is used to nail down the argument. In the penultimate scene, Stan, Kyle, and Cartman are looking at the clone that Stan's sister has just knocked unconscious, when the genetic engineer enters.

> Genetic Engineer: All I ever wanted was to genetically engineer something useful but I failed. Perhaps we shouldn't be toying with God's creations, perhaps we should just leave nature alone to its simple 1 ass schematics.

There are layers of humor. There is the evident contradiction between the genetic engineer's claim that he will be giving up playing God, and the action of shooting the clone, acting God. The question of what sort of thing the clone really is—is it a person or not?—is in the background. Earlier the genetic engineer had asked Stan to find his clone because he alone, with a mind similar to that of the clone, could predict the clone's behavior. What then are we to make of his killing the clone so lightly? What, indeed, is a clone?

This is a quick and nasty reconstruction of the argument. Humor is used to put a familiar line of thought, and it is hard to argue with humor. However, the ways of presenting the argument involve more than just jokes. As with "thought experiments," the absurd situations that evolve are a means of testing ideas. Why not get rid of the disabled children? Why not play with genes? The answers are played out in the absurd vision of a town terrorized by a deviant clone whose level of violence is exceptional even on *South Park.*

We are reminded by the alcohol-induced mating of the elephant and the pig that natural methods of reproduction have their down side and can be manipulated too. In a curious—and almost inexplicable—final turn, the offspring of the match between the elephant and the pig looks like Mr. Garrison. The violence is essential to the story; it is the use of violence that defines good guys and bad guys, the mad and the sane.

The presentation of the argument is multilayered. It is possible to read this episode of *South Park* as a sustained argument against creating new forms of life in general, and of the idea of cloning in particular. The violent behavior of the clone, the insanity of the genetic engineer, the chef's admiration for the beauty of love making, and the boys' ultimate choice in using the natural way to create a potbelly elephant are factors that combine to produce a case against genetic engineering. We would be better off and less violent if we did things naturally, we might say.

However, it is also possible to read the episode as an ironic commentary on the debate about genetic engineering. The schoolchildren are encouraged in their competitive search for the best science project and by the commercial possibilities of marketing a potbelly elephant—precisely those pressures that stimulate scientific exploration. In fact, the whole scientific world is parodied. The genetic engineer is happy to cheat, claiming to have cloned a fish and a rabbit, but, as one of the children observes, the rabbit ears are merely tied on to the fish. He is also prepared to steal genes from Stan and is only worried when the offspring is violent. Again the activities of the scientific world, in general, not just in genetic engineering, are being questioned.

Violence is also seen as natural and not solely a consequence of, genetic engineering. Stan's sister regularly beats him up. Mr. Garrison, the schoolmaster, offers Stan sympathy when he believes that Stan is the victim of abusive parents but ridicules the child when the perpetrator turns out to be the sister. Families are violent, too, and Mr.Garrison's reactions are absurdly inappropriate. Later, he threatens the maniacal clone of Stan with schoolboy penalties: "I know a certain young man who's heading for a detention." Stan sets the clone to fight his older sister. The sister wins. The easy rejection of cloning is complicated: it is clear that not only clones but real people—even children—can be violent.

When the Genetic Engineer simultaneously shoots the clone and sententiously renounces interfering with God, we have a further complication in the argument. Is a clone a person? That raises fundamental questions, of the sort we find raised in *Star Wars* as well, about the problem of how we should treat clones, robots, and human creations. What makes a person someone we should treat as a person? What makes you a person? Why is or isn't a clone a person?

In response to questions of this sort on the web site, one student said of the clone:

> He [the scientist] had to kill it; it was destroying the town; I mean it didn't make a difference if he shoot it or cut its head off; it's not a human. (first-year student University of Canberra, 1998)

However, those who felt that the clone was a human being found this response insensitive. Another student replied, "If it wasn't a cartoon, it would be considered murder." (first-year student, University of Canberra, 1998) In class, we had extended debates on the issues of cloning after watching "An elephant makes love to a pig." Those debates drew on the arguments in the episode. As a starting point for the debate, "An elephant makes love to a pig," does just as well as many more didactic approaches. In this sense at least, *South Park* may be said to be prosocial.

This episode is far from unique, as any *South Park* fan will attest. Each episode picks up and runs with an issue. Perhaps the episode most often cited as prosocial is one dealing with homosexuality. Another interesting episode deals with euthanasia.

Woman: Now blow out the candles, Grandpa.

Grandpa: *(Wheezes)*

All: Hooray!

Man: How does it feel to be 102, Paps?

Grandpa: Shoot me!

Woman: Make a wish, Grandpa.

Grandpa: I wish I were dead.

Man: That's our silly Grandpa.

Grandpa: I'm not being silly, kill me. I'd do it myself but I'm too damn old.

This dialogue alerts us to a number of debates about euthanasia: whether one should have a right to choose to die, and the extent to which the aged should be treated as independent persons with free will. The issue of what it is to properly treat a person as a person is tied up, in quite tantalizing ways, with cloning and with euthanasia. The episodes of *South Park* give those who watch them some idea of what the arguments about these issues are.

MEDIA EFFECTS AND TALKING ABOUT TELEVISION

When on 20 April 1999, two students armed with semiautomatic handguns, shotguns, and explosives conducted an assault on Columbine High school in Littleton, Colorado, 12 students, a teacher and the two attackers were killed, and 24 students were taken to hospital. Appalled, the population of the United States looked for someone or something to blame. The children at Columbine High School, like those at South Park Elementary, were middle-class children with everything to live for. The median household income in Littleton is $ 41,667 U.S. The local government boasts, in a fact sheet it put out after the tragedy, the following:

> Littleton's innovative economic development approach has attracted international attention and been the recipient of a number of prestigious awards and articles in professional journals.... With a highly educated populace, the city has become a center for high tech research and development companies and for medical care.... The nationally accredited Littleton Historical Museum features living history interpreters and attracts 100,000 visitors each year.... Littleton has 42.4 acres of park land per 1,000 population, exceeding the national standard of 10.25 acres. Littleton's 650 acre South Platte Park is one of the largest suburban parks in the U.S., second only to New York City's Central Park. (Littleton Community Network, 1999)

Littleton, the fact sheet makes evident, is not a ghetto or inner-city de-pressed neighborhood. The children lacked nothing. So what could be blamed for their violence? Many commentators sought the explanation in the television culture of the middle classes. They noted the geographic proximity of Columbine High School to the fictional South Park, and the fact that Columbine and South Park shared the prosperous Colorado sub-culture. *South Park* was seen as a symptom of the degenerate televisual culture that gave rise to the event.

Curiously, the press coverage rarely concentrated on what was clearly an essential factor: the alienation of the two boys from the dominant peer group of the school, the sports-playing youth. The children were clearly suffering from the culture of exclusion and bullying, whether physical or mental, which has come to dominate the school atmosphere. Eccentricity is utterly unacceptable within the school context and, in a desperate attempt to find self-assurance, the children went for a marginal culture of violence. School culture, not television culture in this case, was the culprit.

It is an assumption of the television industry that television has an im-pact on children—so that it is worth intervening. Advertising would not, and could not, exist without that assumption, and without advertising, television would not exist. We find the assumption so deeply embedded in the beliefs about television that moral crusaders such as Steve Allen (1999) can simply assert it without question. In an advertisement in the *New York Times* (October 20, 1999) he says, "TV is leading children down a moral sewer." He asks rhetorically:

> Are you as disgusted as I am at the filth, vulgarity, sex and violence TV is sending into our home? Are you as outraged as I am at how TV is under-mining the morals of children...encouraging them to have pre-marital sex...encouraging lack of respect for authority and crime...and shaping our country down to the lowest standards of decency?

As evidence, he asserts: "Since television started around 1000 studies, reports, etc., concerning the impact of TV violence have been published." That is quite true. It is the results of those reports, however, which are highly debatable. In part this is because it is difficult to obtain definite proof that viewing television actually alters behavior, fundamental though that assumption is to both ad agencies and political campaigns.

Complicating any debate about television and children is this vexed question of media effects. The concern about *South Park* can be put, very generally, as a concern about whether the racist, sexist and foul-mouthed style of the *South Park* children might influence the young and whether the random violence that repeatedly ends Kenny's life might be a model for children's behavior. Does media violence promote real violence? The question cannot be answered decisively. Recent summaries explain that there is no definitive evidence for the claims that media violence is a factor promoting real violence. (Federman,1998) Gunter and McAleer give a balanced summary of the evidence, citing studies in which "the evidence in support of the hypothesis that viewing violence leads to an increase in aggressive behaviour is very strong." (Gunter & McAleer, 1997: 114) They conclude:

> The research on the effects of television violence, for example, is voluminous, but far from conclusive.... The fact that there is a great deal of research on the effects of television violence does not necessarily make the case stronger. (Gunter & McAleer, 1997: 220-221)

Cumberbatch (1989)[8] gives a scathing review of the literature, stating that there has never been any decisive experimental proof of the connection between real-life violence and that on television. While empirical studies have attempted to measure the extent to which those who watch violence are violent, their results are mixed. The problems are as many as there are methodologies. Most of the data derive from studies that use ratings as a measure of exposure to television, whereas ratings only measure what people say they have been watching and, in the case of children, what their parents say they have been watching. Many of the surveys were fatally flawed in that experimenters told the parents what the aim of the study was before getting the ratings data. Ratings data are, in any case, no measure of attention; they are a measure only of what is being tuned into on the television. It is evident that much of the time the television is on, those in the room are actually not watching.

Moreover, it has become increasingly clear from studies of those imprisoned for violent crime that those who are violent are not great consumers of television or video violence. Steve Allen (1999), in the only evidence

---

8    I am grateful to John Penhallurick for the reference and for his broad overview of the empirical evidence.

he cites, says:

> An ABC network study found 22 to 34 percent of young felons imprisoned for violent crimes said they had consciously imitated crime techniques learned from watching television programs.

They would, of course. If authorities offer offenders the excuse to blame television for their crimes, it will undoubtedly be taken up. However, properly controlled studies offer little supporting evidence. At times it seems clear that the more violent television watched, the less likely viewers are to be violent—the so-called catharsis effect. Moreover, that research result is also disputed. The only really robust result is that children who watch a great deal of television when young are likely to be those who read more as older children. (Cumberbatch, 1989:10)

The best predictor of violent behavior is not violence seen on television but violence experienced within the family or in the domestic situation in which children are living. There are clear correlations between the childhood experience of violent behavior and violence in later life. There is no good evidence of a correlation between violent television programs and violent behavior, let alone between cartoon violence and violent behavior. Even the slight evidence for copycat crimes has never implicated cartoons or fictional films. Almost all copy cat crimes copy *real* crimes that have been seen on the news, not fictional crimes. If we wish to avoid such crimes, we should ban television news, not cartoons.

For children, as for adults, the impact of real news is far greater than that of violent fiction. Reality checks serve as a filter for how we view television. For Jackson (1998), children like *South Park* because they know it is not real and can enjoy it, while their parents are shocked. "Half the fun is the disgust it produces in others…" (Jackson, 1998). However, she goes on:

> Surprisingly, this generational psyche comes from an understanding that cartoons, films and television programs aren't actually real…. Older people still haven't grasped this idea, something scientists are blaming on the early days of television, when live shows were really live, and breasts were really just breasts. (Jackson, 1998)

While somewhat dismissive of the intelligence of "older people," this is consistent with Rushkoff's point, mentioned earlier, that the impact of cartoon figures, iconic and exaggerated as they are, is because they are not

real. They are fun just because they do not really look or seem like real
people. Cartoons work, in other words, because they are not real. As one
Australian kid said of *South Park:*

> I think if the director of it expressed his views on life in any other way apart
> from animation, he'd be locked up by now, but you know, it's still a funny
> thing to watch. (Quoted in ABC Media Report, 1998)

Children do not take television at face value. There is a process of
largely inchoate evaluation and criticism already in place: the children talk
back. Children talk of *South Park,* at least in Australia, with a mixture of
buzzwords and laughter. They do not analyze or develop the ideas presented on the program, they merely joke. When Robert Bolton interviewed
teenagers on the ABC Media Report (1998) the most articulate responses
were from two boys, one of whom was cited above. The other commented:

> He chops the bloke's head off, it's not very nice. I mean it's a cartoon, it's a
> bit rude for a cartoon when the blood goes—but it's quite funny, other bits.
> (Quoted in ABC Media Report, 1998)

The boy is trying to formulate a criticism but is painfully ill equipped
to deal with the complex questions of why animation should—or should
not—be violent. There is another equally tricky thought: what it is to be
funny and what it is to be rude and the connection between the two. The
child is not given any chance to develop the ideas. Yet those ideas that are
certainly worth exploring.

When given a greater chance to put their views on issues, children can
be far more articulate. In another debate arising from the original *South
Park* episode, cited at the beginning of this chapter, children were asked
about the meaning of Christmas.

**What do words refer to and what do they mean?**
1) Should Christmas have only one meaning, or can it have many meanings?
2) Can the word "Christmas" have more than one meaning?
3) Can the word "good" have more than one meaning?
4) Can a name have more than one bearer? Is there more than one Bill
   Clinton?
5) Is there a difference between the way the word "Christmas" has meaning and the way the name "Bill Clinton" does?
6) Is there a difference between the way a word has meaning and the way

an event, like a ball game, does?

7) Is there a difference between the meaning a ball game has, and the meaning of a religious event? Why?

One student responded:

Q1. I believe that every single word, object, subject or even an action does not have their single unique meaning. Because different people perceive the things are so different based on their perceptions, experience, culture, beliefs and values. So, with these differences, they will interpret the things differently. It is very hard for the world to share a same unique meaning of words, objects, subjects and actions with these differences. (first-year student, University of Canberra, 1999)

This view is what we might call the "Humpty Dumpty" theory of language, since it assumes, as Lewis Carroll's Humpty did in *Alice Through the Looking Glass* (1961), that speakers can individually alter the meanings of words.

"When I use a word," Humpty Dumpty said, in a rather scornful tone, "it means just what I choose it to mean—neither more nor less."

"The question is," said Alice, "whether you can make words mean so many different things."

"The question is," said Humpty Dumpty, "which is to be master—that's all."

The view leaves us baffled about how we could ever understand others' words.

Another student put forward a clever response to this point. Good, she suggests, can have different meanings, but these meanings must have a common core: something good must be desirable.

Q3. When you think of the word good it is always in a favourable sense; it just depends on the degree. So, yes, there is only one meaning to the term good. (first-year student, University of Canberra, 1998)

Others' arguments are less familiar:

Q6. When you think/hear the term rugby union you can visualise all aspects of the game, you do not have to actually be on the sideline to capture the essence of the game. Therefore the meaning of a word holds just as much impact as does the event itself. (first-year student, University of Canberra, 1998)

This is not a compelling argument, but it shows great imagination.

Kids *are* ready to take their television viewing apart and to discuss what they see on television. That, rather than censorship, is the best hope for the future.

There is one bright patch in the conflicting and indecisive evidence about viewing television violence. Among the multitude of studies, few have looked at the influence of talk on the media experience. Johnson and Ettema (1986) suggest that talking about a television program after seeing it, in a school setting, can significantly change the attitudes of the viewers, even over extended periods of time. It seems that talking about television is an effective way to mediate the media effects. Children, when they make sense of television, use what they know about the world and are ready to turn that process back on its head, reinterpreting television programs after they have talked about them. The lesson is that parents who are concerned about the impact of television should speak to their children about what they watch (cf., e.g., Palmer, 1986). It is not television that is the ogre when we talk of the violence of children who watch violent television; it is the violence those children live with daily and the lack of people to talk to. Viewing television violence may accustom viewers to violence; however, there is no proof that being accustomed to violent television makes people violent.

Bart Simpson has the last word. He says to Lisa: "Don't shut your eyes. You'll never become desensitized to the violence that way." (Quoted in Jackson, 1998)

### CONCLUSION

Violence on television is certainly increasing. In the United States there is a curious ambivalence about legislation; there is almost no sex or nudity allowed on television, yet a high level of violence is permitted. This became the focus of the movie (1999) *South Park: Bigger, Longer and Uncut*, in which regulations that limit nudity and allow violence are ridiculed. The movie begins with a vulgar clip of a Canadian movie, *Terence and Philip*, which indulges in toilet humor and foul language. In spite of an R rating, the foursome see the movie and begin copycat swearing. The mothers of South Park, horrified by the language of their children, take the issue to Congress and, becoming "Mothers Against Canada," they send the United

States to war. Robyn Williams was to sing the mothers' theme song, "Blame Canada," in the Oscar ceremony for the year 2000.

In the meantime, Cartman is implanted with a V-chip, which gives him an electric shock when he swears, and Kenny, incinerated, goes to Hell where he finds Satan and Saddam Hussein in bed together. The United States prepares to execute Terence and Philip, the foul-mouthed Canadians. The aim is to clean up America. As one character puts it:

> Horrific deplorable violence is OK so long as people don't say any dirty words. (*South Park: Bigger, Longer and Uncut*)

But the United States loses the war, and Satan takes over until Kenny persuades Satan to go home and to allow the *status quo ante* to return. The children explain that the problem is not the movie they saw but never seeing their mothers, who were off being activists. One of the mothers says, regretfully:

> I was just trying to make the world a better place for children. (*South Park: Bigger, Longer and Uncut*)

The film traces the arguments for and against censorship of television. It allows for limited media effects: the children who see *Terence and Philip* immediately begin to swear. It ridicules, however, the suggestion that toilet humor and bad language might seriously undermine the moral fiber of the country. It touches on the hypocrisy of the military, on the media-oriented planning strategies, and on racism and pomposity in the services. It skirts delicately around the question of the role of family influence in determining behavior, leaving one with the uneasy feeling that children want mothers home all the time. Finally, it drives home the inconsistency of those who aim to protect the young by using violence to avoid swearing.

The film is, of course, about reactions to *South Park*'s own vulgarity and violence. It dramatizes the debates in the press about what counts as prosocial and the value of a show like *South Park*. It plays the familiar postmodern game of reflexivity, taking the debate about *South Park* as the subject of the next program. It makes the points we have been making in this chapter. Cartoons are not seen as real by children; cartoon violence or vulgarity is not at all likely to cause those that view it to become violent or vulgar. Cartoons are, however, a valuable form of social criticism. They have an enormous impact and are remembered long after other events have passed. If we are concerned about the impact of cartoons, we should talk about them. Cartoons can touch on issues of philosophical depth.

The argument of this chapter is not that we should welcome television violence, foul language, or toilet humor. But we cannot censor violence or vulgarity and hope for beneficial social effects. The assumption of those who advocate censorship is that only by censoring violence or vulgarity on television will it be possible to avoid the evil consequences for the young. There is absolutely no evidence to support that view. Censorship is not the answer. The Australian critic, David Marr, puts it well:

> One of the great achievements of the censorship advocates...has been to establish in the public imagination the image of the extraordinarily vulnerable and extraordinarily ingenious child who wanders about the house, barely parented, sleepless at 3 a.m.., looking for mischief and finding it on television...or on the internet. (Marr, 1999:122)

Marr suggests that the waif of the public imagination is a chimera. Children do not learn violence from television. They learn what they are encouraged to learn. What is needed is not more state regulation but more debate about what we already have. After all, if we talk about television, children might even learn how to think critically about it.

# 5                    REASONS TO BUY

## THE LOGIC OF ADVERTISEMENTS

Commercial television does not sell programs to viewers. It sells viewers to advertisers. Newspapers and magazines likewise sell readers to advertisers. Web sites sell users to advertisers. Advertisers pay a high premium to get their message across. Whether a program or a style of news or web presentation succeeds or fails depends on whether advertisers will buy time. The business of advertisers in turn is to sell their message. The implicit message of every advertisement is a call for action from those to whom it is directed. Usually it is a call to buy, but it might also be a call to vote in a particular way or to change behavior or attitudes—to stop littering, for instance. Advertisements only exist because they purport to influence behavior. Nevertheless, the explicit message is rarely an explanation of why it would be rational to buy one product rather than another. Advertisers have become adroit at concealing their aims. Yet, however hidden, the message is always intended to persuade people to act as they might not otherwise act. Advertisements are intended to force people to assimilate a message, then act on it.

The argument of this chapter is that this process in advertising should be seen as rational persuasion and indeed as argumentation. This view conflicts with the received view found in advertising agencies, in academic accounts of advertising, and in the popular folk psychological accounts of how advertising works. Advertising, we have come to believe, works irrationally, catching us unawares. This view is upheld by teachers of advertising, at least for what are called "low-involvement" products. As generally theorized, advertisements are messages designed to induce a process of belief change, which is intended to flow through into action.[1] It is commonplace to distinguish between low- and high-involvement products, and thence of advertisements, where high-involvement products are those for which it is a major decision to purchase, such as buying a motor car; low-involvement products require a lesser commitment, as in buying ice cream. Evidently, what is low involvement for one person may be high for a connoisseur: the choice of a type of chocolate, for instance. The received view is that while advertisements for high-involvement products may require the target audience to reason, the reasoning is only part of the message, and affective components (the feel), are equally important. In advertising for low-involvement products, reasoning is irrelevant: the feel is all.

It is true that some advertisements we all do our best to ignore: these tend to be what are called ads for low-involvement products. The fact that those who view or hear such advertisements do not reason about them is a consequence of the fact that they do not think about them at all. Advertisers have reacted by developing "irrational" ads, ads that grab attention by circumventing lack of interest. The strategy, however, is not irrational. By eliciting reactions, the advertisement is intended to force the potential purchaser to think about and reason about the product.[2] Far from being irrational, low-involvement ads simply involve indirect reasoning. The received view that advertising is irrational is simplistic.

The argument of this chapter is that when we pay attention to advertisements and attempt to make sense of them, what we are doing is making sense of them as instances of argumentation. The advertisement should be seen as an argument directed at an audience, convincing them to act in a certain way. They are, in short, instances of rhetorical persuasion. They

---

[1]   There is a voluminous and very sophisticated literature on advertising effects, very well summarized, for instance, in Batra & Ray (1985).

[2]   Cacioppo and Petty (1980) point out that the extent to which a target is likely to elaborate a message, to make sense of it, depends on a variety of factors, far more complex than the "low-involvement" catch-all would suggest. I would argue that commonsense factors, such as needs and desires, feed in to the extent to which we attend to ads. We reason about the content on that basis.

are, with much rhetoric, rational.[3] This is not to say that advertisements may not fail or use weak arguments. It is to say that the practice of advertising, to a far greater degree than we realize, is based on assumptions that those they address are rational and will act rationally if convinced.[4] Advertisements are implicitly dialogical. An advertisement pits an argument for a product against the adversary: the consumer. Whether for foods, for clothes, for vacations, or for political figures, for programs of public health or for programs to stop drivers drinking, advertisements share generic patterns of argument.[5] It is no part of the argument of this chapter to condone the way we are bombarded with advertisements. Postman (1982, 1985, 1988, 1993) among others has warned of the dangers of advertising. His point that the young are saturated with messages of advertisers is well taken. The argument here is that once we have recognized the dangers, we need to develop strategies to resist the worst effects of advertising. We have at hand skills for criticizing advertisements. The strategy is the familiar process of evaluating arguments. Our reasoning skills are notoriously shaky whether in life, on print or on screen. Advertisers will do their best to gloss over holes in argument, misuse statistics, suggest false analogies. Here I will argue that we can criticize such advertisements in terms of the quality of their arguments.

This chapter seeks out the structures of argumentation in advertisements. It concentrates on the verbal messages of advertisements as the central focus of argumentation. This is not to deny the importance of the

---

3   For this distinction cf. Skinner (1996). In his discussion of Hobbes he argues convincingly that Hobbes returned to rhetoric as a valid part of rational persuasion in his later works.

4   It is evident that the notion of rationality here will need to incorporate the fact that advertisers know that everybody uses heuristics in reasoning (cf., e.g., Kahneman, Slovic & Tversky, 1982) and that certain strategies in advertising rely on formally invalid probabilistic forms. However, my essential point is not that advertisers assume the audience is ideally rational, only that they regard them as rational.

5   Political advertisements and advertisements for products even share particular arguments. A famous campaign for lamb in Australia in the 1980s presented lamb as the multicultural meal, showing people of mixed ethnic background mingling with Anglo Australians. In the early 1990s a candidate who later became Prime Minister, John Howard, used very similar footage of himself to counter suggestions that he was racist.

126 REASONS TO BUY

visual and musical components of the force of advertisements but rather to focus on one element of advertisements that has received relatively little attention. Chapter 6 will deal more specifically with visual argumentation.

<h2 style="text-align:center">REASONING IN ADVERTISEMENTS</h2>

Advertisements are complex and highly sophisticated components of modern life, embedded in a variety of cultural practices, but at the same time communicating across the global village with almost unprecedented effectiveness. George Steiner claims that advertising is the poetry of the modern age. The pure condensation of meaning that was once the province of poetic or religious discourse is now found in the advertisement industry. Highly intelligent (and well-paid) executives spend hours searching for the one pithy phrase, a phrase that will capture the imagination and heart, which will resonate and be sung, whispered or held—often for life. The jingles of childhood seem inexpugnable. One, of very limited poetic worth, went: "Menz makes biscuits a treat/Because Menz makes biscuits that are good to eat." It will, I am sure, remain with me when all else has gone.

In the days of music videos and startlingly high production values of visual television, the qualities of advertisements are legion. The sheer effectiveness of advertisements as memorable images, as semiotic signifiers, as music videos or film clips is itself a matter of academic study. Advertisements appeal to emotions and to the visual and aural senses, and they use a variety of rhetorical devices to achieve their aim. They are frequently intertextual, both in the sense that the one theme will appear in print, television, and billboards and also in the sense that advertisements refer to the genres, particularly of television, with enormous subtlety. Puns proliferate, both visual and verbal, and across the media. The attention to rhetorical devices, visual elements, and postmodernism of advertisements, important though they may be, has distracted attention from the underlying structure and impact of advertisements. It is in the interests of ad agencies to emphasize the irrationality of advertisements, so that their skills in manipulating images seems even more abstruse than they might otherwise appear.

It is part of the orthodoxy of the advertising industry that advertisements have their impact irrationally and that recalling the name or associating the product with a warm feeling is sufficient to sell. There is a dogma that claims that advertising succeeds when it attacks and alters attitudes surreptitiously. It is difficult to evaluate the arguments for the view. Studies of the effects of advertising, generally in the form of surveys, can indeed prove that advertising displaying, say, a baby, causes those who have viewed it to *say* that they feel affectionate. Informants might even claim that their feeling affectionate would incline them to buy the product. But it does not follow that the intention to buy the product *is* a consequence of the feeling. Indeed, the evidence suggests that the intention to buy the product generally precedes the development of what are sometimes called pro or con attitudes (cf., e.g., Ray *et al.* 1973). The advertising companies use attitude surveys to prove the effectiveness of the advertisement in creating a pro attitude; however, the evidence suggests that the attitude in fact comes into existence in response not to the advertisement but to the prompting of the survey.

This is a point worth rehearsing, since the claim that effective advertisements involve irrational appeal is so commonplace. The assumption is that advertisements alter "attitudes" and thereby tendencies or dispositions to behave. Thus, studies of reactions of consumers to advertisements have attempted to identify attitudes with an intermediate stage between viewing, hearing, or reading an advertisement and behavior change. This intermediate stage has typically been seen as a pro or con attitude: that is as a positive or negative feeling. Empirical evidence—namely, asking people about their reactions—is then adduced to identify which component of an advertisement most effectively alters attitude. However, the very existence of attitudes as an intermediate step in changing behavior is a moot point.[6] Music, or humor, or frequency of exposure (but not excessive frequency) can influence pro or con attitudes towards an advertised product, creating "warm and fuzzy feelings." Yet it is difficult to be sure, any role those attitudes might have in changing behavior.

The methods of research in advertising are based on focus groups and questionnaires. Those methods assume that attitudes can be measured and that they are determinate and fixed. Moreover, the assumption is that attitudes causally explain behavior. Yet all that can be measured is what at-

---

6   Cf. e.g., Ray et al. (1973), who argue that messages tend to produce behavioral changes that precede rather than follow changes in attitudes or effect.

titudes the theorist attributes to people on the basis of what they say that
they think. What people say might or might not be true, and even if true,
beliefs might or might not change behavior. Weakness of the will is a
common problem. Attitudes cannot be measured directly: they are at best
explanatory constructs. Evidence for the existence of attitudes is always
indirect.[7]

This is a very general problem with attitude surveys. We attribute attitudes as theoretical constructs to explain behavior, but they take on a life
of their own. Attitudes are taken to be what advertisements alter. The ad
agencies are then in a strong position. Even if behavior does not change,
and the product is not bought, they can survey those who have seen the ad
and say that since the product name is now recognized, the ad agency has
achieved "product recognition." The ad has achieved what is called "cut–
through." Product recognition is supposed to cause consumers to pick a
product without good reason, irrationally, just because the product is
known. Hence the ad campaign is successful as long as product recognition is achieved. There are two problems here. First, why assume that attitude change, not behavior change, is the aim of advertising? And why say
that name recognition is an irrational response? Learning a product name
and being inclined when prompted to say you might buy is far from irrational. Indeed, it requires only minimal rationality.

Advertisements purport to give us reasons to buy. What sorts of reasons are they? A far simpler answer than that proposed by the advertising
agencies is that advertisements are arguments, some good, some bad. The
suggestion is that an advertisement works by offering arguments to the
potential customer. We can make the point with a very simple made-up
example: *Regro can help a balding person to grow hair.* The slogan is set in front
of a before and after image of a balding, then hairy man. A balding person
wishing for regrowth, believing the utterance, and assuming—as would be
natural—that *Regro* is on the market is quite rational to intend on that basis
to buy *Regro*. The underlying argument structure is one in which the advertisement allegedly provides information, which together with knowl-

---

7   I owe this point to Ruth Shrensky, whose Ph.D. thesis on the subject I supervised. It
    is available from the University of Canberra and is titled "The Ontology of Communi-
    cation." She deals with the issue in Chapter 6, "Attitude and Attitude Change."

edge common to the market gives a good reason for buying.

The arguments in real ads are more complex but are nevertheless arguments. When Nike asks us to "Just do it," they are not simply telling us to buy. The phrase has layers of meaning. It could mean do what you were going to do or what you were not going to do. It has overtones of the coach, or the irritated mother, of the inner voice urging you on. It is a cryptic and ambiguous phrase, accompanied by a stylish logo, and it is universally known. Nike advertisements also use images and sound. In this chapter, I put the visual elements of advertisements aside and concentrate on the verbal elements.

How can we transform the Nike ad into an argument? First, we need to allow forms of argument with imperative premises and conclusions. This is not difficult. Imperatives are transformations of more familiar assertoric sentences. So for instance, the command JUST DO IT is a transform of "You just do it," which, together with further enthymematic premises such as "If you just do it, then you (should) buy these shoes," leads to a conclusion, "You should buy these shoes." The conclusion in turn has an imperative transform—BUY THESE SHOES. Stating validity for such transformed arguments is no more difficult—or easy—than for the assertoric versions.

Discerning the arguments in real discourse is far from easy. Most examples of real spoken argumentation are elliptical and require supplementation in order to be evaluated as valid or not, justified or not. Ads are no different. The problem we have with describing advertisements as instances of argumentation is quite general. Linguistic analyses of language do not focus on argumentative structure, whether of imperatives or statements. For instance, perhaps the most sophisticated system of discourse analysis, the systemic linguistic tradition deriving from the work of Halliday (e.g., 1985), discerns three levels of language: the interpersonal, the ideational, and the textual metafunctions of language. Analyses in the systemic tradition give finely detailed accounts of the intent of discourse but cannot focus on the argumentation, precisely because argumentation involves at one time all three functions.[8] The analysis of argument requires at least some understanding of the basic interpersonal structure if, as I

---

8     This point was made to me in 1994 by Dr. Chris Nesbitt, then of Sydney University.

suggest, argument is fundamentally dialogical. It also requires an under-standing of content, in particular of the premises to determine whether the argument needs amplification with further assumed elliptical premises. Moreover, the notion of validity is textual: it involves thinking not just about content but also about the linguistic structure itself. The hallmark of the notion of validity is that the conclusion of a valid argument is true in virtue of structure alone, if the premises are sound. That is a textual or metatextual judgment. Discerning the argument in discourse involves a process of abstraction relative to a norm of complete explicit spelling out of premises and structure and requires all three levels of analysis. This goes beyond the descriptive practices of linguists. It is, of course, a favored oc-cupation of philosophers.

The most convincing model that relates dialogue to argumentation in a non *ad hoc* fashion is due to van Eemeren *et al.* (e.g., 1993). In essence, their view is that argumentation is a social and dialectical practice that is "externalizable." It is possible, using generally motivated linguistic princi-ples along the lines of Searle's (1969) and Grice's (1975) principles of Speech Act theory and meaning to reconstruct argumentative discourse. So, for instance, when Grice's principle that we should be maximally in-formative is not obeyed, it is reasonable to suggest that there may be an implicit argument with a reason against giving more information. Most real arguments require amplification. It is this model of argumentation on which we base the claim that advertisements are arguments.

The view that the audience of television is both rational and critical of the media they view is now widely accepted in media research and applies as well to the print media. The scholars of the active audience tradition (cf. chapter 1) question the assumption that audiences are passive receivers, simply allowing ads to wash over them and have effects of which they are not aware. Audiences who watch television read ads with a critical eye, and their readings are frequently what is called "deviant": unexpected or unpredictable. The same is true if we consider print media. Radway (1984) argues that women read romance stories not passively but actively creating their own responses to the content. The deviant readings are often critical rational assessments.

The notion of an active audience participating in and critiquing the ad-vertisements placed before them shares certain features with social psychologists' account of those subjected to advertising. For instance, when an advertisement takes more time to grasp, whether for intrinsic or extrinsic reasons, then the audience will think about it more and hence will work through the argumentation more thoroughly.[9] Thus print advertisements are more likely than those on television to require and elicit complex arguments. The difference is one of degree, not of kind, but that is the topic of the next chapter.

## A PRINT ADVERTISEMENT

Some advertisements use arguments that are valid, although many do not, but all can be examined for their rationality. Consider the following example of a highly sophisticated print advertisement placed in the *New York Times* of November 1996, by the Fox network. At that time Fox was fighting a battle to gain access to the New York market, controlled, through its ownership of the cable company, by another media giant, the Time Warner Company. Fox wanted Time Warner to offer Fox news on the cable. Time Warner refused, citing that most archetypal of all U.S. institutions, the First Amendment, which protects freedom of speech. In effect, the Time Warner group hoped to protect its own CNN News audiences from competition by citing the First Amendment to the effect that they were not obliged to *say*—that is, broadcast—material they did not wish to broadcast.

Already this was an unusual case, because the First Amendment is more often invoked when someone wishes to say what others do not want them to say. It was this complexity that the Fox advertisement made use of. Far from reducing the complexity of the situation, they exploited it and presented what is, by most counts, a fairly elaborate argument:

**"I'm about to dust some cops off.
Die pig, die pig, die."**

Time Warner used the First Amendment's protection of
free speech in its unwavering support for these lyrics,

---

9    This account is commonly known as the elaboration likelihood model and is taken to show that elaborated messages correlate with more pro, that is positive, attitudes. My own view is that the process of elaboration is one that is best described in terms of argumentation.

> from "Cop Killer," by Time Warner Recording Artist Ice-T.
> After all, profits were at stake.
> Now, Time Warner believes the FOX news
> Channel poses a threat to the Profits of its CNN.
> And this time, Time Warner cites
> the First Amendment to deny New Yorkers
> the right to see the Fox News Channel.
> The First Amendment protects free speech,
> *not* Time Warner profits.
>
> **Support, don't distort the First Amendment**
> **Don't block the FOX News Channel**

This advertisement is striking, not just because of the vagaries of capitalization—and of capital—it exploits. The sheer effrontery of using Time Warner's support of Ice-T's shocking lyrics to grab attention for a competing company has style. So does the irony of Fox accusing other companies of protecting profits by excluding competition. Fox is notorious for its hard-hitting defense of its own monopolies, yet here it is attacking Time Warner for behaving in just the same fashion. The advertisement also uses a complex logical structure to make a rhetorical point.

The advertisement, in short, accuses Time Warner of inconsistency in its use of the First Amendment—the law that protects free speech in the United States. The first subargument claims that:

1)   Time Warner claimed the support of the First Amendment to allow playing of the Ice-T lyrics, and

2)   Time Warner's action was caused by the need to maximize profits.

This is, I take it, a tendentious implication we can draw from "After all profits were at stake." It is the weakest and most rhetorical step in the argument and one whose truth could well be questioned. It follows that:

3)   Time Warner has acted in the past to maximise profits.

1 and 3 suggest, by a weak inductive argument, that the explanation of a past action could well be the explanation of a current action.

4)   Time Warner's actions are now caused by the need to maximise profits.

The second subargument takes 4 and the premise

5) Time Warner claimed the support of the First Amendment to prevent playing Fox news on New York cable

to reach a conclusion that

6) The First Amendment is being used to protect Time Warner profits.

So far, of course, there is no evident inconsistency, for even if Time Warner's actions were caused by the need to maximize profits, their behavior appears to be consistent in both cases. The moral force of the argument depends on two enthymematic or suppressed premises:

7) The need to maximize profits is (in itself) not a good reason for acting.

6 and 7 yield:

8) Time Warner is not acting for good reasons.

The second enthymematic premise attributing misuse of the First Amendment to Time Warner might be

9) It is improper to appeal to the First Amendment except to protect free speech.

This is a debatable premise. Time Warner was operating within the letter of the law, so their action was not legally improper nor inconsistent with the law. Clearly it is not inconsistent *tout court* to use a law which protects free speech under reasonable constraints, as the First Amendment does to prevent playing of one type of material (e.g., incitement to treachery in time of war, or racist jibes) and allow playing of another type of material. Drawing on 6 and 9, we have:

10) The First Amendment *should* protect free speech, *not* Time Warner profits.

In the final call to action we need to draw on a premise that would reasonably be taken to be common knowledge to the readers of the *New York Times*:

11) The First Amendment should be protected (by U.S. citizens presumably).

12) Support, don't distort the First Amendment.

This argument yields the implied conclusion:

13) Do not support Time Warner.

Hence, with the assumption that the only alternative to supporting Time Warner is supporting Fox by not blocking the Fox news Channel:

14) Don't block the FOX News Channel.

Supporting Fox news, the advertisement says, is tantamount to supporting the real intention of the First Amendment.

The advertisement is clearly designed for the *New York Times*. The complexity of the argument structure, whatever the debatable truth of the premises, leaves room for relatively sophisticated readers to fill in the gaps as they choose. Its political force survives the evident inconsistency of one media giant accusing another of greed, through the immensely powerful emotional appeal to the First Amendment. Note moreover that in terms of argumentation this example uses a direct argument structure, the conclusion of which is an appeal to action—supporting Fox. This is a case of practical reasoning. It is rare to find the argument structure of an advertisement so explicit.

A first reaction is that this is a characteristically print media advertisement. The very complexity of form identified here is unlikely to appear in television or radio advertising, since it requires a level of logical and linguistic reflectiveness unlikely to appear on television. Even more, it requires the time, which television viewers lack, to reflect on the argument structure. This conclusion should be rejected, both at the level of the possibilities of argumentation and at the level of the sophistication of audience reaction. What is at the heart of this advertisement is an accusation of inconsistency. It is just such inconsistency that is often attributed to opponents in political advertising on television. Inconsistency in itself is bad enough, but usually there is a further twist—your inconsistency is self-serving. Just as Time Warner was accused of self-serving inconsistency, so politicians are accused of self-serving changes of mind.

Take, for instance, a cartoon by the Australian political cartoonist, Geoff Pryor (1991). A print advertisement, it echoed accusations made on television. In the cartoon, an Australian prime minister, Bob Hawke, is shown as a young radical in 1971 at the time of the Vietnam war, saying

"Bring the Troops Back Home." The next panel shows Hawke as Prime Minister sending troops to the Gulf War in 1991, saying "Your Country Right or Wrong." Below comes lines from the song "The times they are a-changin.'" The cartoon identifies an inconsistency in the attitudes of the then Prime Minister of Australia, in advocating withdrawal of troops from an overseas war on one occasion and in sending troops on another. The Prime Minister might well have replied that there was no inconsistency, since it was not the same war the troops were being sent to and hence there were different circumstances driving his difference in view. We do, however, expect people to be *prima facie* consistent in their views on similar issues over time.

When Fox accused Time Warner of inconsistency, or Pryor accused Hawke of the same thing, the structure of the argument is implicitly dia-logical. The argument assumes that the interlocutor is attempting to defend the action and tries to circumvent possible counterarguments. The inter-locutor of the advertisement—the viewer or reader or consumer—is given an implicit role as an adversary or opponent.[10] We can think of all adver-tisements, I suggest, as a proponent arguing a case to a proposed oppo-nent. In effect we have a debate structure in which the advertiser is the proponent, P, and the buyer or person to be persuaded is the opponent, O. Each has the right to make certain sorts of challenges, with the O being able to request evidence and P in a position to gather new evidence. P and O can each draw out the logical consequences of their own and each oth-ers' remarks. There is thus no rule of strict turn-taking.

In an advertisement for *Regro*, for instance, a balding buyer is resisting the argument for buying a product by asking for evidence. Why buy *Re-gro*?, the notional opponent asks. The response is simple: *Regro* can help a balding person to grow hair. The before-and-after images for *Regro* contain an implicit response to the request for evidence.

The structure of argumentation here is:

1) O: Baldness is irreversible (Premise 1: Assumption).

2) P: Person x's baldness has been reversed using *Regro*. (Premise 2).

---

[10] My own use of terms is based on Lorenzen (1965).

3) So baldness is and is not reversible (Premises 1 and 2, *reductio ad absurdam*).

4) O: Therefore baldness is reversible using *Regro*. (Premise 1 is not true, by *reductio*)

In effect, the argument described in this way draws a contradiction from a supposed assumption of the opponent, in this case the putative viewer of the ad.[11] The contradiction alerts O to the possibility of a reason to withdraw the initial assumption. This argument, together with natural assumptions about a balding person's desire to reverse baldness and his belief that *Regro* will do the trick, will lead to the intention to buy.

1) O: I desire to reverse my baldness.

2) Baldness is reversible using *Regro* ( Premise 4).

3) I should use *Regro* and hence should buy *Regro*.

The dialogical model of analysis of the *Regro* ad is somewhat *ad hoc* but it does, nevertheless, show the implicitly adversarial and confrontational structure many ads do display.

In the cases of accusations of inconsistency, the adversarial role can be made explicit, since there is a butt of the advertisement—Time Warner or Hawke. For instance, revisiting the argument from the Fox ad, we can attribute responses to Time Warner. The opponent is always allowed to ask for evidence for a claim. Thus when premise 2 is put forward—Time Warner's action were caused by the need to maximise profits—O can respond: What is the evidence for 2? Then at premise 6—The First Amendment is being used to protect Time Warner profits— O might again call for evidence. Premise 7 — The need to maximize profits is not in itself a reason for acting—is also debatable, as is 8—Time Warner is not acting for good reasons.

---

11  This account is close to the theory that "cognitive dissonance" forces belief change (cf. Festinger, 1957). It disagrees with the cognitive dissonance account in one major respect. Only salient contradictions with consequences of a particular sort are grounds for belief change—namely, those in which the believer wishes to give up belief in one conjunct.

If premises 7 and 8 fail then this reconstruction of the argument will show it to be unconvincing and strictly speaking invalid. Note, however, that P outflanks O here by never stating the argument that only a desire to protect profits could explain such behavior and by taking it as given. Even if Time Warner could respond directly to the arguments about their use of the First Amendment, they can scarcely reply that they are not driven by profits. The Fox ad wins the round. It wins it not by being irrational but by bringing up elements that, while apparently irrelevant at first, undermine the implicit argument of Time Warner. It is a clever ploy.

Hawke, as Australia's Prime Minister, also appears to lose the argument. He was well known for his rejection of interference in foreign wars in relation to the Vietnam War. Evidently, different reasons were relevant to his support of the Gulf War, notably the impression that Saddam Hussein's attack was unjustified and was itself a foreign attack. However, it was common knowledge that Hawke was also motivated by pressure from the United States. U.S. intervention was common factor in the two cases and, in that respect, Hawke was inconsistent. The use of the tag from a 1960s song, redolent of the anti-Vietnam/anti-U.S.-intervention era, emphasizes this inconsistency. Again, the argument works by outflanking the obvious riposte. Hawke loses.

The dialogical structure of advertisements is always a matter of reconstruction. The reconstruction of the opponent in the advertisement is likely to be tendentious, precisely because it becomes increasingly speculative. We need a generous interpretation of the principle of charity. Having illustrated how it might work in this case, further reconstruction will omit the putative other. However, the dialogical substructure of advertisements is what drives the argumentation.

The level of philosophical complexity of advertisements and the arguments they contain should never be underestimated. A good, cool advertisement is making a range of complex moves that are worth deconstructing, both for the argument structure and for the training in reasoning this provides. Advertising agencies, which specialize in persuasion, are adroit at exploiting underlying philosophical uncertainty as well as pushing blatantly fallacious claims. It will not do, however, to take a simplistic line by denying the force of advertisements and labeling them as immoral, stupid, or ill intentioned. However true such claims may be, they fail to capture the cleverness and attraction of advertisements. Far wiser to begin with the questions: "What does this advertisement argue? Is it valid? Why does it work?"

Television advertisements provide a rich field of examples of all the classical fallacies: from "appeal to authority" to begging the question, from equivocation to affirming the consequent. The most obvious television fallacies, however, must be seen in a context that suggests that while formally fallacious, the advertisement might provide a moderately good reason to buy. This is a consequence of what is a very general truth about television advertisements—they are enthymematic. Spelling out the suppressed premises is often a tedious and unrewarding affair, like spelling out the meaning of a metaphor. Nevertheless, it is worth remembering that much of the force of advertisements derives from the ambiguities and possibilities of elaboration they contain. The general model of elaboration draws on principles of charity to make sense of utterances (Davidson, 1967, 1984 *passim*) together with Gricean principles (e.g., Grice, 1975). The assumption is that where an advertisement appears to be inexplicable or meaningless, we should search for the best fit of meanings, given our knowledge of the world and of linguistic practice. The fit may not be unique. One advertisement may well contain several patterns of argumentation. That is not surprising if we conceive of ads, like poetry and metaphor, as functioning simultaneously at many levels.

Some advertisements have fairly simple arguments. The classical appeal to authority might, for instance, link a sporting star with the breakfast cereal being advertised, suggesting that if you eat the same breakfast cereal you too might improve your sporting ability. This is not always a mere fallacy—appeals to authority are quite reasonable in their place. Indeed, a cereal, recommended by an expert in sporting health might provide a better recommendation than the sheer suggestion that it is great. After all, the skeptical buyer or viewer, in effect, could be seeking any reason to choose one cereal over another. The reasons are not as weak as they might at first seem.

The question of whether an appeal to authority is fallacious is the theme of these questions from the *Reason and Media* web site, which paired snippets of television with discussion pages and spaces for users to respond.

1) If your doctor tells you you have chicken pox, should you believe him or her? Is this an appeal to authority?

2) If your brother tells you he saw a space ship, should you believe him? Is this an appeal to authority?

3) If a very rich man tells you how to make money, should you believe him? Is this an appeal to authority?

4) If an Olympic gold medalist tells you to eat a particular brand of cereal, should you believe her? Is this an appeal to authority?

Another example of an apparent fallacy comes from an Australian advertisement for sugar: "Sugar, a natural part of life." The enthymematic step relies on a premise which suggests that natural parts of life are good for you. It uses this to reach the conclusion that sugar is good for you —so eat sugar! The skeptical buyer might respond that, "Cancer, a natural part of life," is just as true. The argument is absurdly fallacious.

A slightly better reconstruction of the argument might be:

1) You have a choice of natural and artificial sweeteners (assumption)

2) All else being equal, natural is better (assumption).

3) Sugar is natural.

4) (4) So buy sugar.

Appeal to a principle of charity makes better sense of the advertisement than harping on invalidity.

Consider a Mexican example. It is an advertisement for a beer called, in Spanish, *Dos X* lager. It shows an image of a refrigerator, opening first to show it filled with beer, opening again with less beer, then again with more beer.[12] The punch line is, "Now you understand the evolution of species."

---

12   Dos X, Two X, is a Mexican beer. The difficulty in interpreting the ad is one shared by mother-tongue Mexico City residents. The Australian beer, Four X, was also part of a highly successful and allusive advertising campaign, of which the punch line was "I can feel a Four X coming on." The ambiguity in this case was somewhat easier to

This is open to a range of interpretations. It may mean that *Dos X* has proven, by its ability to survive, that it is the best—it has achieved natural selection. From the point of view of the advertisement agency, intentional ambiguity such as this grabs attention and ensures impact. In part such advertisements are driven by the washback validity of advertisement companies' evaluative methods. It is normal to test advertisements for 'cut-through,' or the extent to which they are remembered by focus groups of viewers. Advertisements that are difficult to understand and thus tantalizing may be more memorable than others.

The very fact that the punch line is tantalizing suggests that it might not be possible to find a unique elaboration. Thus we need to draw again on our principle of charity to make sense of the *Dos X* advertisement. Why would the advertisement give us reason to buy? One version might be:

1)  The advertisement shows lots of beer passing through the fridge.

2)  If people drink a lot of *Dos X*, it must be a good beer to drink.

3)  *Dos X* must be a good beer (from premises 1 and 2).

4)  So I, too, will buy *Dos X* (if I want beer).

This is not compelling, but it alerts us to a possible structure of argumentation. Advertisements can indirectly suggest how to behave by making indirect claims about others' behavior.

This is particularly true of lifestyle advertisements. The Apple advertisement, "Think Different" is designed to remind consumers that although PCs dominate the market, a different product might have advantages. The advertisement is both possibly ungrammatical and definitely elliptical for "think different thoughts."[13] Its impact derives in part from its open-endedness. What does it mean to "think different"? Is it the same as thinking differently or not? With Apple positioning itself to be the minor

---

untangle than in the Mexican case: no mother-tongue English-speaking Australian past puberty could be in doubt as to the meaning.

[13]  I owe this interpretation to Ruth Shrensky who suggests that the use is elliptical. It is an adjectival not an ungrammatical adverbial use of "different." She cites Washington Irving, "they who drink beer will think beer," for another related use.

player in the personal computing domain, how is it locating its market? In a sense, this is a paradigm lifestyle advertisement. Reconstructing the argument without the cumbersome notional skeptical buyer, we could suggest:

1) People who think different, such as the Dalai Lama, Einstein, and others, are good.

2) So thinking different is good.

3) People who think different, such as the Dalai Lama, Einstein, and others are associated with Apple computers.

4) So, if you are associated with Apple computers, you will be like people who think different, such as the Dalai Lama, Einstein, and others.

5) (5) So you will be like the Dalai Lama, Einstein, and others.

Even if it were true that you would be different if you were to be associated with Apple, it certainly does not follow that you will be anything like the extraordinary people shown.

Again exercises can help clarify the concepts at play here. These come from the *Reason and Media* web site. They are designed to force students to work out for themselves whether there is a difference between thinking different and thinking differently. As a result of the exercise, students should realise that language is often used flexibly and that there are often no predetermined meanings which phrases have in advance of being interpreted. It is possible that the phrase "think different" means no more and no less than "think differently."

**Thinking different and thinking differently**

1) You decide to buy a pair of gym shoes just like the ones your favorite basketball player uses but unlike the ones your friends wear. Are you thinking differently?

2) You have an assignment in art, and your answer is different from everyone else's. Are you thinking different or differently? What if the assignment were mathematical?

3) All your friends are going skiing for their vacation, and you want to stay at home. Are you thinking different or differently?

4) Your family votes for one party, but you don't agree. Are you thinking different or differently?

5) You are looking for the remote control that is lost. You decide to look in the kitchen, a long way away from the television set. Are you thinking different or differently?

Ungrammatical slogans can often have a strong impact. Chomsky (1957) explained that "'colorless green ideas sleep furiously" is nonsense but is grammatical sense. "Think different"' is sense, but it is ungrammatical or elliptical. Slogans designed to catch your attention often do so by making you stop and wonder what they mean. Often they are ambiguous, with two or more possible meanings. The first of the examples below was used in the successful political campaign in Australia in 1974, after which a left-wing government replaced a conservative government that had ruled for some 25 years.

**"It's time."** This can be taken to mean:

Change now!

Start now!

We have had too much!

The second example is the Nike ad:

**"Just do it**." This can be taken to mean:

Do what you were going to do.

Do what you were NOT going to do.

These are just a few of the many possible interpretations of the two slogans. Their ambiguity means that any reconstruction of an argument is a reconstruction of just one path through that advertisement. The further paths based on other interpretations will need separate reconstructions. This is a consequence we have no choice but to accept. Ads are ambiguous and argue at a number of levels. Just because an advertisement contains arguments that are multileveled, it does not mean the ad does not contain argumentation—only that the argumentation we discern may not be unique.

Coke advertisements associate a particular lifestyle with those drinking Coke, with the implicit suggestion that if you drink Coke you will also be young, elegant, and lively. Even if we accept that "If you are young and lively and beautiful, you drink Coke," it is an invalid step—affirming the consequent—to infer that "If you drink Coke, you are young and lively and beautiful." It is clearly invalid to infer that drinking Coke will *make* you young and lively and beautiful. However, children certainly recognize this fallacy as do advertising agencies. The Sprite advertisements in Australia drew on children's skepticism, saying "Drinking Sprite will not make you a good basketball player. But it will refresh you." The very existence of the debunking form of advertisements shows how aware we are of the logical weakness of advertisements. It also shows us that we should be aware of the levels at which the argumentation is functioning.

Coke ads, like the Nike and the Sprite advertisements, may be invalid, but they are more than that. They are multiply ambiguous. If we are well aware of the fallacies, why do we like the advertisements, and why do we keep on buying? Partly, the answer is that ambiguous phrases draw our attention and avoid the obvious. The Nike campaign, "Just do it," exploits ambiguity to draw attention. It does not simply *tell* us to buy the shoes. One reconstruction might go:

1) When we buy training shoes, we want to buy the same sort as everyone else—we will try to buy what others buy.

2) In the absence of other good reasons to pick one brand over the other, pick the brand you think others will pick, and assume that they do the same.

3) We all know we all watch television and the Nike advertisement.

4) So we all know we all know the Nike brand.

5) So the best strategy is to buy Nike.

Another might be:

1) Nike shoes are expensive.

2) Just do it—the expense is worth it.

3) So I will just buy Nike.[14]

---

[14] I thank an anonymous referee for a version published as an article in *Argumentation* for this interpretation.

Such chains of reasoning are rarely made explicit, but they do provide reasons for acting as the advertisement suggests and buying Nike.

For this reason, criticism of the impact of advertisements on the lives of children must allow for a high level of complexity, rather than debunking advertisements. This does not mean we have to *accept* a pattern of consumption dictated by advertisements. Rather, conceiving of advertisements as arguments gives us the right—and indeed the obligation—to question how good the arguments are. Do they follow? Should we buy? Once we have found the best possible argument, we examine the truth of the premises. In the case of this version of the Nike argument, we would want to ask why children should use the same trainers as others and why they want to be like others. We might ask what the costs are to those who produce the goods.[15] Advertisements are not just a necessary evil of capitalism, they are also parts of the culture that can be criticized.

## A CASE STUDY: IMAGES AND STEREOTYPES

Lifestyle advertisements make an implicit appeal to stereotypes. Feminist critiques have denounced the consequences of such stereotypical images that portray what is considered to be desirable in regard to body shape, clothing, or behavior. Stereotypes, for instance, may be disastrous if they influence a young woman's view of what is a normal body shape.

A publicity campaign in Mexico City for the upmarket department store, Palacio de Hierro (The Palace of Iron), is an extraordinary example of the formation of gender-based stereotypes. The images of elegant young women are accompanied by slogans like: "What makes the difference between a child and a woman? The phrase 'I have nothing to wear,'" or "There are two things a woman cannot avoid: crying and buying shoes," or "It's not so much whether it suits me or not, as whether I've been seen in it before," or "No man can answer these questions: 'How do I look?' and 'Do you love me?'"

Each of the advertisements ends with the slogan "*Soy totalemente Palacio*": "I am totally Palacio," suggesting that everything about the young

---

15    Indeed, the recent difficulties of Nike about their use of cheap labor suggest that just
      such questions have been asked by consumers.

women in question—style, attitudes, and looks—could be purchased from the department store. The campaign has been very successful, with a pay-off in merchandising. Moreover, there have been numerous anecdotal reports of young girls, 11 years old and up, longing to be adult, saying plaintively, "I haven't got anything to wear and I cry and I like buying shoes."

The advertisements have inserted themselves into the social fabric of the "fresas" (strawberries) of Mexico City—the young upper-middle-class spenders—to such an extent that there is a notable change in the ways they conceive of growing up. To evaluate the impact of the advertisements properly would require a major sociological study, but the existing evidence suggests that the advertisements have had an impact on social reality. There is an association between maturity, consumerism, and the forms of seductive childishness characterized by crying, or by such lines as "I have nothing to wear." There are, of course, economic issues at stake here, but there are also philosophical questions about the ways in which women are represented in our society and the impact that such representations have on the self-concept of women, men and children. The rites of maturity, once belonging within the province of the family and the private domain, have become consumerized and made part of the public domain—an affair not just for the growing adult and her family but for the entire public sphere.

Consider the following extract and questions from the *Reason and Media* web site:

### Stereotypes

Racial conflict often derives from stereotypes. When we have certain simplified generalizations about groups, we are using stereotypes. Some are harmless. Others prevent balanced judgment of evidence. What would make a stereotypical generalization true? When would it be sensible to use a stereotype?

1) You are trying to save an endangered species of lizard and you are told that they tend to live in sandy burrows under gum trees. Is this a stereotype? How would you establish it as true? Would it be sensible to use this stereotype in your actions?

2) You are looking for someone who stole a car. You are told that young unemployed men are more likely to steal than other groups. Is this a

stereotype? How would you establish it as true? Would it be sensible to use this stereotype in your actions?

3) Your are trying to save the language of a small Aboriginal group and you are told the group lives in small settlements around a certain mission. Is this a stereotype? How would you establish it as true? Would it be sensible to use this stereotype in your actions?

4) You are told that South Africans have a characteristic accent. You are trying to identify a South African in your group. Should you use the accent clue? Is this a stereotype? How would you establish it as true? Would it be sensible to use this stereotype in your actions?

5) You are told that people with a certain accent are less educated than those with another accent. You are choosing a new employee. Should you listen to the accent? Is this a stereotype? How would you establish it as true? Would it be sensible to use this stereotype in your actions?

6) You are told that people with a certain skin colour are less educated than those with another skin colour. You are choosing a new employee. Should you take skin colour into account? Is this a stereotype? How would you establish it as true? Would it be sensible to use this stereotype in your actions?

Students' reactions show their attempts to terms with the notion of stereotypes:

In Regard to Q.4 I believe that this is a very tough situation. But I believe that this is NOT a stereotype but the accent is more of a cultural distinction than anything else. It is a determining characteristic of a nation. Most nations and its inhabitants have a distinct sound to their voice and speech. It would be ignorant of us to believe that we would use stereotypes to identify a person. (first-year student, University of Canberra, 1999)

Though stereotypes can often be degrading and insulting they are often useful and necessary to help us identify certain people and situations. (first-year student, University of Canberra, 1999)

Stereotypes, while we may not generally agree with them, will inevitably exist in our society. (first-year student, University of Canberra, 1999)

The points of the final two students are well taken. It is easy to criticize stereotypes of females. Yet we are dependent on stereotypical classifications to understand the world. Students in Mexico City were reluctant to criticize the campaign for Palacio de Hierro. They loved the indirectness and savviness of the campaign and the advertisements, which had become a talking point for the middle-classes of Mexico City. The image of women was, as one male student pointed out (graduate student, Universidad Ibero-Americana, 1999), more progressive than in other advertisements for clothes. They show the power of women in manipulating their weaknesses to their own advantage. So, for instance, in "No man can answer these questions: 'How do I look?' and 'Do you love me?'", in which a woman is shown standing in front of a blackboard covered in mathematical formulae, there is a subtle suggestion that women create the questions to baffle men. In another advertisement, with an image of Batman on a motorbike, the line runs, "Luckily, we're the weaker sex/The good thing is, he carries the shopping." Men provide the brute force, which women then manipulate to their advantage.

More recent ads have gone further to penetrate the mature audience. An advertisement for online shopping at the store runs:

There are three ways of getting over depression:

1) Stay at home

2) Go shopping

3) Do both.

Again, the advertisement offends norms of what it is appropriate to say in a public place. In middle-class Mexico, depression is regarded as a shameful illness. Shopping your way out of depression is itself a form of the illness. Yet the advertisement, by making explicit reference to depression, paradoxically empowers those women for whom such illnesses are unmentionable. Another ad, also directed at a mature audience, shows a woman making herself up and asks "Who is the vainer? The one who thinks she is fine as she is?" The implicature, that it is less vain to use Palacio products, is a twist, a joke to justify expenditure, at once self-mocking and self-serving.

These are lifestyle ads, with premises of the form of superficially shocking remarks. When we are asked who is vainer or told that all real women say, "I've got nothing to wear"; that women cannot avoid crying or buying shoes; or that men never know the answers to the questions "Do you love me? " or "How do I look?," we are playing a game of being sophisticated. The lifestyle ad takes these smart remarks as premises and goes on, roughly

1) Palacio de Hierro is cool enough to use those types of remarks in ads.

2) I recognize that others recognize that Palacio is cool.

3) In the absence of other reasons for identifying a store as stylish, the fact that the ads of Palacio are cool suggests them.

4) If I want to go where I think others will go to be stylish, I go to Palacio.

At best, the argument provides weak inductive grounds for shopping at Palacio. Expressed this way, the crucial step is the truth of the first premise. Is it true that "I've got nothing to wear" is a smart thing to say, or that men's baffled reaction to certain types of questions is a sign of power for women? After working with the advertisements, one student said that the suggestion that women could not avoid crying and buying shoes was a serious reversal of the process of encouraging women to become professionals in Mexico. That reaction, however, is not the end of the matter. The Palacio ads have also empowered some women, allowing them as shoppers to talk about their choices and creating a sense of the fun and devilry of doing as they choose.

The Palacio advertisements have had a disproportionate effect in Mexico. They are beginning, however, to create a groundswell of reaction. One ad, for instance, shows a woman holding a frog and saying:

Every day there are fewer princes. Luckily there are more Palaces every day....I am totally Palacio.

In the entrance to a leading art gallery, Galeria Carilllo Gil on the Avenida Insurgentes, in September 1999 a huge poster greeted the visitor:

All the time there are fewer Palaces. Luckily we don't all want to be princesses. I am totally iron.[16] (punning on the name of the store, Palacio de Hierro or Palace of Iron)

---

[16] Cada vez hay menos palacios. Por fortuna, no todos queremos ser princesas. Soy totalmente de Hierro.

Advertisements exposed widely enough begin to create their own counterarguments.

## POLITICAL ADVERTISING AND BEING REASONABLE

Each of the strategies and fallacies identified in this chapter can be found in political advertising, which is slick and very thin on content in the modern democracies. This is the complaint of many who are concerned about the impact of television and the new media on the fabric of society. Sartori (1998), for instance, talks of the way that television has disempowered the individual. He argues that we have been reduced from *homo sapiens* to the state of *homo videns*, people who can no longer know, but only watch, as uncritical onlookers.

The commercialization of the political process is at the heart of Sartori's concerns. By turning politics into advertising campaigns, we have turned voters into consumers. As consumers, voters are seen as irrational and dangerous; they are to be manipulated, not convinced. The consequences are obvious in political campaigning. Politicians develop a repertoire of techniques for not answering difficult questions. Perhaps the most effective of these is irrelevance, in which a reply to a question on health care is deflected by raising unrelated issues. At times a politician responds either by questioning the assumptions of the question or the motivation of the interviewer—possibly justifiably but generally only to evade. Political advertising raises these strategies to an art form, avoiding questions and relying on evading issues. Negative campaigns are very successful in this environment, because they do not require a commitment. When Dr. Hewson, the Australian Liberal Party leader, led a campaign to win government in 1993, he took a campaign of action—a consumption tax[17]—to the electorate. His party lost the election which in Australia, with the Westminster system, means that he was not elected. His successor, John Howard, won government for his party on the basis of purely negative campaigns directed against his opponent. At no stage did he mention the consumption tax, but once in government he reintroduced it. His negative

---

[17]  A consumption tax is the tax familiar in the U.S. as the tax placed on goods after purchase. In the U.K. it is called the value added tax, VAT, and in Mexico IVA.

campaign was extremely successful, if misleading about the tax strategy of
the party. Negative campaigns are, on the face of it, fallacious—just because someone else is rotten, it does not follow that the opposition is better.
But it is a clever strategy for evading responsibility and for avoiding the
danger of frightening or offending part of the electorate with your own
policies.

The crudest examples of the genre of political advertising can be found
in countries new to political controversy. Consider the example of Mexico,
which had had over 70 years of one-party rule until the 2000 election. The
ruling party, the Institutional Revolutionary Party (PRI), had never toler-
ated debate or dispute about the political process in any shape or form.
The final PRI president, Zedillo, gave up the custom of *dedazo*, that allowed him to appoint a successor behind closed doors. In 1999 the PRI
candidates, no longer assured of winning, had to fight out issues in what
would be called in the U.S. a primary campaign. The advertisements were
vitriolic, and the first-ever televised primary debate was full of *ad hominem*
arguments. The entire country was shaken by the advertisements of one
candidate named Madrazo. Using a second sense of the candidate's name,
which is an argot word meaning thump, the ad went:

> Dar un madrazo al dedazo.
> Give a bash to the dedazo.

Curiously, the campaign was criticized for vulgarity, for being a gringo
import, and for being inappropriate. It was never criticized for the contradiction inherent in it. Had the *dedazo* been in force, there could have been
no campaign and hence no ad of this type. The content of the ad itself was
never rationally scrutinized.

There is no doubt that there is much that is objectionable in political
campaigns, especially as they endeavor to avoid rational debate. But does
this mean that political ads in fact persuade irrationally? There are many
theories to explain why people do not act in what is taken to be their best
interest; and why they vote not intelligently, but for emotional and irrational reasons (cf Page, 1996). The voters, claim the theorists, are under
the spell of the spin doctors. However, voters, gullible though they are, are
not quite as irrational or passive as some would suggest. The assumption
that voters can be manipulated is the culmination of the attitudes criticized

earlier in the paper, in which it is taken as given that we citizens—or better, consumers—are incapable of rational choice. That view can be contested on two fronts. It takes a very narrowly conceived vision of being rational, and it is self-fulfilling.

If we conceive of reasoning skills and reason in terms of a formal mathematical system, then indeed, no amount of battering with formal conclusions is likely to persuade. However, there are alternatives to this narrow view of reasoning. Reasoning can and should be conceived as intersubjective: good reasoning is a result of fitting the reasons to the audience. Moreover, reasoning skills are used in dialogue. Only rarely do we construct arguments or analyze them as a solitary activity. Reasoning is not something we do in isolation.

Argument is embedded in a social and dialogical context. It is not surprising that we tend to believe people we regard as attractive, competent, and charismatic figures and those whose attitudes and style resembles our own. Such people are credible for good reason. For instance, if a politician sounds uncertain, however good the arguments are, we tend to doubt the message. There are reasons for the snap judgments. Few of us have time to examine all of our beliefs all the time. If we find someone who shares our basic beliefs recommending that we vote in a certain way—or even drink a certain drink—it may be very efficient just to take their advice. Neither should the nervous politician be given the benefit of the doubt too quickly. A nervous politician will not put a case as well as one who is confident. Hence there is a good reason to vote for the more confident candidate. The crucial point is to subject that metalevel assumption itself to criticism.

Much human activity appears irrational or difficult to understand. People are frequently convinced by views that appear incomprehensible to others. Nevertheless, such disagreement about what is rational or logical is possible only in the context of massive agreement. If a person were to act completely illogically, he or she would be regarded as mad. If someone were to claim to believe a view that is, from our perspective, totally unreasonable and inexplicable, we would have to assume that this person had misunderstood the claim or, as Wittgenstein says in a discussion of these cases, "we should regard him as demented."

It is far too easy to accuse another person, or even another sex, of irrationality. Women's discourse structures are different from those of men.[18] Their supportive uncompetitive forms of discourse do not appear to conform to the model of rational conversations. One of the concerns of feminists has been that rationality, as presented in the formal logical models, excludes women and defines the rational as nonfemale (Lloyd, 1993). Certainly, there is a long tradition of defining men as rational; women as irrational. Possibly female forms of conversation may have contributed to this stereotyping. As argued in chapter 2, there is no reason why being reasonable should require competitive modes of talking. The female styles of talking may well be as rational as those of men.

Advertisements, particularly those that are political, should be seen within the context of a broader notion of reasoning. Not only are political advertisements extremely powerful and hence worthy of analysis but they are also crucial to the democratic process. The subtlety and density of the arguments used in advertisements should not deter us from assessing the argumentation. The view that advertisements are irrational has become self-fulfilling.

Once we are convinced that advertisements cannot be assessed on a rational level, we are left defenseless in the political debate. The only reactions sought from the electorate are primitive reactions of liking and disliking. Televised political debates are assessed not in terms of the content of the views put but in terms of how the populace reacts. In Australia, a studio audience in political debates is equipped with an electronic joy stick with a positive and negative direction where they can mark their approval of the candidates. The resulting "worm," a graph of approval or disapproval, is shown at the same time as the debate, cutting across the bottom of the screen. The behavior of the worm has become the most important political test of the candidates. The only other issues that receive attention are the questions relating to the body language and confidence of the candidates.

Obviously, this is a travesty and a magnificent piece of self-advertising on the part of agencies who assist in political campaigns. On the basis of the observation that the electorate may have reactions that are not predictable, advertising companies argue that the electorate is irrational. In fact,

---

[18]   cf e.g., Tannen, D. (1991) and Thorne, B. Kramarae, C & Henley, N. (1983).

electorates may be fickle and difficult but they are not irrational. As citizens, we all need more training in how to assess the impact of political advertising, but we do not need to be told we are persuaded against our better interest. We need to be trained to use our wits better against the very sharp and subtle forms of argument that are being directed at us.

## CONCLUSION

Why do advertisements work? We have been told that arguments act on our subconscious, persuading without engaging the consumer rationally. The assumption of irrationality is wrong. I have been arguing that we should begin with the assumption that advertisements contain arguments, arguments that we can assess. If the premises are not true or the argument does not follow then, even with our very best attempts to be charitable, it is unlikely to be sensible to act on the advertisement. The conclusion simply does not follow.

It is no part of the argument of this chapter to suggest that advertisements cannot change the meaning of products, creating an aura in which a soap powder symbolizes care or a drink like Coke represents a lifestyle. The argument is that this process should not be regarded as irrational. At times the manipulation of meaning is diabolically clever, at times crude; but it is never unconscious. It is the result of a process of ratiocination that is worth untangling. Advertisements are worthy of intense critical scrutiny. Identifying the structures of argumentation in advertisements may not be the only form of critical scrutiny we need to give them, but it is an important form.

Let us finish with another excerpt from the *New York Times*. Below an image of a young punk figure with pierced nose and dark glasses is the following text:

> The bad news is, he's the sole heir to your jewelry collection.
>
> The good news is, there's still time to cash it in for an around-the-world cruise.

It is an advertisement for Windsor Jewelers, a firm that specializes in recycling jewelry. The advertisement leaves a great deal to the imagination—the evident lack of a beloved heir and existence of the ne'er-do-well nephew, for instance. It comes from a cultural context in which there is no expectation that heirlooms should be kept. It is crudely appealing to materialism or making as if it is doing so. The implied argument is obvious: if you own jewelry, it might be worth more than you think. Come to Windsor Jewelers and find out. The conclusion is the intention—if not precisely to buy in this case—at least to go to the shop. The advertisement works by requiring us, the readers, to make a series of reasoned steps. The ad gives us reasons to sell. The question is how good those reasons are.

VISUAL ARGUMENTATION IN ADVERTISEMENTS

On 5 October 1999, the back page of *The News*, the English-language
newspaper in Mexico City, consisted of a full-page ad for the U.S. bank,
Citibank. In the top righthand corner of the advertisement, a bank note in
the shape of a butterfly appears to be leaving the page, trailing a faint blue
jet stream. The image is reminiscent of the many images of chaos theory in
which the flight of a butterfly in one part of the world has catastrophic
consequences elsewhere. It appears to refer to the effects of NAFTA, the
North American Free Trade Agreement, in the Mexican market. The entry
of U.S. banks was part cause, part consequence of the disastrous privatization of the Mexican banking sector just before the fall of the peso in
1994, but coming together with NAFTA, this has had an important impact
on the Mexican economy. Curiously, in an ad for a U.S. bank in Mexico,
the bank note is the Australian $20 note—a note that is technologically far
in advance of the currencies of North America in its use of plasticized paper and watermarks but that is scarcely familiar in the context. At one hit,
the advertisement suggests global access, together with potential for cataclysmic change. It is global, decentered, and elusive—the perfect postmodern announcement.

   The text is minimal. It reads "renewal, growth, freedom" in red text in
lowercase, then on the lower righthand part of the page, the logo appears
in blue text, upper case "CITIBANK" and then in variable point bold lowercase "**where money LIVES.**" This has overtones of chaos theory, of the

freedom from rational constraints that is implicit in "living money." The
nominalized "renewal," "growth" and "freedom" appear to be intended to
categorize not just money but also the life of the investor in Citibank.

The advertisement combines many of themes of this chapter. It is a
print-based advertisement but depends crucially on visual impact. While
visual, grasping its force requires complex ratiocination. We, the consumers, are not simply invited to compare the performance of Citibank with its
rivals or even to take its record as a reason to invest. The reasoning is more
complex and contextual than a simple comparison. The complexity resembles the style and presentation of a television advertisement. The viewer is
invited to reconstruct a possible argument, drawing on specific contextual
knowledge and assumptions about the role of advertisements.

The view that advertisements, and particularly visual advertisements,
are arguments is at odds with the popular account of advertising as irrational. In Poster's terms, an advertisement of this type

> stimulates not an object choice, a cognitive decision, a rational evaluation,
> but works at other linguistic levels, to produce the effects of incorporation
> and attachment between the viewer and the product…[it] works with simu-
> lacra, with inventions and with imaginings. (Poster, 1994: 177-8)

These are familiar claims, dealt with at some length in chapter 5. Advertisements, it is said, together with a large portion of the electronic media, do not function rationally. We find such views throughout the
literature dealing with the transformation of society through technology;
from both sides of the pro- and contra- new technology divide, and indeed,
from both post- and premodernists. Here we concentrate on the visual
elements in advertisements.

This chapter takes up in detail those issues that have been touched on
tangentially in earlier chapters. Lurking behind the debates about the role
of the media, and about television in particular, is the view that the newer
media are utterly different in kind from the familiar print media. Techniques designed to analyze print are accordingly considered to be quite inappropriate for the newer media. Notably, there have been many who
have claimed, as Poster does above, that the newer media do not rely on "a
rational evaluation."

Television has been demonized; its impact, even if unmeasurable by
ordinary testing, assumed to be very profound. Those whose views are

criticized in this chapter argue that the impact of television is due to the nature of the medium. Television is visual and hence cannot function in the rational logical way that language functions. Television moreover interferes with the development of the self; it reconstructs our identities within its own framework.

In this and the following chapter, these two metalevel concerns about television and the new media in general, are taken in turn. The chapters will have a different structure from earlier chapters, relying less on the examples and responses of students and more on argument itself. In this chapter, the ideas of the previous chapter—that advertisements contain argumentation—are developed. The scope of the argument is broadened to the claim that there is visual argumentation. Understanding visual texts requires using the same sorts of skills we use in interpreting verbal texts. This is not to say that visual literacy can be reduced to, or is equivalent to, verbal literacy; just that similar techniques, and most importantly similar levels of rationality, are required.

## VISUAL LITERACY

There is a long tradition of teaching "media literacy" and of other skills designed for the new technologies: "computer literacy," "technology literacy," "visual literacy" and the whole swag of literacies dubbed by Tyner (1998: 63): "multiliteracies." The view that what is needed is a more critical response to the media is often associated with the campaigns for "media literacy." That label is not used here for a number of reasons. First, programs of media literacy have been associated with a condescending tone toward the media—with the beliefs that ads are rubbish, soap operas are stereotypical, news is trash, and cartoons are idiotic. Those beliefs are simplistic. They are often associated with the "critical" tradition of concerns about the media. That tradition, while it gave rise to a powerful research tradition of great value, assumed just as firmly as empirical North American traditions did that the audience had no choice—the content they were offered influenced them in spite of their own interests and concerns.

A newer tradition of media literacy associated with the "active audience" research model has also grown up.[1] This is far more sensitive to the

---

1   I have discussed the tradition at length in chapters 1 and 5, but here refer to Master-

interpretations of those who view television, at times to such an extent that criticism becomes impossible. Between these approaches lies the middle view that we need to be sensitive to the interpretations of those who view television, but at the same time leave room for criticism. That middle view has not found a voice in the media literacy tradition.

There is a second assumption among those who work on the media. It is that the newer media require and evoke new ways of thinking: new skills entirely at odds with the skills used to think about verbal and written texts. For instance, radio and television, being aural and visual, are quite different in kind from written media. This view is taken from both sides of the technology debate. Technophobes such as Postman (1993) decry the impact of television and the new media, suggesting that the linear patterns of thinking may be undermined by the immediacy and impact of television and that hot links on the Internet also fail to encourage the development of logical thinking skills. The general argument is what might be called technological relativism—a form of neo-McLuhanism—because it argues that how we think and see the world depends on the technologies of communication available to and being used by us. Postman, for instance, calls on Eisenstein's (1983) finely worked analyses of the impact of print to suggest that television, with its plethora of clues, limits the imagination and the demands made on the viewer. Print, on the other hand is both "linear" and demanding; the imagination is working double-time to think through images given in language while at the same time interpreting the logical links explicit in written language.

Prophets of the new media, including Douglas Rushkoff, mentioned in chapter 4, share Postman's assumption that television alters reasoning skills, but they welcome the consequences. Rushkoff (1997) talks of the expectations of young viewers and of their inability to tolerate linear patterns of television viewing. He claims that the addiction to channel surfing and highly complex television programs is evidence of the sophistication of what he calls "screenagers." As he sees it, television has changed as "the linear story just broke apart as the programs reached turbulence." (1997:45)

---

man & Mariet's summary (1994) of the European research, Aufderheide's summary (1993) of the North American research and the work of ATOM (The Australian Teachers of the Media in Australia), among others.

Rushkoff characterizes the new viewing style of youth in terms of their abilities to "navigate chaos." (1997:100) He spells this out in terms of the youthful skills of recognizing the fractal patterns that chaos theory identifies, in which a pattern at one level is repeated at other level, in much the way that the seemingly irregular pattern of a coastline seen in broad view is repeated at ever more detailed levels of focus. What appears to be random can be understood and predicted by chaos theory, and that is the sort of understanding, he believes, that characterizes children who surf channels. They can see a pattern, identify content from a fragment of television, and keep moving.[2]

For Rushkoff, we must replace "so called rational thought, linear thinking, and empirical repeatable evidence" (1997:18) with chaotic nonlinear thought, and "nonlinear stories [which] don't define causes and effects, heroes or villains, good or evil." (1997:66). As he later explains:

> We also need to replace the parable with a storytelling form more suitable to a real world based on chaos…a more self conscious recapitulated experience. (1997:223)

In these ways, for critics from both sides of the fence, there is an intimate connection between the medium whereby we receive communication and the possibilities and ways we think about it. The new age of television and the Internet will no longer be the age of the printed word—of the critical thinker and of the individual—but will be one of the image and multimedia—of the chaotic thinker and of the fragmented identity.

The association between the linear display of sentences—the stability of the word on the page characterized by print—with critical thought and individual authorship is at the heart of much of the debate about television and the new media. This chapter deals with the question of the role of critical thought in visual media. The final chapter touches tangentially on the idea of individual authorship. The issue of whether the interpretation of visual images in advertising and the media is irrational is rarely debated directly in the literature. Far too often, there is an uncritical assumption that there is one canonical form of linear reasoning that is paradigmatically

---

2    Rushkoff's use of chaos theory is both very suggestive and highly metaphorical. He draws on elements from the mathematical theory of chaos, together with more broadly based issues of genre and form.

found in print. This chapter argues against that view. Being reasonable is fundamentally a feature of discourse and action, not of written linear texts. It is only a contingent feature of our culture that extended patterns of reasoning do normally appear in print. Reasoning, in the broad sense, is closely linked to descriptions of how we act and rationalize our acting in the world. It is also fundamentally linked to discourse. Framing the rules whereby we extract arguments from extended passages of print, let alone of television, is difficult, as is determining the rules of good reasoned discourse. But this does not mean it is impossible to do so.

The next section identifies the claims and assumptions that underlie the view that advertisements and other elements of the media are irrational. It is argued that underlying these claims are a series of assumptions about reasoning that are themselves unfounded, namely, that reasoning is linear and unemotional. The second section turns to the issue of visual reasoning and its relationship to nonvisual reasoning. Some, but not all, visual images are best seen as arguments. The argument of the chapter is thus designed as a pincer movement on claims that the visual component of advertisements is irrational, first arguing that a full-bodied conception of reasoning means that much of what is called irrational is not and then arguing that certain cases of visual advertisements can be read as argumentation.

## REASONING IN THE NEWER MEDIA

The view that the newer media in general, and advertisements in particular, are incompatible with reason is commonplace. The strategy of this section is to identify the assumptions of three versions of this view, which are identified as separate theses 1, 2, and 3. After defining a notion of reasoning, the assumptions that bolster the three theses are rejected. Theorists generally hold all three theses together to form a network of related views. Nevertheless, it is illuminating to consider them independently. In the following section I will put forward three further positive theses, replacing those I reject here.

The theses concern the *meaning* of elements of advertisements, and they move from the particular to the general—from the meaning of elements, or images, through the meaning of segments to the emotional meaning.

*Thesis 1: The meaning of elements of advertisements is not rational.*

This is a common view, one version of which says that advertisements are not rational but actually function to persuade the viewers irrationally by creating structures of meaning, or signification, in which the product and the consumer are identified.

This thesis is so widespread, even in the industry itself, as to be accepted as common knowledge. It is identifiable in Barthes' (1972) classic work on the impact of advertisements. Using soap powders as an example, Barthes argued that although these were simply harsh chemical cleaners, their meaning had been transformed through advertisements so that they are perceived as soft, gentle, and loving, like the mothers who use them. Judith Williamson's text *Decoding Advertisements*(1981) takes the analysis further. She suggests that:

> …in providing us a structure in which we and those goods are interchangeable, they are selling us ourselves. (Williamson, 1981:13)

A variety of semioticians have developed and refined the analysis to the extent that is widely argued that symbols used in advertisements, like images in the electronic media in general, act not to refer to reality, but are, to use Baudrillard's word "simulacra." The assumption here is that simulacra and second-order signifiers function irrationally.

*Thesis 2: The meaning of nonprint-based forms of communication is irrational.*

This thesis, often associated with the first thesis above, is the claim that nonprint-based forms of communication are nonrational, nonlinear, and even chaotic. One version is that understanding advertisements and understanding the newer media require nonrational processes of thought.

Inclining toward such a view are theorists as various as Poster (1994), Postman (1985, 1993), Rushkoff (1997), and Sartori (1998). Their assumption is that print is uniquely well-suited to argument.

*Thesis 3: The impact of advertisements is emotional and hence irrational.*

Again this thesis is associated with the first two theses above, but it has a long history independent of postmodernism. The claim here is that the newer media, especially television, evoke emotional reactions in viewers that are unmediated by reason. The argument is particularly strong with respect to advertisements, where the psychological literature on persuasion is invoked.

The *locus classici* of this view can be found in the *Republic*, in which Plato said that music and poetry should be banned because he believed them to be liable to evoke emotions and hence lead people astray. The general wisdom of advertising theory agrees with Plato, but it reverses the argument. In order to lead people astray, we should evoke as much emotion as possible. Emotions, it is assumed, are irrational. Television, given its costs and the style of impact, tends to appeal to emotions and is thus the most powerful and expensive way to advertise.

To assess these three theses we need a working definition of what is rational or reasonable. That is in itself a major undertaking, for notions of rationality vary. In this context, rationality needs to be conceived very broadly, as it was presented in the previous chapter. Davidson (1984 *passim*), for example, argues that an act is rational if it "makes sense" to attribute the action to a person while understanding her language, her circumstances, and her desires. In this approach, being reasonable is essentially attributed to a group of language speakers, in order to make sense of their behavior from our own point of view.

Within this broad approach to the notion of rationality, reasoning may be described in different ways. It can be seen as responsive to preexisting norms, or as deriving from the practices of interpersonal behavior and based fundamentally in discourse. In either case, patterns of rational interaction can be described—and indeed formalized—by logical systems, but the formalization is always best seen as an attempt to regiment a description of human behavior. Some theorists assume that there are transcendent critera of rationality; others prefer an emergent conception of what is reasonable as a product of the process of debate. In either case, the notion of being reasonable is linked primarily to the ways we understand human behavior and, crucially, debate. Reasoning is not a print-based activity, nor is the notion of rationality print based.

Here we attempt to transpose to visual communication the model of van Eemeren *et al.,* (e.g., 1993) as sketched in the previous chapter. The strategy is to seek to apply a structure of reasoning and of argumentation to the visual elements of advertisements in particular. That necessarily requires a translation into a system of argument that is generally language based. It is also necessary to amplify the visual elements of advertisements. The model of reasoning as requiring amplification is now widely accepted. But given that amplification is accepted for spoken argument, why should we expect anything different of the rationality of images?

## SIMULACRA—SECOND-ORDER SIGNIFIERS—FUNCTION IRRATIONALLY

Let us apply this model of rationality to the assumption of the first of the views outlined above, namely, that simulacra, and second-order signifiers, function irrationally. Very often the claim that certain practices are irrational really amounts to the claim that to make sense of the practice requires a certain type of amplification. Many of the symbols used in advertising are highly contextual and elliptical. To make sense of them, we need to amplify their role. Amplification may consist in explaining the role of the symbols, for instance in the way that Barthes, Williamson, or Poster give extended (print) explanations of the role of advertising symbols. To say that the use of images, colors, and elisions in advertisements is designed to shortcircuit rational evaluation and encourage "incorporation and attachment" (Poster, 1994: 177) is to claim a rational etiology for the use of such elements. In short, the fact that we need to spell out how signs are used in advertising is not the same as to say that their use is irrational; rather it is to rationalize their use.

Moreover, the first view can be interpreted more broadly along the lines suggested by Baudrillard (1983), as mentioned in chapter 1. He argues that the televisual image becomes a "simulacrum": an object more real than any extra-televisual entity. His arguments on the social role of the image are complex and convincing. There is no doubt that reality and televisual space are interpenetrating, that image is taking precedence over function. But is this process irrational or even any more irrational than any use of referential terms? Baudrillard seems to suggest that some elements of language, of images, or of the televisual repertoire refer unproblematically to the real world. What then would he say of the concept of beauty? Was that, even before television, ever more than a simulacrum? The fact that society has ontological difficulties is scarcely new. Religion specializes in the process of creating simulacra. There is nothing uniquely irrational about the process of creating televisual or advertising simulacra, although the forms of simulacra are being propagated in a unique, and possibly uniquely worrying, way. Nor is the careful analysis of the dangers of televisual reality in any way irrational.

So much for the assumption underlying the first thesis. What then of the second thesis, that print is uniquely well-suited for logical thought and for reasoning, since it is linear, displayed on the page, and stable? If this claim is correct, then the preceding argument is vitiated, for however much we spell out the meaning of a signifier in print, we are doing so in an alien medium, not that to which the signifier primarily belongs. We return to that argument in the next section, but for now let us concentrate on the essence of the second claim, that print is linear and uniquely well-suited to argument and reasoning.

Dialogue, not print, is the basis of argumentation. It is not our practice of writing arguments that is at the heart of being rational; it is our practice of essentially interpersonal debate—of justifying ourselves to others. Argument is linear only in a metaphorical sense. It is a metaphor to think of time as a line. Arguments, whether written or spoken, take time to scan. Insofar as we analyze arguments, their linear appearance, as a coherent argument presented in steps, is generally misleading. A full explanation of the argument will nearly always require amplification and/or cases in which two or more alternatives are considered. It is not a coincidence that branching "natural deduction trees" are such a useful format in logic and that versions of topological spaces are used in some formal semantics. Arguments are often messy. The models developed by van Eemeren normally display the branches of argument on a page, but they are far from unidirectional and linear. Print gives us the formal techniques for representing validity, since it allows the representation of argument structures, but the argument structures themselves are no more print based than the arithmetical relations A>B, B>C, so A>C are essentially print-based relations. Insofar as the relations A>B, B>C, so A>C relate anything, they relate classes of objects, normally numbers, and only by extension anything at all in print.

It is true that the stability of print has made reflective criticism of argument possible. The newer media, such as television and the Internet, being less permanent than printed books, contain arguments that would not get past a print editor. The gatekeepers of the Internet, when they exist, do not play the role of a good print, radio, or TV editor in correcting apparently irrational material. But can we blame the medium for this? It is true too that the reactions of viewers of television and the user of the Internet are less easily controlled than those of book readers. Television viewers, flicking through channels, pick up, as Rushkoff puts it, the fractal patterns of self-similarity between two different programs. However, this is not to say that television viewers are irrational. In effect, television encourages a sort of argument by analogy; a recognition of similarities in one respect that leads the viewer to assume similarities in another respect. Argument by analogy is just another perfectly rational form of argument. Rushkoff is correct in saying that the process of seeing the analogies is more "chaotic" than in print media, precisely because media such as television, with music, print, voice, and image, allow many more branching possibilities than does print. But irrational? Surely not. After all chaos theory is rational; it is just harder to grasp than simple linear relations.

At the risk of overdoing the argument, we can also apply this case too to "hot links" on the Internet, which are, Postman points out, essentially like picking up tangents, taking a new route through the data. This, too, is rational; it is just that it is less easy to regulate than the route taken through a book by an obedient student. Those who have worked through old card files and footnotes have taken the perfectly rational path of links—these are just links rather cooler and more arduous than those offered by the Internet.

There is certainly a core of truth in the claim that the newer media are not linear in the way that traditional narratives were linear. Games like the new genre of hyperfiction,[3] allow the player to choose the pathway and to retrace pathways. Life *is* linear, in the sense that it is irreversible: effects follow on causes. In the newer media, such as the Internet, we can go back, let the story take another path, begin the game again.[4] But in this sense argumentation is reversible as well: arguments are designed to be replayed, and new pathways to conclusions are constantly being devised.

What is implicit in much of the debate about the irrationality of the

---

3   e.g., hyperizons http://www.duke.edu/-mshuma te/hyperfic.htm

4   I owe this point to Greg Battye.

newer media is the fact that the they have a high level of redundancy. Ordinary language is also redundant insofar as messages can be grasped by
competent speakers from just a part of a phrase or from a defective text or
utterance. However, the degree of redundancy is much higher with the
newer media. Television is massively redundant with its messages repeated
both in language and across codes, from images to music. One segment of
an ad, or one episode of a soap opera, is enough for a seasoned viewer to
get the picture. But we must recall that the process of guessing or discerning the meaning is a complex and highly reasoned one, if unconscious;
seasoned viewers draw on knowledge and use analogy and induction to
make sense of what they view.

It is also true that the newer media often exploit ambiguity and levels
of meaning. The interplay of visual, spoken, and written texts in television
and on the Internet have given rise to what Barthes would call a "floating
chain of signifieds" (1977: 39), that is, a multiplicity of meanings and
readings. So, for instance, in the Citibank ad discussed at the beginning of
this chapter, there are levels of meaning which may or may not be appreci-
ated by the consumer. The cross-referencing with the famous image of
chaos theory—the butterfly whose flapping wings on one side of the world
may have major repercussions on the other—is part of the meaning but
only part. The New Age phrasing itself reinforces what is anything but a
New Age message—to bank with Citibank, a bank that just a few years
ago was being publicly derided on every New York subway station for
mistreating its workers.

The phenomenon of multiplicity of meaning, however, also exists at
the level of language. In a finely tuned poem, metaphoric and literal
meanings proliferate. Even with less elevated examples of print, the process of interpretation notoriously demands sensitivity to levels of meaning
and to the vagaries of context and intention. There is nothing unique about
the newer media in this regard, just an acceleration of a familiar process.

## EMOTION IS IRRATIONAL

Far more serious to the defender of the rationality of the newer media
is the role of emotion. The third and final thesis is that emotion is irrational. Since emotional response is the aim of much advertising and much

television, that response is consequently irrational.

At least since Hume, it has been argued that emotion is irrational or inconsistent. It has been said that the fact that written languages divorce the word from the immediacy and emotionalism of the moment allows the written text to distill the rational. A written language requires imagination to visualize or recreate emotion; it cannot recreate emotion the way a film or spoken poem may. Written texts leave a space for recapitulation and for reconsideration; they allow a gap between the first emotional response and a composed and rational reaction. Television short circuits that gap, flinging out fireworks of emotion, and advertisements and visual advertisements operate the same way.

We cannot dismiss this final thesis too rapidly. Seeing a television program *is* more immediate than reading. Considered rationality takes time, time that is rarely given in the television news report, or the online chat room. But emotion is not in itself irrational. The very understanding of reasoning proposed above builds in emotions—we make sense of others as rational only by making a guess at their desires, at what is driving them, and then assuming they are like us in acting rationally to achieve their ends. Emotions are premises in and conclusions of arguments. An image that horrifies does so for good reason. Understanding why an image horrifies may require a great deal of amplification. It may be very difficult to find the premises, the triggers of certain sorts of reactions, but reasonable they had better be if the spin-doctors' and ad agencies' claims to be able to direct emotional reactions have any force. How else can we guess what others may be feeling and what might persuade them to act, except by guessing at their beliefs, often about values, guessing at their desires and then arguing back to find what might motivate that type? We reason, in short, both about the emotions and by using the emotions.

Advertisements are no more or less irrational than any other medium of communication.[5] They are used for communication and understanding what others mean, linguistically or nonlinguistically. This requires a complex series of reasoning activities. In understanding the force of a gesture or an utterance, we have to assume much about another's intentions; about

---

5   This is a claim about the nature of communication. A person may act irrationally as a result of any communicative act.

their use of codes and their beliefs concerning those with whom they communicate. To count as communication, the process must involve an elaborate process of reasoning rather than an irrational leap in the dark. This does not mean, of course, that the messages that advertisements contain, or the ways they want you to act, are moral or justifiable or in the best interests of consumers. It merely means that the communicative act is not irrational.

Thus, while each of the three theses described on page 161 contains important insights, visual advertisements do involve reasoning, or, to be more precise, argumentation. The images contained in advertisements serve in the argumentation, as do the emotional reactions they elicit which can be both premises and conclusions in argument. Moreover, the principles of reasoning are not importantly different from those used in print- or oral-based reasoning.

## VISUAL REASONING

Not all images involve argumentation. Indeed, most do not. Images in advertisements carry dialogical weight, in part because of the context and the generic style of advertisements. But is there a specific form of visual reasoning and can it be reduced to a linguistic form, or is it purely visual and independent of language? There is a substantial body of literature on the meaning of visual symbols, but, for the purposes of this chapter, we consider only those that provide a tentative basis for a theory of visual argument. Again, these can be identified as a network of three theses, though perhaps better regarded as suggestions.

*Thesis 4: Images may function as speech acts.*

Mitchell (1994) suggests that there is a "pictorial turn" in postmodern culture to images in place of language. After a century characterized by the "linguistic turn," the argument goes, at the level of both practice and theory, we have now reached a time in which the pictorial image and the possibilities of representation it presents are central.

> On the one hand, it seems overwhelmingly obvious that the era of video and cybernetic technology, the age of electronic reproduction, has developed new forms of visual stimulation and illusions with unprecedented powers.

> On the other hand, the fear of the image, the anxiety that the "power of im-
> ages" may finally destroy even their creators and manipulators…has become
> a technical possibility on a global scale. (Mitchell, 1994:15)

For Mitchell, the pictorial turn is as rational,[6] as highly culture bound, and
as complex as the print culture.

> There is, *semantically* speaking…no essential difference between texts and
> images…there are important differences between visual and verbal media at
> the level of sign types, forms, materials of representation, and institutional
> traditions. (1994:161)

Images need a general theory of semiotics to explain their force.
Mitchell's approach sets him apart from those who merely identify meanings of particular symbols. He is concerned with the complexity of pictorial meaning, with its structural and metalevel import. Pictures, he thinks,
may have the force of a speech act and, indeed, have had so since the beginning of human communication. The change is that we now have an increasing dependence on the image, which we need to understand on its
own terms. His argument is that we cannot reduce the meaning of the
pictorial component to the linguistic.

*Thesis 5: Images are to be interpreted in terms of their culture- specific semiotics.*

The suggestion that images have their own semiotic system that is not
parasitic on that of language is implicit in Mitchell and has been made explicit in theories of social semiotics, especially in the field now known as
"discourse semiotics" (e.g., Kress & van Leeuwen, 1996). Systemic linguists such as Halliday (e.g., 1985) offer a classification of the functions of
language in terms of ideational, textual, and interpersonal roles. In line
with the Halliday perspective, Kress and van Leeuwen identify the ideational, the textual, and the interpersonal metafunctions of a semiotic mode.
The first of these essentially describes the representative function. In the
case of visual images, Kress and van Leeuwen distinguish narrative and
conceptual ideational modes. Images, that is, can tell a story or put forth an

---

6    This is so, even as we accept that Mitchell is investigating the "paradox" of the picto-
     rial turn expressed by the two views mentioned here. There is no paradox without rea-
     son.

analysis or both. Kress and van Leeuwen identify each of these functions with characteristic modes of pictorial presentation. The Citibank ad is essentially a conceptual analysis—a representation of how money lives.

At the level of the textual metafunction, Kress and van Leeuwen concentrate on the meaning of compositional elements of the image. They argue that in Western cultures with a left to right writing mode, the page has been divided. They summarize their analysis with a diagram (1998: 621) slightly simplified here.

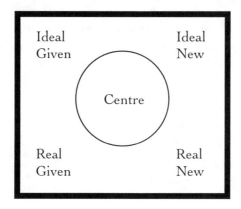

The left-hand side of the page tends to be the given, the top the ideal. Thus an advertisement like the Citibank ad would be analyzed as having significant left-right/up-down meanings. Perhaps we might say that the given of renewal, growth, and freedom on the left leads up to the top-right, money-patterned butterfly symbolizing the future.

Within the *interpersonal* metafunction, Kress and van Leeuwen discuss the ways in which a viewer is positioned relative to the image. In the Citibank ad, we are positioned as onlookers. Here the viewer is being persuaded, by visual argument, to buy. It is an instance of what I call visual argumentation. While we have of necessity translated the code into language, it is in essence not a verbal, but a visual, code.

A systematic approach to the force of images within a particular context does not consist in merely dubbing a linguistic function with a nonlinguistic substitute. The visual codes have their own functions. The aim is to show we can spell out the code, which is essentially visual and spatial, not linguistic.

*Thesis 6: Images and metaphors contain their own argumentation structure.*

The suggestion that images and metaphors contain their own patterning of argumentation is made explicit in Johnson's influential book, *The Body in the Mind* (1989). The particular argument of interest here is his suggestion that schemata, whether linguistic or nonlinguistic, allow us to "have a world." A schema is for Johnson "...a recurrent pattern, shape, and regularity in or of the ongoing ordering activities." (1989:24)

Thus a pattern of images, or a metaphorical model, may serve as a schema and determine how we experience our world as comprehensible. Images or metaphors drive argument, so that reasoning is not purely propositional but may be visual. In an earlier work, Lakoff & Johnson (1980) pointed out the visual component of much language about argumentation—we "point out issues," "see an argument," and so on. Argument is both imbued with and embedded in the language of visual discrimination. Johnson argues that thought itself is irredeemably metaphoric.

Putting the theses 4, 5, and 6 together, one can envisage the case for visual reasoning. The visual impact of images, at least in certain specified contexts, should not be explained as irrational or unreasoned. It is based on, and derives from, reasoning at a visual level. Certain images contain and give rise to complex patterns of reasoned thought; patterns that are intended to be discerned by the viewer and that modify or determine the communicative act. This implies that there is a logically significant structure in the visual "utterances."[7] Both Kress and Johnson give guidance as to how we might discern such a structure. The structure must be resilient enough to support an argument: with amplification, it must be possible to show how elements of the visual might correspond to, or play the role of, premises and conclusions. A full exploration of such a scheme is beyond the scope of this chapter; however, we can test the idea against the Citibank advertisement described at the beginning of the chapter.

## THE CITIBANK AD REVISITED

The linguistic component of the Citibank ad is "renewal, growth, free-

---

7   It is no part of the suggestion here that we deduce the meaning of images from "bare particulars." We deduce in seeing the images (cf Wittgenstein, 1953:2, para xi.)

dom" and "Citibank: Where money lives." This is susceptible to analysis
within well-motivated linguistic theory or theories. Within argumentation
theory, the verbal text would be read as dialogical: as making an argument
to the consumer, who can be taken to be the other voice in advertisements.
This is not *ad hoc*. The genre of advertisements often uses the imperative, or
locutions in which "you" refers to the consumer, to make that a characteristic generic type. The conclusion then, given the linguistic and extralin-
guistic context, in which banks are competing for custom in the Mexican
market, is obvious: "Bank with Citibank."

Now we need to amplify the argument contained in the elliptical
premises, in order to reconstruct the argument. First, consider the nominalized "renewal, growth, freedom" with a link to Citibank, "where money
lives." How do we reconstruct an argument here? Clearly renewal,
growth, and freedom are, in any context, desirable. The premise might
read: you desire to have renewal, growth, and freedom. However, given
the context, Citibank: "where money lives," the argument might better be
put: you want your money to renew, grow, and be free. The implicit inference is then based on: if you want your money to renew, grow, and be free,
bank with Citibank. Then, by *modus ponens*, we get the conclusion to bank
with Citibank.

The analysis does not explore the metaphorical shift that is implicit in
the notion of renewed or free money—free from what? Tax? Nor have we
analyzed the implication that not just your money but *you* will be renewed,
will grow, and be free if you bank with Citibank. Again, there is far more
to be said, for the use of the butterfly is symbolic of freedom as well as
beauty within a well-attested set of advertising traditions. Only by the full
process of reconstruction with an imaginary interlocutor could we trace
through those implications. Nevertheless, we have the beginnings of a
dialogical process that yields argument.

The visual argumentation is far more difficult than the verbal to analyze in a systematic way, precisely because it lacks the framework of linguistic behavior. Language gives the resources for displaying argument. It
provides the very notion of truth essential in descriptions of validity in argument. Sentences or utterances are true[8]; images are representations—a

---

8   The particular notion of truth at play here is not important; what is important is the

quite different relation. We can understand a sentence and not know whether it is true or false. We can see an argument is valid and, not knowing the truth of the premises, can doubt the truth of the conclusion. We can see that an argument containing propositions p and q and with a structure:

If p then q

p

So q

is valid in virtue of the structure of the argument together with the meaning of the operator "If...then. " "If...then" is, in the traditional formulation, a truth functional operator. The meaning of that operator is what licenses the structural move, but we are licensed to identify the operator because it is used across a wide range of linguistic activities. Discerning the meaning of "if...then" is not *ad hoc*.

What is a visual equivalent? In the example given by Kress & van Leeuwen (1998) of the meaning of quadrants of a written page in Western culture, there is a *prima facie* plausibility to the claim. We might agree that, in the cases analyzed, the left-right direction leads from past to future, while the upper half as ideal is contrasted with the lower real. However, a great deal of evidence would be required to make the case watertight. In the Citibank ad, the logical meaning of the quadrants is plausible but debatable. The ad writer may be unconsciously playing on the fact that the butterfly on the top left is ideal and future oriented, but it is unlikely that it is assumed that the consumer recognizes that the placement of the butterfly has that meaning.

Thus the precondition of communicative intention seem to be lacking. The embedded intentions necessary for communication are of the form:

I use this, intending to mean *x*, and intending that another takes me to be using this to mean *x*, and intending that another recognizes my intention (and so on.)[9]

---

fact that there is some notion—assertability, justification, or the like—that is needed in an account of linguistic behavior and is not necessary to describe the use of images.

[9] This model of communicative intentions is based on the work of specifically Schiffer (1972) on meaning. It is Gricean in its basic form.

That is, we communicate assuming that others share our repertoire of meanings. But is this true of visual communication? Do we have shared visual meanings as we share language? Can visual imagery be as explicit as language, given that the structures of vision are so much less obvious than the syntax of language? The difficulty is one that has led many to question the whole concept of the meaning of an image and the semiotic theory that has been of such currency. Semiotics, it has been argued,[10] mistakenly assimilates linguistic and nonlinguistic meaning, failing to recognize the unique force of linguistic structure in meaning generation. Chomsky (1957) explains the role and power of structure in language and Frege (e.g., 1952) demonstrates the role that structure has in argument. How can we suggest that images have the sort of structure that language so evidently possesses?

However, images may be part of highly complex structural networks, some parasitic on language, others not. In the Citibank ad, the reference to chaos theory and the fact that the butterfly is constructed from an Australian $20 note may not be picked up by many of those to whom the ad is addressed. Nevertheless, the references are part of common knowledge within the global community, as is knowledge of the chaotic impact of the NAFTA free trade arrangements on Mexican banks. So the visual component of the ad has common meaning and common meaning structures, which can be translated into an argument structure. For instance, we might explain the reasoning as follows:

> The butterfly is made of an Australian $20 note, and the butterfly represents Citibank, so the assumption is that Citibank deals in Australian money, so Citibank is an international bank, but I want to be part of an international bank (assumption ), so I will bank with Citibank.

In this argument, the premises are at least plausibly true, as are the conclusions. A similar set of arguments might link:

> A butterfly's movements in one part of the world can cause chaos in another. This image associates a butterfly with banking in Mexico. The butterfly could shake Mexican markets. There is a banking crisis in Mexico (assumption). We can avoid the crisis by relying on international banks (assumption). Citibank is international (see above). So I should bank with Citibank.

---

10   e.g., Pettit (1977).

The argument is that we can identify visual arguments that support and reinforce the reconstructed verbal argument of the advertisement. The reconstruction is verbal, but this is not to say that it is essentially linguistic. It relies on knowledge and use of nonlinguistic meanings.

Visual reasoning exists. It is profoundly important in the way we react to the world. As visual reasoning becomes more deeply embedded in the cultural artifacts of the newer media, it is increasingly important to discern the reasoning patterns implicit in images. But we should not merely attribute meanings to images in an *ad hoc* fashion. The analysis of the argumentation structure of images must be well motivated and generalizable. The model of argumentation analysis then should be the analogue of the processes of reconstructing argumentative linguistic discourse.

## CONCLUSION

The newer media are characterized by the interplay of image and text, of voice and cultural cross-referencing. Theorists discussed in this chapter have argued that the impact is irrational. The argument here is that the impact, far from being irrational, is, in fact, highly rational. The newer media make more demands than ever on reasoning skills, insofar as they embroider the verbal text with arguments of a purely visual kind. Arguments in the newer media draw, as arguments always have, on the common knowledge about the world, the texts, the genres, used by a community. Those who construct arguments in the newer media, including those who construct advertisements, play a highly sophisticated game using visual representation: suppressing premises, misleading and bringing the opponent in the argument up short. None of this should be a surprise. The basic styles of argumentation have persisted since Socrates confounded his interlocutors with his dialectic. Images and metaphors have always had a role in argumentation, just as analogy and inductive reasons have. Argumentation and reasoning is a complex human behavior, but its complexity should not drive us to call it irrational or to abstain from attempting analysis.

We can see reasons. Let us turn finally to another ad from the Mexico City press, this time a quality broadsheet, *Reforma* (14 July 1999). This is an ad for a Samsung mobile phone, which has been used in many countries and languages.[11] This text is in argument form, roughly translated:

> Sometimes, small things are more striking.
> Moreover, these things recognize your voice, and are friendly, orderly, intelligent and good-looking.
> It's coming!
> Samsung Electronics.

We might add an elliptical premise or assumption, "You want electronic equipment that is small, recognizes your voice, is friendly, orderly, intelligent and good-looking." Given the claim that Samsung offers the product, we get the conclusion to buy the Samsung cellular phone.

The message is, however, far more complex. The image shows a man unclothed to the waist, the lower half of his body covered with text. A pony-tailed and rather startled, fully-dressed woman is looking through a magnifying glass at what is hidden by the text. Is this small and "impactante"? The sexual innuendo proliferates the meanings of the written text, making a series of sexually colored claims about small members, about those which recognize your voice, are intelligent and so on. The *double entendre* clearly serves primarily to grab attention, but it also has argumentative force. We might reconstruct a series of arguments at this point, using the style of a semiotic theorist but now placing it in the context of argumentation.

First the ad is narrative rather than conceptual in terms of its ideational function. It tells a story. The story carries its meanings in terms of the diagonal lines drawn across the image, from the woman's eyes, through the magnifying glass to the unseen focus of our glance. Next, the image in its interpersonal function is an instance of what Kress and van Leeuwen call "demand pictures": images which call on the viewer to act. Women are invited to look, and then to buy. Finally in terms of the textual function, the rather conventional division of the ad into an upper half with an image,

---

11   In Spanish the text is:
     A veces es más impactante que sea pequeno
     Y además reconoce tu voz, es amigable, ordenado, inteligente y el más bonito
     ¡Próximamente!
     Samsung electronics

the lower half with text, here has a particular meaning. Recall that the upper half of an image is the ideal, the lower is the real, while the left is the given, the right the new. The woman in the top left quadrant thus is seen as the ideal and new, the undressed male is the ideal given element of the design. The real, both given and new, is hidden behind text, as if for reasons of modesty.

The ad is set in a social context in Mexico, where men are still the major sexual predators. The image of the young woman as sexual investigator, resembling a naturalist on the lookout for a rare series of beetle, resonates in that context. She is indeed the ideal and new style of woman. The image of the woman inspecting the man contributes to the shock value of the ad. Reality, the ad suggests, may be hidden but significant.

Implicitly the ad is aimed at women, as the new group of buyers of equipment. The ad asks in effect that the woman make a choice of sexual partner. Previously such actions were restricted to men. Not only can women choose, then, they should and do want to. There is an argument by analogy. You, a woman, have the right to choose your man (and his equipment). Similarly you, a woman, have the right to choose your electronic equipment. The conclusion then is that you, a woman, should choose Samsung.

Here, the visual message supplements and overrides the verbal argumentation, giving a twist to the story. But the twist is no less rational for being a twist. You may need a magnifying glass to see it, but a reason is there to be seen.

# PUBLIC FACES
# IN PRIVATE PLACES

## The Public/Private Divide and Identity

Private faces in public places
Are wiser and nicer
Than public faces in private places.[1]

W. H. Auden's lines bring out the distaste many feel at the parading of the private affairs of public figures. Yet television specializes in putting public faces into that most private of places: the home. Public figures themselves use television to gain entry into the home to create their own identities and mold those of the voters they woo. This chapter deals with the way the divide between what is public and what is private has been recast under the impact of the new technologies. In particular, it concentrates on the ways personal identity has been transformed by the newer media, both television and the Internet, and the impact that this has had on the possibility of defining the self.

The very notions of the public and the private are under pressure. Newer technologies undermine the borders between the public and private spheres, leaving many of our most deeply felt intuitions floating in cyberspace. Public figures, while decrying the invasion of their privacy, exploit the access television gives to private homes and emotions with the consequences ranging from bathos to tragedy. On the one hand, the opinions of

---

[1]    Quoted in Alan Bennett, 1994: 49.

private individuals with no relevant expertise are elevated to profundity by an appearance on talk-back television. On the other hand the lives of public figures such as Diana, Princess of Wales, are left with no private space at all, even in death.

In *The New York Times*, Bruni (1997) cites a number of cases in which the private affairs of public figures in the United States have been publicized, with their agreement—the personal details of their families are cited by the politicians themselves. Ruth Messinger, the Democratic candidate for mayor of New York, for instance, began her unsuccessful campaign by revealing that her daughter was not only gay but also a mother. "I think people like to know that their elected officials are not plastic figures but real people," she said by way of explanation (Bruni, 1997: B2).

In this chapter, we deal with notions of the public and private as they are used in the media and as they have influenced the discussion throughout this book. We trace a very brief etiology of the notions, then analyze the concepts in more detail, dividing them into subconcepts, before dealing with the changes in each concept under pressure from new technologies and globalization. Finally, we return to the mediated self and the transformed public sphere in an attempt to reinstate the moral intuitions those concepts instantiated.

## PUBLIC, NOT PRIVATE; PRIVATE, NOT PUBLIC

Each chapter of this book has charted a crossing of the line between the public and private in some senses. While once the major public events of the world were those that were real, at least in the sense of being really important, now it is the private events that are seen as real—to use Messinger's terms, "real, not plastic." The transformation of the notion of reality under the impact of television was the theme of the first chapter. When tabloid style news takes over from the "public" broadsheet tones of the network news bulletin, what is happening is an invasion of what had been seen as a public space by the mores and style of private gossip. That question was the theme of the second chapter.

The place for discussion of major changes in the moral codes of a society is no longer the church or state, but popular soap operas, as it is in the case of *Mirada de Mujer*, discussed in the third chapter. Here, there is a re-

verse infiltration of the private domestic space of the soap opera into public debate. The same is true in debates about censorship and cartoons such
as *South Park*. The claim that there are some things that should not be said
publicly is precisely a claim about the limits of what is public and what is
private. *South Park* is shocking because it breaks the conventional divide.

Advertising, too, transgresses the public/private divide. When the
Mexican press shows a suggestive image of a young woman inspecting a
young man's equipment, as the Samsung ad does, it is shock that demands
attention. The shock comes from the sense that what is said publicly is
really a private matter. The distinction between the public and private is at
the heart of moral intuitions and of the sense of what can be said in the
media. What is private should not be publicized, at least not if we wish to
preserve some sense of personal integrity.

Nor is the realignment of the public/private divide just of theoretical
concern. That divide is fundamental to our moral intuitions. The links
between the self and what is private are deeply embedded in Western culture. The moral codes that underlie much of the debate about television
and the new media are driven by a network of beliefs about the role of the
domestic private family sphere as the appropriate space for defining the
individual and personal morality—of the public sphere as a space for im-
posing a rational public grid on the private selves. Television, in this sense,
disturbs the division.

Habermas' discussion of the public/private divide (Habermas [1962]
1989) has served as the basis of the debate as it has been applied to the
media.[2] In *The Structural Transformation of the Public Sphere*, Habermas
identified the personalization of the public sphere as a danger:

> The public sphere becomes the sphere for the publicising of private biogra-
> phies, so that the accidental fate of the so-called man in the street or that of
> the systematically managed stars attain publicity, while publicly relevant de-
> velopments and decisions are garbed in private dress and through personal-
> isation distorted to the point of unrecognisability. The sentimentality
> towards persons and the corresponding cynicism towards institu-
> tions…curtail the subjective capacity for rational criticism of public author-
> ity. (Habermas, 1989: 171-172)

---

2    cf., e.g., Kress (1986), Lumby (1999), Meyrowitz (1985), Poole (1989), and critiques
     in Robbins (1993).

These remarks illuminate a particular tension that television has brought to the fore, between the public sphere and the domain of the private self. In the post-Cartesian West, the notions of the self and of the private are closely intertwined: the self is just the part of the universe to which we have privileged private access. The public world, at least in Habermas' terms, is a space of rational impersonal debate where disembodied reason can be applied to public communal matters. Television both reflects and abets the shifting boundaries of the self, the public, and the private.

The dichotomy between what is public and what is private is problematic not only in television but also, more broadly, across a range of issues. The debate about the characteristics of the public sphere has, to a certain extent, reached stalling point, when it has become natural simply to deny that the distinction even exists. I suggest that it is not so much the distinction that we should abandon but the spatial metaphors which dominate our thinking about the public/private divide. The immense force of the spatial images that dominate our understanding of this can best be illustrated metaphorically.

Consider an Australian example. Australian government policy is written in Canberra, a capital which, in the words of Jan Morris (1980: 7), resembles those other created capitals such as Islamabad, Brasilia, and Washington in its bleakly and highly regulated artifice of architecture. In Canberra, the regulatory environment is pervasive. There is a continuum from the clean and tree-lined streetscape, liberally scattered with bike paths and traffic lights, where roads are constantly dug up, to the constantly revised and "transparent" policies of the bureaucrats whose houses line the streets. The analogies proliferate. One of the most curious features of the Canberra streetscape is the lack of front fences. It is, in fact, against the law to have any front fence, other than a "growing hedge." This excludes brush, wood and all other ways of screening the house and garden from public view. Indeed, the only really effective barrier allowed is the exotic hedge of pine, which major media barons such as Rupert Murdoch use to shield their Canberra residences from the outside world.

The point of this extended analogy lies in the setting of a particular contrast: that between the public world of the street, in this case the transparent open front of Canberra, and the private domain of the rear garden, used for hanging out the wash.[3] Canberra is a city that places a high value on transparency and a high value on the public. The back garden/front garden divide is, as it were, a divide between the public and the private domains. It is a divide between what counts as part of the public world, open for regulation and scrutiny and available for debate, and what is the realm of the private, of the family, the region of life that is not meant to be open for government legislation or other scrutiny. Metaphorically speaking, it is this front garden/back garden divide that television invades. The public world of the television enters and penetrates the private space of the house and back garden, while revealing and making transparent back garden "private" affairs to outsiders. *Neighbours*, the highly successful Australian soap opera, deals precisely with the way that neighbors, whose relations belong to the public world of the street, can and do become part of each others' private worlds. The soap was the first of a huge range of programs that exploited the metaphor of the public/private divide. *Neighbours* was successful because it reflected the interpenetration of the public and private spheres, a process television itself encourages. Its success is evidence that it was placing itself at the edge of issues of more than theoretical interest—it showed how the public/private divide could be bridged. The actors in the soap offended almost unrecognized taboos and provided new visions of living a private life in public.

We have come to think of the public/private divide as a given, as a univocal division that divides the world into just two spheres—what is properly speaking public and what private. We are then shocked at any transgressions of the borders. It is this division of the public and private that needs to be examined.

## CONSTRUCTING THE PUBLIC/PRIVATE DIVIDE

It is worth summarizing a number of factors that contribute to the way the borderlines are laid between the public and private realms. First, the

---

3  A sustained argument that modern architecture itself emerges from the merging of the public and private domains and assimilation of the principles of the mass media can be found in Colomina (1998). She examines the work of Le Courbusier and Adolf Loos. Her arguments fit well with the thesis of this chapter—that the notions of the public and private changed significantly over the 20th century.

conception of the public/private divide is essentially a Western conception, deriving from the ancient Greek and Roman polities. The distinctive spatial metaphors in which we describe the distinction—the public realm or domain, the private space of the home—may be traced to those sources. On one side of the divide in Greek and Roman life was public life, the life of the agora or forum, and in the case of Rome, the Senate, and of the streets in which men debated the affairs of the State, regulated the law of the land, began wars, and debated issues of trade. On the other side was domestic life in which women played a major role directing the life of the family and the regulation of domestic morals as well as the management of the domestic economy. Often, since this involved the management of farms and major households, this was not an inconsiderable undertaking. The conflict between public and private morality becomes clear in *The Apology*, when Socrates, accused of perverting the youth by leading them to a discussion of morality, is condemned to death by the State. He chooses to drink hemlock rather than flee because he sees his private life as inextricably linked to his public life in the State. That view is in stark contrast to the Christian maxim to "render unto Caesar what is due unto Caesar; render unto God what is due unto God." The maxim tells us to pay taxes to the state but to practice an individual religious life in separation from the obligations to the state. Private religious life is seen as properly independent of the public life of the state.

Both the Socratic and the Christian views can be found in the models of the public and private that were developed by the emerging Western nations. Notice that in both cases, the conception of the public is a conception of what is liable to public regulation. It is the extent to which law is seen to apply that delimits the public realm. Cartesian dualism, by drawing a line within the private between the mind and the body, reinforced the Christian separation. Thereby arises a distinction between the private, certain if disembodied *cogito*, and the possibly mistaken but corporeal and extensive body. That divide let loose on Europe the possibility of radical skepticism and doubt about the external world. It also provided a justification for the separation of a narrow private space from the public domain. The public sphere, then, became a domain utterly distinct from the private space of the home, and the even more private space of mental life.

In this scheme of opposition between the defenders of the private and of the role of the State, Habermas' (1989) ideal public sphere offers a middle way. The ideal public sphere is the domain in which participants in the social process can engage in debate about the public good. The notion of a public sphere is of a space in which public debate governed by rules of rationality is protected. In chapter 2, we noted that critics such as Fraser (1993), Benhabib (1992) and Iris Marion Young (1990)[4] have argued that Habermas' public sphere is unacceptably narrow in conception. The model of rational debate is one of informed and competent debaters coming together to put their views, presumably articulately and rationally. It excludes those who are voiceless and marginalized, and it is insensitive to the need for empathy, for an ability to change and see the world as oppressed groups do. Even so, the model of informed debate does give a perspective for the understanding of the role of the private individual in the public sphere.[5]

This cursory survey is designed to bring out the factors that are germane to the dual difficulty of establishing an identity in the framework of the newer media and of defining a space in which the self is "private." Philosophical problems exist precisely because such issues are emotionally loaded. What counts as private is both deeply felt yet inchoate in a range of cultures. The sense of outrage that attends a breach of privacy is partly a result of the profound links that exist between our notion of what is private and of what constitutes the self.

The immediacy and visual force of television as medium has allowed the public world to invade both the home and the inner mental world in an unprecedented way. It is this feature of television that has driven much of the criticism of the new medium. When Postman (1982) talks of "the disappearance of childhood" or of a culture that "amuses itself to death" (1985), his concern is that the public world has invaded the private spaces of domestic education. The theme of the inversions of the public and private aspects of culture is a theme that Meyrowitz (1985) examined in some depth. Lumby (1999: 57-58), while less quick to condemn the assimilation

---

4    Robbins, 1993, summarizes debates on Habermas.

5    Thompson (1998) describes a way of reinstating the Habermasian public sphere with a less narrow model of rationality. In this chapter, as in chapter 3, I draw on her work.

of the public and private spaces in the modern tabloid press, endorses Meyrowitz's analysis.

As Lumby makes clear, it would be simplistic to condemn the personalization of the public sphere too rapidly. The "higher truth" of the broadsheet and the traditional news bulletin had an inherent bias toward established interests—toward those who were in command of the public forms of rhetoric—thereby reducing those on the margins, whether for reasons of race, gender, or educational difference, to near invisibility. The television talk shows empower private individuals in a society to take a voice and to participate in the public sphere, even if this is now a public sphere very different from the Habermasian ideal. Oprah Winfrey's talk shows provide another, more personal, narrative route to an understanding of the world—a route that in some sense is preferable since it includes those minorities, such as women and African Americans, who are implicitly excluded by the WASP tones of the older-style evening news bulletin.

Nevertheless, the uncertainty about what is public and what is private is a profoundly unsettling consequence of modern culture.

## PERSONAL IDENTITY

There are important consequences in the changing faces of the public sphere, including the privatization and the increasingly soapy character of the public domain. Not only does it affect how those citizens who view television understand public affairs, it also determines how viewers develop their personal sense of identity.

It has long been a commonplace of theorizing about television that viewers' apprehension of how the televisual world is constructed determines to some extent their view of themselves. Paradoxically, theorists from the empirical perspective who followed, for instance, the effects of propaganda, and critical theorists, who deplore the alienation imposed by television, share an assumption that media effects are direct and immediate and impose a given image of the world on viewers. Those who concentrate on the reception of television in their turn frequently assume that viewers bring a ready-formed self to the act of viewing television. Identity is not formed independently of the media. Identity is in part formed through the media, just as the media is shaped through the participation and expectations of the audience (Alasuutari, 1999).

Television images and models do have some effect on the viewer's self-concept. That effect is best gauged by concentrating on the audience rather on than the message, but it is an effect nonetheless. For instance, Jane Shattuc's (1997) study of TV talk shows and women looks at the meanings particular audience segments create through the talk show and the ways in which the myths of the home and hearth have been reinstated by the genre. Yet Shattuc is unequivocal: the talk shows do have an effect on the ways a certain group of American women perceive themselves.

The stereotypes of the talk show, the domestic sitcom and the soap opera have not only formed the self-image of the viewers but they have also created the images of politicians. As Messinger says, politicians have to be seen as "real, not plastic." By a mysterious semantic shift, to be real now appears to mean to be like a soap opera character, with a gay daughter, perhaps. The natural tendency to guard one's privacy has become "plastic." No public figure can be real unless their private proclivities are up for public view.

Identity becomes difficult to establish. It is only by voicing, preferably loudly, a personal and private truth that one becomes "real." The popularity of talk shows and talk-back radio witnesses the importance viewers now place on having their own say, on becoming "real," not plastic, themselves. Socrates warned against "the unexamined life," suggesting that a sense of self would elude those who did not consider their choices philosophically. These days, the dictum would be better expressed as a dictum against "the unpublicized life." A private self is not "real" or validated until made public.

This said, there is a curious anomaly in the attitude toward the revelation of the private self in public. At the same time that the fashion for public coming out has taken hold, the rhetoric of invasion of privacy by new technology has increased. In one sense, then, the invasion of our privacy, whether by noise or compuuter access to our bank records, is the converse of the personalization of the public. Discussion of the invasion of privacy is an intensely emotional and heated debate. Privacy inherits a range of philosophical problems associated with the self, self-definition, and the self in a group. Those philosophical problems exist precisely because such issues are emotionally loaded. What counts as private is deeply felt yet inchoate in a range of cultures. The sense of outrage that attends a breach of privacy is partly a result of the profound links that exist between our notion of what is private and of what constitutes the self.

While we have become increasingly inclined to broadcast private matters, we are increasingly wary of those who might gather and broadcast private facts without our permission. What counts as private has altered significantly. The self, defined as it is partly in terms of the notions of privacy, is also under pressure as the boundaries of the private domain shift. On one hand, the public sphere, represented more and more vividly through the newer media, casts issues in a highly personalized fashion. On the other hand, the privacy of the private domain is contracting. Computer data bases make possible invasions of privacy that were hitherto impossible. Direct marketing companies already accumulate detail on a range of preferences and choices made by consumers in order to target new markets. The information can be horrifyingly misused. Data matching for purposes other than that for which the data was originally collected has been outlawed in principle in many countries, but policing such a regulation in the new technological age is well nigh impossible.

New technologies recast the boundaries of the self. The Cartesian conception of the self continues to provide the fundamental structure of Western morality and understanding of the world. If the Cartesian "I think therefore I am" is the basis of our understanding of ourself, then what I think is also my private business. No one else should have the access I do to my thoughts, at least unless I choose to reveal them. On the Cartesian model, being a self is constituted by having reflexive thoughts about yourself as a thinker. If we are our thoughts, then any attempt to undermine our possession of the products of our mind is an outrage.

We are uneasy about invasion of privacy insofar as the public stories enter our private world and in so far as our private stories are publicized. There are serious taboos against the assimilation of the public and private areas of life, taboos that are associated with the fact that our identities are defined differently for the two spaces: as public figure or as private being. To extend Appadurai's (1993) evocative phrase, overlapping mediascapes are at play here, and our unease is a result of geological fault lines at the division of the public and private domains. Yet the public and private domains are themselves shifting, dividing into a variety of different categorizations. To speak of one dividing line, as if it were an impenetrable fence, and to conceive of the extensions of the notions of public and private as mutually exclusive, simply confound the problem. Yet the notions are of such historical importance that they cannot simply be dismissed. We have long tended to think of the public/private divide as univocal, with there being just one distinction. In fact, there are many.

## DIVIDING UP THE PUBLIC/PRIVATE DIVIDE

The public and private spheres are typically defined in opposition to each other. Like the Canberra garden, any space is either public and open to scrutiny or private. Much of the debate also assumes that the public/private divide is univocal — that in any case in which we distinguish the public and the private, there is just one notion of the private and another complimentary notion of the public. This is absurd. Notions of the public and private are various, if interwoven, with quite different moral intuitions turning on the different notions. Within the range of different concepts of public and private in play, several are particularly germane to the questions of the impact of the newer media. It is these notions that are disentangled here.[6]

In this section seven different views or notions of the public/private divide are distinguished. Confusion between these notions has led to very muddled debate about the importance of "identity" in the context of the newer media. In the next section, I show how these interweaving notions have been put under pressure by forces of globalization and by the introduction of new technologies. The conceptual space charted here has been much discussed, with important scholarly works raising and debating the questions. The conceptual grid here is intended to focus on how differing notions of public and private can dissolve into each other, alter under pressure, yet continue to influence moral intuitions. The notions of the public and private outlined below are not exhaustive, nor are they mutually consistent. They are part of the families of uses of the terms. Those uses are at times contradictory and inconsistent.[7]

---

6    There are of course many other notions of the public and private in different spheres, over and above those I list here.

7    This model is based on earlier work (Slade 1997).

*Notion 1*

The first notion associates the public with the political. The public is the government, as opposed to private individuals. The legislative bodies of the state are the public sphere, in this sense, with responsibilities to legislate for the "public good."

*Notion 2*

The second notion links the public with a sense of national identity. The private is then defined as the complement of the nation—as the local or regional, in some cases, as ethnic or interest groups in others, or as citizens.

*Notion 3*

The third notion links the public with the state administration and civil service, and the private is the market economy. This notion has both a descriptive and a normative version. The flavor of the normative version depends on political preference. One view is that the public is what should be owned and regulated for the public good, in order to control the rampant selfishness of the private market, and the contrary view holds that the private domain is efficient and hence should be allowed to manage the economy.

*Notion 4*

Here the public is associated with a sense of "community" as opposed to government and "private" enterprise. The public in this sense constitutes a broader notion than any of the earlier definitions. "Public radio" in the United States is public in this sense. The private is then demonised as noncommunal.

*Notion 5*

The fifth notion evokes the ideal public sphere as conceived by Habermas (1989), in which the members of the public debate rationally what is the correct thing for the state to do. The private then becomes a space protected from public debate; a context in which it is not necessary to be rational.

## Notion 6

The sixth distinction contrasts the domain of the family and the house with the public world. The private domestic space then becomes a space in which the outside world has no right of entry. Associated with this notion of the private domestic domain are a series of further subdivisions of senses of the private. First, the feminine has traditionally been identified as the domestic and private (e.g., Young, 1990), while the masculine is identified as the public. Secondly, the private domestic space has also been identified with a style of language. What Bernstein (1971) calls the restricted code is the language of the home. The elaborated code is the language of public debate.

## Notion 7

Finally, there is the dualist conception of the public as the corporeal world, the private as the private inner world of reflection. This dualism can be characterized as Cartesian insofar as it assumes that ideas are the one inalienable property of individuals. It carries over to most broadly dualistic models and to the metaphors of the privacy of the imagination and of inspiration.

Debate about issues of the media and identity typically slide from one to another of these distinct but related notions. Consider the first category, in which the notion of the private individual is opposed to the political. It is this notion that is at play in the "Render unto Caesar" Christian maxim, which calls on private individuals to act publicly as citizens in terms of taxation but privately in religious matters. When critics call on the government to legislate or censor the media, whether television or the Internet, they are conceiving of the government's moral imperatives as a public body in relation to the private citizen. Implicit is the idea of the government as guardian of the morals of the citizens. There is also an assumption that the media imposes attitudes on users or—to use the much-derided hypodermic model of the media—injects attitudes into users. Much of the debate about television and the Internet is predicated on this view of the public good. Access to citizens via the airwaves, the Internet, or the press is portrayed as the space of regulation, however impossible new technologies have made the task of regulation. On the other hand, citizens as private individuals are portrayed as powerless and incapable of making decisions for themselves.

Much of the regulation of the media is driven not just by this first notion of the public as the state, but also by the second notion of national identity.[8] Lord Reith was quite explicit in his charter for the BBC in which the media were to educate, by which he meant that the media should raise the populace to be British. The public media of European states had a similar brief, however differently they conceived their nations. The same remained true throughout much of the development of media regulation laws in the twentieth century. National content laws, which call for a given level of, say, Mexican or Australian content on television, are regulating (notion 1) with the implicit aim of developing a national consciousness (notion 2). In Australia, for instance, regulations explicitly required the media to develop a national consciousness. Radio and the post were seen as devices to develop a sense of nationhood in a far-flung country, and provisions for equal access for those outside metropolitan areas were built into the concept. Even today, in the debate about the privatization of the national telecommunications company, Telstra, the major political issue is the question of cross-subsidies to rural areas. Those cross-subsidies were part of the drive to give equal access in order to build a national consciousness.[9] Here the individual is seen as requiring state aid to develop an awareness of the self as a member of a nation. The mediated self is to be formed as a member of a nation, and that, so this view goes, requires legislation.

Support for community media, in the sense of notion 4, on the other hand, calls on different imperatives and a different notion of the public. Here the public is no longer the monolithic nation but the various ethnic groupings. The private individuals, in this sense as members of a community or of an ethnic group, require in turn their own legislative framework

---

8    Price ( 1995: chapter 3) has a discussion of these issues, that draws a range of distinctions between the ways Europe and the United States have—and have not—legislated to ensure that a national identity was promoted by television.

9    Cf., Lewis, Slade, Schaap and Wei (1994) for analysis of these issues in a comparison between Australian and Taiwanese regulation of cable television and also Cunningham & Turner (1997 eds *passim*) for a history of the Australian experience.

to develop their identity. It is not enough to have an identity within the nation—one's other communal identities also need mediated support. The notable Australian example of this is the outstanding state-subsidized television network, SBS (Special Broadcasting Service), which broadcasts programs from across the world in a variety of languages. It is this network, curiously enough, that has *South Park* as its most highly rated program ever.

The partisans of neoliberalism, characterized in the third notion of the public/private divide, set themselves against these notions of the public and the public good as the mechanisms appropriate to the state. Just as Adam Smith saw competition as the best mechanism for ensuring benefit to the populace, so neoliberals see a deregulated media as best for those who consume it. The state's role should not be to control the media, only to intervene to avoid excessive monopolization. The regulatory regime of the United States has always been of this kind; most states are, however reluctantly, following this model. It is a model that suits the great television companies well, for the only constraint on what is offered is then what is, as measured by ratings, popular. The impact on the identity of the consumers is no longer a responsibility of the provider of the media nor of the state—that is the choice of the consumer.

At this point, the slippage from the private individual as citizen to the private individual as consumer is complete. The fifth notion of the "ideal public sphere" as described by Habermas is an attempt to incorporate individual citizens into public debate once more and to give them a voice. As was pointed out in chapter 2, however, characterizing the public sphere in the terms of rational debate can itself be exclusionary. How can those who are silenced by lack of education, or by gender or race, for instance, hope to participate if rationality is defined as being able to use the tones of traditional public debate? We should not abandon the Habermasian ideal, but rather we should modify it so that it is no longer exclusionary.

At the same time that rationality should be broadly conceived to include all that is normally thought of "domestic" or "private" language—as referred to in the sixth notion. In Bernstein's (1971) distinction between elaborated and restricted codes, class differences are marked by differing uses of linguistic forms. Those of lower class have access only to the syntactically impoverished restricted codes of the domestic scene, while those of higher classes have, he claims, access both to the restricted code and to the elaborated, formal codes of public life. In terms of the distinctions above, the restricted code is the language of the private sphere; the elaborated is the language of the public sphere. In effect, broadening the notion of rationality to include utterances in restricted code, as I suggested in chapter 2, permits the use of private domestic language in the public sphere.

This is precisely what has happened with the tabloidization of the press. The language of the public domain has shifted to an increasingly restricted register: the register of the domestic sphere. What has been lost in the process is the need for a critical view of what is said. I argued in chapter 2 that the real danger of the tabloid press is not that it uses the language of the private sphere. The real danger lies in the loss of critical perspectives. The language of the public sphere can just as well be restricted as elaborated in code, but if it is to function as a public sphere, we cannot dispense with the critical questioning attitude towards all that is said.

The revised public sphere in the sense of notion 5 should draw on elements of the private domestic sphere. When the private is thought of as "domestic" or "individual," it has positive connotations. However, when opposed to communal or national interest, or to the space of rational debate, the private in this sense has connotations of irrationality, selfishness, or narrow personal aims. Confusion about how public figures should behave has followed the elision of the two notions of public—public as state and public as nondomestic, cold and unloving. We should be clear that the public sphere requires the thoughtful and critical but not necessarily pompous or cold attitudes of this domesticated public sphere.

Notions of the private as the individual (notion 7) are particularly important in Western cultures. Feminist critiques of this notion of the self have focused on the disembodiment, the genderlessness of the Cartesian self. That is crucial, but there is a more subtle and even more pervasive use of the Cartesian model of the self in discussion of media effects. Much of the debate about the impact of television and its ability to pervert the minds of youth is predicated on the idea of a young and disembodied mind waiting to be imprinted with beliefs.[10] Even recent studies of "embodied" children watching television, playing, and making their lives around the television set assume that it is the self-behind-the-viewer that is the focus of study. It is this self that comes to the fore as the individual needing protection from the media, as though an individual with no media experience were somehow purer and less corrupted than those with such experience. It is at this point, too, that we find the most passionate appeals for state regulation. This notion of the private self also drives the concerns about intellectual property and privacy—concerns which, we have seen, have become increasingly acute as new technologies invade the private domain.

It is important to recognize that we are in a time of conceptual change. Even in the clearest forms of the public/private distinction, the application of the concepts to new cases is problematic—our intuitions are frequently inconsistent. Should we allow what otherwise appear to be invasions of privacy to detect tax fraud? Or to detect homicidal maniacs? Should we treat pay television as a public good, since it uses the airwaves, or as a private contract between supplier and subscriber, since the viewer pays? New technologies alter the very concepts under discussion, so that moral intuitions are at sea.

These moral intuitions are under pressure not just from technological change, but also from globalization. Each of the contrasts above are specific to the Western culture. To take but one example, the sense of being a private individual, rather than an identity with links in society whose rôle is to fulfil a network of obligations and duties, is anathema in traditional Chinese thought. As Hui *et al* put it:

> In the Confucian moral order only the Emperor had subjectivity (*zhen*)...*Du* is a...term for individual; it means eccentric, isolated. (1993: 603)

In a society with such a view, intellectual property law may translate as mere selfishness.

What should we do about the semantic delinquency of these terms?

---

10 Strictly speaking, the conception of the self in television research is not of course Cartesian, but a *tabula rasa* model of the young child waiting to be formed for good or evil. In the interests of brevity, I have elided this subdivision of the notion of the private as the self.

The shifts of meaning in the notions of public and private are not, in themselves, difficult to chart nor are they dangerous. As Wittgenstein (1953) pointed out in his later works, it can be futile to try to define too closely the meanings of terms. The notions of public and private, Wittgenstein might suggest, each carry with them a family of usages and a family of meanings. Yet, in recognizing the family of uses, we should be wary of the families of misuses of the terms. The notions of public and private are central to our view of the world and fundamental to the ways we talk about media. Only by careful negotiation of these multiple notions of the public and private can we hope to clarify the complex moral issues of identity and the newer media.

## NEW TECHNOLOGY AND GLOBALIZATION

Understanding the impact of newer technologies as well as the intuitions we have about the ways these technologies should be regulated depends on our ability to extend familiar concepts to new circumstances. The pressure on the notion of the public on one hand, and privacy and of personal identity on the other, comes from two directions. New information technology actually alters the landscape of what is private, allowing unprecedented access to data by a number of bodies, both government and nongovernment. At the same time, the globalization not only of the market but of the technologies themselves means that it is impossible to regulate just at the national level. Issues of regulation further complicate the question. Since the private is very often defined as just that portion of experience that should be immune from regulation, and hence by definition unable to be regulated, the problems with the regulation of privacy have been particularly acute.

Globalization has a particular effect on the notion of the private individual. As we seek global regulatory structures to handle technologies that respect no boundaries, the very notion of the public alters to a global public. This, in turn, leads to the private being defined as the complement of the global public—namely, the national publics. Hence, there is no space for the role of the individual as the private. Consider again the categories in turn.

## Notion 1

The public is transformed at the global level into the international publics such as the European Union and United Nations. The private then becomes the former public bodies, namely, the nation states which are members of international organizations. The individual is then neither public nor private but nonexistent.

## Notion 2

The public corresponds at the global level to transnational identity. One example is the European case, in which the transnational identity of European citizenship is touted as an identity that needs to be developed. The difficulty is that either there is no space for genuine individuals, or there is no space for other national identities. Venturelli (1993) has argued that the problem in Europe is a notion of citizenship that is transnational and leaves no room for component—ethnic or national—identities.

## Notion 3

The correlate of the public as the state administration and the private as the market economy also has a global correlate. At the international level the public is "the global" in terms of global administrations. The correlate of "private" individuals is then those states or companies that have a role as members of the globally administered marketplace.

## Notion 4

The public as community corresponds at a global level to the global public—the individual people of the world. Yet again, there is confusion about what is not public in this sense—paradoxically, governments and private enterprise become "private" together.

## Notion 5

The model of the public realm as an ideal has been explicitly applied by those who wish to speak of a transnational public sphere, such as the United Nations, the European Union, or other major international bodies. Once again, the correlate of the private individual becomes the member states. The difficulty is that of finding an equal voice in a domain that is *de facto* English speaking, based on economic rationalism, and implicitly male.

*Notion 6*

The sixth distinction, contrasting the domain of the family and the home with the public world, applies to the international level when countries who wish to reject international scrutiny tend to label internal affairs as "domestic."

*Notion 7*

The Cartesian dualist conception of the public as the corporeal world and the private as the private inner world of reflection carries over to the national and international domains, with the use of metaphors such as "the body politic" or "the regulatory bodies of the General Agreement on Tariff and Trade" (Foreign Affairs and Trade, 1994).

Notice that these conceptions of the transnational public sphere leave little room for the concerns about the individual and privacy, precisely because states, not individuals, provide the inverse of what is public. There are no genuine individuals as players in the transnational public sphere as it is conceived here. Individuals are, of course, the representatives of the various national players in the international bodies such as the United Nations. However, they do not represent themselves but their nations. This conception of the transnational public sphere also leaves little room for a differentiation between states in terms of how the public/private divide is constructed.

The consequences of the elision of the private citizen in international law can be seen in Australia. As a signatory to The General Agreement on Tariffs and Services, (GATS), Australia has agreed to a considerable amount of protection of intellectual property and copyright protection (Foreign Affairs and Trade, 1994). Yet, these laws only protect commercial companies or patents. There is no protection of the individual in terms of intellectual property. Underpinning the belief that we have a right to the products of our own mind—our e-mail, our literary production, our knowledge about ourselves—is the assumption that the self should be inviolable in certain ways. Yet the very idea of the self has been dissolved into the concept of the nation of which we are part. This shift is then inherited by the national regulatory bodies.[11]

---

11   Only in 1996 did the Australian government devise privacy legislation to apply to pri-

Not only globalization but also new technologies alter the landscape. Consider the notions now in reverse order, as they apply to our intuitions about privacy. The final notion, of the disembodied Cartesian self, underpins much of our thought about intellectual property and knowledge of the self. If we are our thoughts, then any attempt to undermine our possession of the products of our mind is an outrage. Turkle (1995) charts the manifold ways in which computer users conceptualize the computer as an extension of the self or the various selves construed in MUDs (multi-user dungeons or domains—cyberspace regions where players adopt identities) and argues that identity itself is being recast through the use of the computer. The Cartesian self is shattering under the impact of technology. Yet the intuitions that draw on privileged access as the source of selfhood remain dominant.

If someone breaks into your files on a computer or even matches data about you from a number of different sources, it is as if your mind has been exposed. Implicit in much of the talk of privacy on the Internet is a conception of the computer as an extension of your private mental space. It is also behind those who defend pornography on the Internet—censoring the Internet is like censoring private thoughts. Furthermore, international copyright and intellectual property law ignores the question of individual ownership of ideas. As outlined in GATS, international copyright and property law is powerless to address infringements of intellectual property except when that property belongs to a company. (Foreign Affairs and Trade, 1994) There is still no viable international intellectual property law covering individual ownership of ideas, nor laws governing what is owing in a personal sense to a creator of an idea.

Turning to the penultimate category of domestic space (notion 6), the Internet and even the telephone have altered how we conceive of the home. We can surf the global Internet from our home computers—the world is no longer kept out. Moreover, gender has come to be recognized as important in studies of the impact of technologies yet has only just begun to be seen as a factor. The assumption has always been that participa-

---

vate companies within the domestic sphere and that was only, according to the Privacy Commissioner (O'Connor, 1996), because private enterprise saw the need for legislation to increase their business.

tion is disembodied and hence ungendered—resembling a Habermasian ideal public sphere (notion 5). This is clearly not the case. Studies of the telephone show how women use the technology differently from men (Moyal, 1984). Recent studies, such as Gillard *et al.* (1995) have laid out the different ways that women use newer technology. Spender (1995) describes a utopian vision of the Internet, which she calls "Nattering on the net." All these cases put into doubt the assumption that individual private participation in new technologies is ungendered, as if the Internet were just another version of the "ideal public sphere."

With the fourth notion of public as a community, new technology has had a paradoxical effect, creating a new global public community. This has come to represent the interests of the "private" individuals who, as citizens or consumers, cannot otherwise have their views heard in the global marketplace. For instance, there is an emerging sense of the global community on the Internet, an unregulated body. Curiously, individuals, through communities on the Internet have developed a real ability to make themselves heard. New technologies not only disturb and invade the private sphere but they also create new areas of privacy, new modes of speaking and reaching the public sphere.

The government, the nation state, and the public service (notions 1 to 3) similarly, and in a paradoxical fashion, become less public and, accessible to individuals with the new technologies. The Internet gives unprecedented access to government; public servants can actually be quizzed on line about policy. The voices of the politicians have, under the impact of the television, become more domestic, more like soap opera and "private" than they were in the era of the great "public" speakers. The government clothes its actions in a personal voice, the voice of the home, whatever the political message is and is thus personified.

The moral of the lesson of the porosity at the edges of the public/private divide is not that we should somehow tie down and reallocate the terms. They are part of a language and are developing with it. As new technologies emerge, so do new needs, and we use what we have at hand to serve those needs. However, we do have to be wary of leaning too heavily on the terms—of assuming that what is public is good (or bad), that the private is selfish or self-fulfilling.

## THE PUBLIC SPHERE AND IDENTITY, RECAST

Pressure on the public/private divide has led to the reaction that perhaps we should jettison the concepts of the public sphere on the one hand, and of the private self on the other. As Robbins (1993) suggests in *The Phantom Public Sphere*, the notions of the public sphere are so various and twisted that their very existence is questionable. That is certainly the postmodern strategy when it comes to the inverse notion; the notion of the private individual. The model of the fractured, dispersed self is found in theorists across the tradition, associated with talk of the loss of the individual author of the earlier written tradition.[12] Foucault, in particular, traces the historical reconstruction of the notion of the self, and its relation to the broader categories is what can be known. Foucault's analyses trace in detail the "archaeology" of the shifting boundaries of the self, drawing out the consequences of the Cartesian transformation on the Western idea of a knowing subject. Feminist critiques of the Cartesian self of Western philosophy concentrate on the disembodiment of the self and its suspicious lack of gender. Others are concerned with the self and the impact of new technologies. Poster (1990, 1994), for instance, argues that electronic writing is a symptom of the loss of the authorial identity, since documents are multiply rewritten leaving no trace of the hand of the writer.

This chapter traces the convergence of these two lines of thought, one relating to the self, the other to the public sphere, to their dual definitions. The idea of the public sphere is required to serve as the justification for governmental and international intervention; to develop national identities; to develop democracy; and, at the same time, to be alternate to the domestic or to the irrational. This is too great a burden for any single notion to carry. The private, on the other hand, is the individual citizen, the feminine, the irrational, the personal and the creative. That, too, is an excessive burden for one concept to carry.

When we talk of the public, we need to come clean about which public we mean. The public sphere must be redefined, concentrating on the skills of debate and criticism of ideas, but now including the ideas from the

---

12   e.g., Derrida (1987), Foucault (1973, 1977), Gergen (1991), Lloyd (1993), Miller (1993,1998), Poster (1990, 1994).

newer media. In particular, we need to think of how and why we regulate the products of the newer media and why that regulation is or is not in the public interest—in whatever notions of public we might appeal to. Regulation might not be the only route to salvation. It might be more effective to spend time and money developing the new and transformed styles of debate about the media.

What, then, of the other side of the public/private divide? The self as we know it has too many aspects to be covered by any single aspect of the notion of the private. The self ranges from the "knowing subject" through the creator of the computer file to the embodied domestic, from the participant in the public sphere, through the citizens to consumers. The fracturing and dispersal of the traditional self is inevitable. The postmodern strategy is to embrace the consequences and accept that the Cartesian assumption that there is a unified self is simply mistaken. There is, they suggest, just no such thing as the unifying *cogito*. They give up on the self as unified, as the centre of reason and moral decision. The idea that we should reject the unifying consciousness of the self is not unfamiliar. Hume, after all, notoriously argued in 1739 that, although he could sense the self as the bearer of impressions, he could not sense the unifying consciousness independently of those impressions (1962: 238-249, Book 1, Part IV, Section 6). The ever-retreating sense of a self as a bearer of ideas, but of no idea in particular, is certainly mysterious.

Yet there is still a place for a notion of a self. As users of television, Internet chat rooms, or teleconferencing facilities, we have both a sense of self and play roles of which we are reflexively aware. It is either trite or mistaken to say that one person consists of different selves when involved in these activities. One person takes responsibility for the actions that he or she performs. Our fractured and multiple identities can be sheeted home. We create our own narratives and our explanations of our behavior. Television, the Internet, literature, family, friends—and no doubt genes— all play a role in the story we tell ourselves about who we are. We can no longer stick to the old certainties, but that does not mean that we cannot examine how we constitute ourselves critically.

It is this process which is necessary as we try to navigate the shoals of the shifting public/private divide and the notions of the self which are associated with it. It is not necessary to abandon the conceptions of public and private and of the self and the moral intuitions so deeply associated with them. We can take a middle way and explore and remap the overlapping notions of the self and the private as they shift under the impact of new technology.

The conceptions of the self as moral agent resemble in some ways the conception of the self as body. Even over the last generation the conception of the body has altered. The public sight of a unclothed body on film has, for instance, lost the sense of taboo, and that has shifted how we related to our own nudity. Like the body, the self as moral agent is a historically and socially constructed self. It is not and cannot be devised *a priori* in Cartesian fashion from facts about the nature of consciousness. Moral agency is tied not just to a moral order but also to the possibilities of action, for instance, of taking responsibility. If people are unable to control the purposes to which their credit records, health records, phone conversations, or e-mail are put, they are not able to act as free moral agents and take responsibility for their actions. If information privacy is not recognized as possible by a community, the notion of the self as moral agent will alter. There are links between the self and public responsibilities. The newer technologies have recast those links, but they have not destroyed them. There is a new self to be mapped.

The mapping takes many forms. Television itself, as we saw with *South Park*, is a prime site for reflexive comment on its impact. So, too, is the Internet. However, let us finish with an example from that earlier technology, literature, which has offered for generations the imaginative space to explore notions of the self. David Malouf, perhaps Australia's greatest living novelist, makes vivid how notions of privacy in the house have changed since his childhood.

> ...you sleep, in the humid summer nights, outside the sheet with as little clothing as is decently allowed; and yet privacy is perfectly preserved. A training in perception has as much to do with what is ignored and passed over as what is observed. (Malouf, 1985)

Malouf goes on to describe that archetypal private space, the bathroom, and its transformation; a transformation that goes hand-in-hand with the transformation of the body.

> It is a distinguishably different body, then, that goes up that step into the old fashioned bathroom and strips itself to view....For our bodies are inven-

tions....The rooms that serve these bodies reflect them. Modern bathrooms are secular shrines. Under all these brilliant lights the body is apotheosised....This is a holy of holies....Old style bathrooms...were the product of a simpler economy....What you practised before their brutal plumbing and beaten tin walls, in the spirit of dour austerity, was the virtue that was next to godliness; and was most nearly a virtue when you did not linger over it. You did what you had to do briskly, efficiently, and you never locked the door. (Malouf, 1985: 56-58)

Here, the interweaving notions of privacy, access, and control are charted through a change. The body itself, the public face, alters as the structures of living change. So, too, does the nature of privacy itself. Yet there is a recognizable continuity, functional and ethical, between the privacy of the wartime household and our more modern equivalent, just as there is between the body of the 1940s and of the present.

## CONCLUSION

This book is a contribution to the project of restructuring just one aspect of the ideal public sphere. Critics of the newer media complain that they have had the effect of silencing criticism, of turning the citizen into *homo videns*, or of making us all "illiterate boobs sitting around the television." These claims are exaggerated. But to the extent that the concerns of critics about television and the new media are justified it is not just the fault of the media. It is our fault. It is we who are reacting to and using the newer media. We need to reestablish critical skills using the languages and visual styles of the newer media themselves. We cannot sit back and wait for a return to the style of the print media. We must develop critical views of the ways we see our society. That will involve a new and more domesticated vision of the public world. We do not need to accept the worst of the tabloid and personalized public debate. We can ask for more and ask others for more. Our talk about soap opera, ads, and cartoons already contains the seeds of the methods we need to develop further. What we have to do is analyze the argumentation and moral premises of ads and soap operas and cartoons. We need, in short, to apply philosophical skills to the newer media.

The issues of this book, however, are not just those of the larger public sphere. How we conceive of ourselves depends on our ability to negotiate the newer media and to develop a critical response to it. It is here that we return to the opening themes of this chapter. Television has achieved a restructuring of the nature of the public moral agent. No longer is a public moral agent one who acts well in the public domain. Instead, the dominant model of public moral agents is of those who reveal their private moral lives, however flawed. The danger lies not in the revelations of the private lives of public figures, tawdry though they may be. The danger lies in the loss of the ability to criticize and develop a principled reaction to the events. When the possibilities of debate about action are curtailed through the impact of newer technologies, we may indeed be brainwashed. Television and the new technologies mediate action and identity, but at the same time have effectively silenced the means of questioning the identities that emerge. We must refuse to be silenced.

Socrates said: "He who will fight for the right...must have a private station and not a public one." (*The Apology* 32a;1970: 70) As television and the Internet turn every private dwelling into a public space, a "private station"—a position from which to take a critical point of view—must be redefined. That is the aim of this book.

# AFTERWORD

## PARADOXES AND POPULAR CULTURE

Paradoxes pervade popular culture. One successful program on Australian television is called *Unreal TV*. Despite its name it is most certainly a "real" televisual event. It occurs at 6 p.m. on week nights on the network, as advertised in the *TV Guide*. It is discussed by those who watch it. What is more, the events shown are real. They are clips of the unexpected, normally untelevised events that occur when making television programs. In fact, they show the reality behind the creation of reality in television. It is called "unreal television" partly because "unreal" still has overtones of "cool," but partly because real TV production creates a reality so real that it makes the production process seem "unreal." The label captures the angst that arises as we become aware of the ways that television constructs reality.

It is reality television, a style of television that has burgeoned over the 1990s and reached its apogee with the cult of *Survivor*, "the highest rated summer series in TV history" (*Newsday*, 2000). The show took the commonplace fantasy of a shipwrecked group stranded on a desert island and played it out with real people, that is to say people who were not actors. There was no script, no direction, just carefully edited filmed real events. As one article puts it

> *Survivor*, the well-produced, irresistible, inessential and insanely successful hybrid of fantasy and reality, has changed television forever. (*New York Daily News*, 18 February 2000)

What is striking about the success of *Survivor* is that it plays with the complex notion of reality itself. Just as the students who enjoy cartoons enjoy the philosophical game of deciding what makes the cartoon real or not, so the viewers of reality television identify with the double game of events that are real and yet at the same time televisual.

When reality television began, with shows like *Cops*, it was a professional business, skirting the fine line between news and entertainment by involving the audience in the search for criminals. At the same time, however, the attraction of reality television of a different sort was emerging. Camcorder footage (Dovey, 1995) became the new fad, and unprofessional video clips, badly lit and subjectively handled, replaced the professional "transparent" image created by the camera teams. The private and personal space of the home video gave a sense of genuineness to the new fad. It was as if the Platonic concerns about the transparency of television mentioned in the first chapter of this book were being directly addressed by reality television.

At the same time, there is another element in the attraction of camcorder footage. The enjoyment is partly voyeuristic, insofar as we are watching what was not designed to be broadcast. That element of voyeurism transposed but still essential in the success of *Survivors*. We are seeing real people, but they are aware of the filming. Rather than a silent voyeur, the viewer is implicated in the very construction of the fantasy reality. In a debriefing show, *Survivors–Reunion*, following the *Survivor* series, two of the players claimed that their mutual attraction as seen on the televised view of events on the island, was "not real." They claimed that they had made it up because it seemed the sort of thing viewers would expect.[1] The unease viewers feel when they hear such an admission is an unease that derives from the tension underlying reality television. How can we be sure that reality shows are *really* real? There is a paradox at the heart of reality television.

*Unreal TV* makes the paradox of reality television explicit. Is unreal

---

[1] There is a burgeoning on-line literature on *Survivor*, (cf. the *Survivor* web site) as well as much press commentary (e.g., Boal, 2000). Samela Harris' (2000) article is one of the best of the journalistic commentaries. I am grateful to Greg Battye for discussion and ideas on reality television.

television real or unreal? If it is real, then it is unreal, and *vice versa*. Of course, it is easy to dissolve the paradox here, for *Unreal Television* is just a misnomer — it is real footage of real events and only unreal in the sense that it was not intended to be broadcast. Yet, the very fact that a paradox lurks in the background of the title is interesting. Magritte's paintings of pipes and apples labeled "Ceci n'est pas une pipe" or "Ceci n'est pas une pomme" ("This is not a pipe" or "This is not an apple") have a reading in which the message is just strictly true — the images are not actually pipes or apples but *images* of them. Magritte is making a point about the process of representation, forcing us to think what he might mean by presenting an apparent paradox. *Unreal TV* plays on the edge of paradox similarly and intentionally, alerting us to the possibility that all is not as straightforward as it seems.

*Unreal TV* is pitched precisely at the feature that Nehemas (1988), claiming a Platonic ancestry, identifies as the morally worrying feature of popular culture: namely, its transparency. Like all reality television, *Unreal TV* gets its bite from coming clean about the lack of transparency of television. Unlike the other forms of reality television, *Unreal TV* wears its heart on its sleeve. It shows the paradoxical nature of pretending to be a transparent image of reality. It thus throws the viewer back to a recognition of the lack of transparency of the medium. That is, it seems, a philosophical riposte at the viewer: an invitation, at the very least, to reflection.

This book begins with the films of the nineties that embodied the philosophical uncertainty at the heart of the mediated experience. I mentioned the Silver Production 1999 film, *The Matrix*, in which the world is illusion, a construction by a malicious power, in which we, the people, only believe that we are acting freely and perceiving the real world. Here, too, we have the possibility of paradox. It is worth recapitulating the plot to see just how the paradox emerges.

The virtual reality, composed of a Sydney cityscape filled with New York subway stations, is manipulated by the computers themselves. A visionary father figure, Morpheus (Laurence Fishburne), can see what is really happening and leads a select group into the future to fight the manipulators. The group reenters the virtual reality of what is, for them, the past, via comfortingly old-fashioned 1930s bakelite telephones, and there act out video-game battles with the hidden and flexible representatives of the malign power. The game is being lost, until Morpheus and a fey New Age seer identify the "one"—the elect figure, Neo (Keanu Reeves). While modestly unsure of his own power, Neo reenters the virtual reality game of the past and destroys Smith, thereby, one is led to gather, freeing the world. Neo is at once the Judeo-Christian prophet and the romantic love figure—taken to his greatest feats of bravery by a kiss to his sleeping figure by the female lead, Carrie Ann Moss. The story lines converge in mythic power, playing off video-game culture, comic-strip appearances, religion, and fairy tale.

The story line also draws on philosophical tradition. The plot is a version of Descartes' argument that all our beliefs about the external world might be in error. It also raises a plethora of philosophical problems; problems about how we know that we are not deceived by our senses. The paradoxes emerge when we consider virtual reality and the past. Could the world really be virtual reality? If the virtual past reality has no effects on the present or the real world, why would it be a matter of concern to Morpheus? If past reality does have causal effects on the real world, then surely there is a paradox inherent in changing it? If Neo reenters such a previous world, virtual or not, and alters it, how can that not affect the future of which he is part? How can being killed in a virtual reality game have effects in reality? The film leaves these problems unresolved but, as with *Unreal TV* or Magritte's images, the impact and success of the film derive in part from the suggestion of impossibility. The plot lines of the popular film skirts the edge of paradox intentionally, mobilizing the interest the paradoxes generate.

Paradoxes of levels have long been the staple of philosophy. The Cretan liar who says "this statement is a lie," is telling the truth if he lies and lying if he is telling the truth. In *The Matrix* we have a related problem— can we really think that "I am in virtual reality"? If we can, then the truth of that thought implies that our actions do not have real consequences. Only if we are thinking virtually that we are in virtual reality, can the consequences be real. But in that case these consequences should be virtual, not real.

The problem resembles that of the paradoxes Russell first discovered in Frege's mathematical system—the so-called paradoxes of set inclusion. Is the set "the set of all sets which are not member of themselves" a member of itself or not? If it is, it is not, and *vice versa*. One solution is that adopted by Russell (1937). He outlawed the set inclusion axiom that allows us to generate such sets as "the set of all sets which are not members of themselves," saying, in effect, that such sets are not possible, because they cross levels. We cannot talk about all the sets of this type because the totality of such sets can only be conceived by going, as it were, outside the system. To translate this into notions of reality, can we think within virtual reality that it is not real? We can, of course, from a point of view outside virtual reality think of it as unreal, but we cannot simultaneously think of virtual reality as real and virtual.

That solution is not satisfactory. There is a good sense in which we can say to ourselves "this is unreal" and be telling the truth. Events can be at one time both real in one sense and not in another. However, the paradox of virtual reality in the *Matrix* is stronger than such anodyne forms. In the film, there must be real causal connections between what happens within a virtual game and what happens outside it. The players can have nightmares about what happens in virtual reality without offending the laws of physics. But there is also apparently backward causation from virtual reality to real reality. And that seems to be just not possible.

The paradox keeps us watching, however, ever aware of the possibility of absurdity. In logical theory, paraconsistent logicians[2] claim that the outright rejection of the paradoxes is itself a mistake. For paraconsistent logicians, a statement such as that of the Cretan liar can be both true and false at the same time, so long as the classical logical consequences do not follow. In classical logic, where there is a rule that from a contradiction anything whatsoever follows: a contradiction collapses the system. If any statement can be both true and false, then all can. For paraconsistent logicians, this does not follow. A contradiction can exist in the system, without a collapse. In effect, paraconsistent systems seal off the true contradictions and allow them to exist in the system. Certain paradoxes are just part of the world.

For others,[3] paradoxes are best seen as calls to action, as an indication that we need to expand the universe of discourse and look again. With the

---

[2]   Cf., e.g., Priest (1987).

[3]   Here I follow Dummett (1977, chapter 2).

set paradoxes, for instance, the problem is the definition of the set of all sets. We can assume that each time we apply the predicate "set of all sets that are not members of themselves" we thereby expand the universe of discourse, so that the totality of *all* sets is indefinitely extensible. Since we cannot ever define the extent of sets, the set of all sets not members of themselves is itself constantly expanding as one uses the universal quantifier "all." The universe is not contradictory, so much as ever in flux. On this view paradoxes allow us to see the universe as extending indefinitely. A paradox is more like a call to action—evidence that we need to keep questioning.

There is a danger of misusing notions that are fundamentally philosophical and logical in this context. I suggest, however, that the sense of the paradoxes of justification informs much of the modern angst and the popular culture that derives from it. When Goodwill thrift stores in Ottawa label themselves and proclaim in an ad "Goodwear, it's not a label, it's a Headspace" (cited in the *Ottawa Citizen*, Harris, 1999) and go on "It's a virtual thing"(Harris 1999), then proclaim that there is a "Goodwill philosophy," I suspect that the paradox of the nonlabel is self-conscious. The underlying problems of paradoxes of self-reference are in the back of the writers' minds.

So too are we aware of the problems of justifying reasoning. In "What the Tortoise Said to Achilles," Lewis Carroll (1895) asked how we can ultimately justify our logical moves. He was pointing out the paradox of logical inference. Any justification must itself use logic and hence needs justification. How can rules of inference be justified, and if they can, what justifies the justification? Priest's (1979) solution is to distinguish entailments, which must be justified, from inferences, which, as instances of human rule-governed behavior, need no justification. His argument is that practice yields the bedrock that avoids the regress. Of course, if practice is to provide the bedrock, it cannot be any old practice. We all know we make mistakes in inference. The logical practice that is the final justification of inference must be a practice that has been scrutinized, criticized, and debated.

There is a paradox in justifying our sense of reality, rather like that which Carroll identified. How can we ever be sure that we are real? Any reassurance will reassure only if it is real, and that is what is in question.

We cannot keep on seeking reassurance of reality, that we and our practices are real, forever. The best we can do is rest with our examined practices. We can treat as real what we choose, but we should be aware that we are doing so and be prepared to defend the decision.

This book opened with the question of what is real, and why television and new technologies have forced us to reconsider this. Philosophical questions of this sort are ones viewers are quite capable of debating and, in fact, wish to debate. Here we find the media itself, in films such as *The Matrix* and *The Truman Show*, exploring the philosophical landscape, pushing the edges of the notion of the real to its limits.

There are philosophical issues embedded in television and the newer media. Like the Cretan, we think "everything here is a lie" but simultaneously examine the issues, think through consequences, and talk. We think that all elections are manipulated, and we are being manipulated too. The reaction should not be to retreat but to attempt to keep one step ahead of the manipulation. Advertisements manipulate us, we know, yet we both enjoy the way that agencies catch us unawares and at the same time criticize the process. Cartoons such as *South Park* play the game of being one step ahead, commenting on the comments, criticizing the game of television itself. As viewers, we appreciate the humor and take in the complexity of the ethical argument.

New technologies have undermined and recast the ways we interpret the world and the sense of how we should behave. The clear dividing lines between public and private spheres have been dissolved. We have our privacy invaded and our public lives circumscribed by private details. Yet we and our children are also agents in the global universe, voters and decision-makers. We can escape the virtual reality matrix, the televisual world, and indeed, we are constantly doing so. That does not mean we have to reject television or video games or attempt to insulate ourselves from the world. That would be disastrous, even paradoxical. Television and computers are *part* of the world, even as they alter and change the ways we interact in the world. What is important, I suggest, is to examine even more carefully our own ways of managing the newer media. That is a philosophical task.

We do not need to impose philosophical debate. Philosophical questions seem to be the order of the day. Consider a final New York gleaning,

from a department store called Barney's. I was wandering in the store
when I saw a huge sign: **Philosophy.** It was a trademark for a range of
cosmetic products—and I quote here from the publicity booklet:

> **the naked truth** spf 15 is a revolutionary new product that takes the notion
> of tinted moisturisers to the next generation...so we're stretching the truth a
> little. after all perception is reality **(philosophy** sales booklet, Barney's,
> 1996: 30)

Even more tantalisingly we are told:

> **Logic:** what is reasonable and what is not reasonable when it comes to skin
> care. **(philosophy** sales booklet, Barney's, 1996)

The title page of the booklet reads:

**philosophy** is a fundamental physical science divided into

five areas.

aesthetics

our color division

logic

our skin care division

metaphysics

our fragrance, bed and bath division

ethics

our charity division

epistemology

our book and music division

**(philosophy** sales booklet, Barney's, 1996: 2)

Philosophy has become one of the tricks in hand of the new advertisers. Surely, then, it is time to turn philosophical skills and traditions to the
job of examining the media who make so free with philosophical issues?

# BIBLIOGRAPHY

ABC (30/7/98). "The Media Report," *Radio National,* with Robert Bolton. *http://www.abc.net.au/rn/talks/8.30/mediarpt/mstories*

Adatto, K. (1990). "Sound Bite Democracy: Network Evening News and Presidential Campaign Coverage, 1968 and 1988," *Research Paper R2.* Cambridge, Mass.: Joan Shorenstein Barone Centre on Press Politics and Public Policy, Harvard University.

*Aerial Magazine* (September 1998). "Watch Out They're Coming for You," pp 6-7.

Alasuutari, P. (ed.). (1999). *Rethinking the Media Audience.* London: Sage.

Allen, R. (1985). *Speaking of Soap Operas.* Chapel Hill: University of North Carolina Press.

Allen, R. & Smith, M. (eds) (1997). *Film Theory and Philosophy.* Oxford: Clarendon Press.

Allen, S. (1999). "TV Is Leading Children Down a Moral Sewer," *New York Times* 20 October 1999, B4 advertisement.

Ang, I. (1985). *Watching Dallas.* London: Methuen.

Ang, I. (1996). *Living Room Wars: Rethinking Media Audiences for a Postmodern World.* London: Routledge.

Appadurai, A. (1993). "Disjuncture and Difference in the Global Cultural Economy," in B. Robbins (ed): *The Phantom Public Sphere.* Minneapolis: University of Minnesota Press. pp 269-296.

Aufderheide, P. (1993). *National Leadership Conference on Media Literacy Dec 7-9, 1992.* Queenstown, Md: Washington DC Communication and Society Program, Aspen Institute.

Bandura, A., Ross, D. & Ross, S. (1967). "Imitations of Film Mediated Aggressive Models," *Journal of Abnormal and Social Psychology*, 66 (1), pp 3-11.

Barnes, J. (1999). *England, England*. New York: Vintage.

Barthes, R. (1972). *Mythologies*. Trans. A. Lavers. London: Paladin.

Barthes, R. (1977). *Image, Music, Text*. Trans. S. Heath. London: Fontana.

Batra, R. & Ray, M. L. (1985). "How Advertising Works at Contact," in Alwitt, L. F. & Mitchell, A. A. (eds)(1985). *Psychological Processes and Advertising Effects*. Hillsdale, N. J.: Erlbaum.

Baudrillard, J. (1983). *Simulations*. Trans.P. Foss, P. Patton, & P. Beitchman. New York: Semiotext(e).

Beckenham, A. (2000). "Sex, Science Fiction and Cyberspace," thesis submitted to the University of Canberra in fulfilment of the degree of Master of Communication.

Behar, J. E. (ed).(1997). *Mapping Cyberspace: Social Research on the Electronic Frontier*. Dowling: Dowling College Press.

Benhabib, S. (1992). *Situating the Self: Gender, Community and Postmodernism in Contemporary Ethics*. London: Polity Press.

Benitez, S. (1997). *Bitter Grounds*. New York: Hyperion.

Benn, S. & Gauss, G. (1983). *Public and Private in Social Life*. London: Croom Helm.

Bennett, A. (1994). *Writing Home*. London: Faber.

Bennett, T., Emmison, M. & Frow, J. (1999). *Accounting for Tastes: Australian Everyday Cultures*. Cambridge: Cambridge University Press.

Berger, A. (1992). *Popular Culture Genres*. Newbury Hills: Sage.

Bernstein, C. (1971). *Class, Codes and Control*. London: Routledge and Kegan Paul.

Bernstein, N. (1997). "Lives on File," *New York Times*, 12 June 1997, A1, B14, B16.

Bilbenny, N. (1997). *La Revolución en la Ética*. Barcelona: Anagrama.

Boal, M. (2000). "Smile, You're on *Lord of the Flies*, The Million Dollar Castaway," *The Vil-*

*lage Voice* 27 October 2000. http://www.villagecoice.com/issues/9943/boal/shtml

Braithwaite, J. & Drahos, P. (2000). *Global Business Regulation*. Cambridge: Cambridge University Press.

Bruni, F. (1997). "Gay Daughter, Political Asset: Messinger, in Trend, puts the Spotlight on a Relative," *New York Times* 3 March 1997, pp B1, B2.

Buckingham, D. (1987). *Public Secrets: East Enders and Its Audience*. London: British Film Institute.

Buckingham, D. (1993). *Children Talking Television: The Making of Television Literacy*. London: Falmer.

Buckingham, D. (ed.). (1993). *Reading Audiences: Young People and the Media*. King's Lynn: Manchester University Press.

Buckingham, D. (1996). *Moving Images: Understanding Children's Emotional Responses to Television*. Manchester: Manchester University Press.

Buckingham, D. (ed.). (1998). *Teaching Popular Culture: Beyond Radical Pedagogy*. London: UCL Press.

Buckingham, D. (2000a). *After the Death of Childhood: Growing Up in the Age of Electronic Media*. Malden, Mass.: Polity Press.

Buckingham, D. (2000b). *The Making of Citizens: Young People, News and Politics*. London: Routledge.

Cacioppo, J. T. & Petty, R. E. (1980). "The Effects of Message Repetition and Position on Cognitive Response, Recall and Persuasion," *Journal of Personality and Social Psychology*, vol 37, pp 97-109.

Calabrese, A. & Burke, B. R. (1992). "American Identities, Nationalism, the Media and the Public Sphere," *Journal of Communication Inquiry* 16, pp 252-273.

Canedy, D. (1997). "P. & G. is Seeking to Revive Soaps: Shaking up TV Serials as Audiences Dwindle," *New York Times* 11 March 1997, pp D1, D4.

Cantor, M. (1983). *The Soap Opera*. Beverly Hills, Calif.: Sage.

Carroll, L. (1895). "What the Tortoise Said to Achilles," *Mind* NS IV.

Carroll, L. (1961). *Alice Through the Looking Glass*. London: J M Dent.

Carter, B. (1997). "Watching the Watchers: Neilsen Taking Heat for Drop in TV Viewing," *New York Times* 13 October 1997.

Cavell, S. (1982). "The Fact of Television," *Daedelus* 111, pp 77-99.

Chandler, D. (1999). "Children's Understanding of What Is 'Real' on Television: A Review of the Literature," *http://www.aber.ac.uk/-dgc/realrev.html*

Cheney, L. (1988). *Humanities in America: A Report to the President, the Congress and the American People*. Washington: NEH.

Chomsky, N. (1957). *Syntactic Structures*. The Hague: Mouton.

Chomsky, N. & Herman, S. (1994). *Manufacturing Consent*. London: Vintage.

Citibank Advertisement (1999). "Renewal, Growth, Freedom," *The News* 5 October 1999, Mexico City.

Coles, R. (1997). *The Moral Intelligence of Children: How to Raise a Moral Child*. New York: Random House.

Colomina, B. (1998). *Privacy and Publicity: Modern Architecture as Mass Media*. Cambridge, Mass.: MIT Press.

Commission of the European Community (1988). *The AudioVisual Media in the Single European Market*. Luxembourg: Office for the Official Publications of the Community.

Commission of the European Community (1990). *The European Community in the Audio Visual Field*. Luxembourg: Office for the Official Publications of the Community.

Corbett, E. (1990). *Classical Rhetoric for the Modern Student*. Oxford: Oxford University Press.

Cumberbatch, G. & Howitt, D. (1989). *A Measure of Uncertainty: The Effects of the Mass Media*. London: John Libbey.

Cunningham S. & Jacka, E. (1996). *Australian Television and International Mediascapes*. Cambridge: Cambridge University Press.

Cunningham, S. & Turner G. (eds) (1997). *The Media in Australia: Industries, Texts, Audiences*. Sydney: Allen & Unwin.

Davidson, D. (1967). "Truth and Meaning," *Synthese* 17, pp 304-323 (reprinted in 1984).

Davidson, D. (1984). *Inquiries into Truth and Interpretation.* Oxford: Oxford University Press.

Davies, M. M. (1997). *Fake, Fact, and Fantasy: Children's Interpretations of Television Reality.* Hillsdale, N. J.: Lawrence Erlbaum.

De León, A. (2001a). "Se acaba el drama...empieza la comedia," *Reforma* 26 January 2001, p 1E.

De León, A. (2001b). "Su juez: el público," *Reforma* 30 January 2001, p 1E.

Dennett. D. (1981). "Where Am I?" in D. Dennett, *Brainstorms.* Sussex: Harvester Press. pp 310-323.

Derrida, J. (1987). *From Socrates to Freud and Beyond.* Trans. A. Bass. Chicago: University of Chicago Press.

Dovey, J. (1995). "Camcorder Cults," *Metro,* 104, pp 106-109.

Dummett, M. (1975). "The Justification of Deduction," *Proceedings of the British Academy,* vol LXI, pp 201-232.

Dummett, M. (1977). *Elements of Intuitionism.* Oxford: Clarendon Press.

Dummett, M. (1978). *Truth and Other Enigmas.* London: Duckworth.

Dummett, M. (1993). *The Seas of Language.* Oxford: Clarendon Press.

Eemeren, F. van & Grootendorst, R. (1992). *Argumentation, Communication and Fallacies: A Pragma-Dialectical Perspective.* Hillsdale, N. J.: Lawrence Erlbaum.

Eemeren, F. van, Grootendorst, R., Jackson, S. & Jacobs, S. (1993). *Reconstructing Argumentative Discourse.* Tuscaloosa: University of Alabama Press.

Eisenstein, E. (1983). *The Printing Revolution in Early Modern Europe.* Cambridge, Mass.: Cambridge University Press.

Ellis, J. (1982). *Visible Fictions.* London: Routledge & Kegan Paul.

Evans, G. (1982). *Varieties of Reference.* Oxford: Oxford University Press.

Federman, J. (ed) (1998). *National Television Violence Study. http://www.ccsp.ucsb.edu/execsum.pdf*

Fernández, C. & Paxman, A. (2000). *El Tigre: Emilio Azcárraga y su Imperio Televisa,* Mexico City: Grijalbo.

Festinger, L. (1957). *A Theory of Cognitive Dissonance.* Chicago: Row, Peterson.

Fisherkeller, J. (1998). "Learning about Power and Success: Young Urban Adolescents Interpret TV Culture," *The Communication Review.* vol 3, no 3, pp 187-212.

Fiske, J. (1987). *Television Culture.* London: Methuen.

Fiske, J. (1994). *Media Matters: Everyday Culture and Political Change.* Minneapolis: University of Minnesota Press.

Fitzgerald, K. (1994). "The Truth Comes Out: Trend Is Clear as Marketers Place Truth in Ads, Product Name," *Advertising Age,* vol 65, no 43.

Foreign Affairs & Trade (1994) *Uruguay Round Outcomes: Services* Canberra: AGPS.

Foucault, M. (1973). *The Order of Things: An Archeology of the Human Sciences.* New York: Vintage.

Foucault, M. (1977). *Discipline and Punish : The Birth of the Prison.* Trans A. Sheridan. Stanford, Calif.: Stanford University Press.

Fraser, N. (1993). "Rethinking the Public Sphere: A Contribution to the Critique of Actually Existing Democracy," in B. Robbins (ed) *The Phantom Public Sphere.* Minneapolis: University of Minnesota Press, pp1-32.

Frege, G. (1948). "On Sense and Reference," *Philosophical Review,* 57, pp 209-230.

Frege, G. (1950). *The Foundations of Arithmetic.* Trans. J. L. Austin. Oxford: Blackwell.

Frege, G. (1952). *Translations from the Philosophical Writings of Gottlob Frege.* Trans. P.T. Geach & M. Black. Oxford: Blackwell.

Fuentes, C. (1998). "La Primera Telenovela Global," *Reforma,* 27 January 1998, p 7A.

Gabriel, T. (1996). "Decoding What Screen Agers Think About TV," *New York Times* 25 November 1996.

Garnham, N. (1990). *Capitalism and Communication.* Oxford: Sage.

Geraghty, C. (1991). *Women and Soap Opera.* Cambridge: Polity Press.

Gergen, K.J. (1991). *The Saturated Self: Dilemmas of Identity in Contemporary Life.* New York: Basic Books.

Gibson, W. (1984). *Neuromancer*. London: Grafton Books.

Gillard, P., Wale, K. & Bow, A. (1995). *Privacy and Control: Social Indicators of Interest in Future Telecommunications*. Melbourne: Telecommunications Needs Research Group.

Gitlin, T. (1983). *Inside Prime Time*. New York : Pantheon.

Govier, T. (1987). *Problems in Argument Analysis and Evaluation*. Dordrecht: Foris.

Grice, H.P. (1957). "Meaning," *Philosophical Review* 66, pp 377-388.

Grice, H. P. (1969). "Utterer's Meanings and Intentions," *Philosophical Review* 78, pp 147-177.

Grice, H.P. (1975). "The Logic of Conversation," in P. Cole & J. Morgan (eds), *Syntax and Semantics*. New York: Academic Press.

Guerrero, C. (2001). "Teme Robles a Narcos" *Reforma* 26 January 2001, p B1.

Gunter, B. & McAleer, J. (1997). *Children and Television*. ed. 2. London: Routledge.

Gutman, A. (1987). *Democratic Education*. Princeton, N J: Princeton University Press.

Habermas, J. (1989 [1962]). The *Structural Transformation of the Public Sphere*. Trans. T. Burger. Cambridge, Mass.: MIT Press.

Habermas, J. (1987). "Discourse Ethics," in S. Benhabib & D. Cornell (eds), *Feminism as Critique*. Minneapolis: University of Minnesota Press.

Habermas, J. (1992). "The Unity of Reason in the Diversity of Its Voices," in J. Habermas, *Postmetaphysical Thinking*. Cambridge Mass: Polity.

Halliday, M.A.K. (1985). *An Introduction to Functional Grammar*. London: Edward Arnold.

Hallin, D. (1994). *We Keep America on Top of the World: Television Journalism and the Public Sphere*. London: Routledge.

Hare, R. M. (1952). *The Language of Morals*. Oxford: Clarendon.

Harris, G. (1999). "Goodwill Gets Competitive," *Ottawa Citizen*, 13 May,1999, p A3.

Harris, S. (2000). "Ugly Reality Challenges the Net," *The Advertiser*, 5 July 2000, p 18.

Hawkins, R. P. (1977). "The Dimensional Structure of Children's Perceptions of Television Reality," *Communication Research*, vol 4, no 3, pp 299-320.

Hodge, B. & Tripp, D. (1986). *Children and Television: A Semiotic Approach*. Cambridge: Polity Press.

Hoover, S., Venturelli, S., & Wagner, D. (1993). "Trends in Global Communication Policy-Making: Lessons from the Asian Case," *Asian Journal of Communication*, vol 3, no 1, pp 103-133.

Hui, W., Lee, L. O. & Fischer, M. J. (1993). "Is the Public Sphere Unspeakable in Chinese? Can Public Spaces (gonggong kongjian) Lead to Public Spheres?" *Public Culture*, vol 5, pp 598-605.

Hume, D. (1962 [1739]). *A Treatise on Human Nature*. London: Fontana Collins.

Hyperizons http://www.duke.edu/-mshuma te/hyperfic.htm

Jackson, K. (1998). "Gen X Are Incapable of Being Shocked," *Sydney Morning Herald*, 28 September 1998.

James, H. (1963 [1892]). "The Real Thing" reprinted in Edel, L.(ed) *The Complete Tales of Henry James*. vol 8, pp 229-258. London: Rupert Hart-Davies.

Johnson, J. & Ettema, J. (1986). "Using Television to Best Advantage: Research for Prosocial Television," *Applied Social Psychology Annual*, vol 8, pp 143-164.

Johnson, M. (1989). *The Body in the Mind: the Bodily Basis of Meaning, Imagination and Reason*. Chicago: University of Chicago Press.

Kahneman, D., Slovic, P. & Tversky, A. (1982). *Judgement Under Uncertainty: Heuristics and Biases*, Cambridge: Cambridge University Press.

Katz, J. (1997). *Virtuous Reality: How America Surrendered Discussion of Moral Values to Opportunists, Nitwits and Blockheads like William Bennett*. New York: Random House.

Klite, P., Bardwell, R. A. & Slazman, J. (1997). "Local TV News: Getting Away with Murder." *Press/Politics*, vol 2, no 2, pp 102-112.

Kress, G. (1986). "Language in the Media: The Construction of the Domains of the Public and Private." *Media, Culture and Society*. vol 8, pp 395-419.

Kress, G. (ed.). (1988). *Communication and Culture*. Sydney: UNSW Press.

Kress, G. & van Leeuwen T. (1996). *Reading Images: The Grammar of Visual Design*. London: Routledge.

Kuhn, T. (1962). *The Structure of Scientific Revolutions*. Chicago: University of Chicago Press.

Lacey, N. (1993). "Theory into Practice? Pornography and the Public/Private Dichotomy," *Journal of Law and Society* (special issue on feminist theory and legal strategy). A. Bottomley & J. Conaghan (eds), pp 93-113.

Lakoff, G. & Johnson, M. (1980). *Metaphors We Live by*. Chicago: University of Chicago Press.

Lembo, R. (1997). "Beyond the Text: The Sociality of Image Based Viewing Practices," *Cultural Studies: A Research Volume*, vol 2, pp 237-264.

Levinson, S.C. (1992). "Language and Cognition: the Consequences of Spatial Description in Guugu Yimithirr," *Working Paper no 13*. Canberra: Cognitive Anthropology Research Group.

Lewis, D. (1969). *Convention*. Boston: Harvard University Press.

Lewis, G. & Slade C. (2000). *Critical Communication* ed.2. Sydney: Prentice Hall.

Lewis, G., Slade, C., Schaap, R. & Wei, J. H. (1994). "Television Globalisation in Taiwan and Australia," *Media Asia*. vol 21, no 4, pp183-189.

Lipman, M. (1974). *Harry Stottlemeier's Discovery*. Upper Montclair, N.J.: IAPC.

Lipman, M. (1976). *Lisa*. Upper Montclair, N.J.: IAPC.

Lipman, M. (1978). *Suki*. Upper Montclair, N.J.: IAPC.

Lipman, M. (1980). *Mark*. Upper Montclair, N.J.: IAPC.

Lipman, M. (1981). *Pixie*. Upper Montclair, N.J.: IAPC.

Lipman, M. (1984). *Kio and Gus*. Upper Montclair, N.J.: IAPC.

Lipman, M. (1985). 'Thinking Skills Fostered by Philosophy for Children, " in J.W. Segal, S.F. Chipman & R. Glaser (eds) *Thinking and Learning Skills*, vol 1, pp 83-108. Hillsdale N.J.: Lawrence Erlbaum.

Lipman, M. (1988). "Critical Thinking: What Can It Be?" *Educational Leadership*, pp 38-41.

Lipman, M. (1991). *Thinking in Education*. Cambridge: Cambridge University Press.

Lipman, M. & Sharp, A. M. (1979). *Philosophical Inquiry: Instructional Manual to Accompany Harry Stottlemeier's Discovery*, 2 ed.. Upper Montclair, N.J.: IAPC.

Lipman, M. & Sharp, A. M. (1980). *Writing, How and Why: Instructional Manual to Accompany Suki.* Upper Montclair, N.J.: IAPC.

Lipman, M. & Sharp, A. M. (1980). *Social Inquiry: Instructional Manual to Accompany Mark.* Upper Montclair, N.J.: IAPC.

Lipman, M. & Sharp, A. M. (1984). *Looking for Meaning: Instructional Manual to Accompany Pixie.* 2nd ed. Upper Montclair, N.J.: IAPC.

Lipman, M. & Sharp A. M (1983/1984). *Ethical Inquiry: Instructional Manual to Accompany Lisa.* Upper Montclair, N.J.: IAPC.

Lipman, M. & Sharp, A. M. (1984). *Wondering at the World: Instructional Manual to Accompany Kio and Gus.* Upper Montclair, N.J.: IAPC.

Littleton Community Network (1999). "Columbine High School Tragedy Fact Sheet–May 28 1999" http://www.littleton.org/LCN/governe/news/GOANcolu.htm

Livingstone, S. (1990). *Making Sense of Television: The Psychology of Audience Interpretation.* London: Butterworth.

Livingstone, S. (1992). "The Resourceful Reader: Interpreting Television Characters and Narratives," in S.A. Deetz (ed) *Communication Yearbook 15*, pp 58-90. Beverly Hills, Calif.: Sage.

Lloyd, G. (1993). *The Man of Reason: 'Male' and 'Female' in Western Philosophy.* 2 ed. London: Routledge.

Local (2000). "El televisor, un integrante más de las familias." *Diario Yucateco*, 26 December 2000, p 13.

Lorenzen, P. (1965). *Métamathématique.* Trans J.B. Grize. Paris: Mouton.

Lumby, C. (1997). *Bad Girls: The Media, Sex and Feminism in the '90s.* Sydney: Allen & Unwin.

Lumby, C. (1999). *Gotcha.* Sydney: Allen & Unwin.

McCann-Erikson (1996). *Creative Presentation to the Authenticity Brief for Coca-Cola.* unpublished brief. Mexico City.

MacColl, S. (1992). "Conversation and Dialogue—Not Just What You Say but How You Say It," in R. Reed (ed): *When We Talk: Essays on Classroom Conversation*. Fort Worth, Texas: Analytic Teaching Press, pp 75-86.

McDonald, S. (1998). "Tales from the Park Side," *TV Guide*, March,1998. P 6.

McLennan, D. (2000). "Love My Shorts, Not Eat My Shorts," *Canberra Times, TV Guide*, 6 March 2000.

McQuail, D. (1987). *Mass Communication Theory: An Introduction*. 2 ed. London: Sage.

Malouf, D. (1985). *12 Edmonstone Street*. London: Chatto & Windus.

Marr, D. (1999). *The High Price of Heaven: A Book About the Enemies of Pleasure and Freedom*. Sydney: Allen & Unwin.

Masterman, L. & Mariet, F. (1994). *Media Education in the 1990's Europe: A Teacher's Guide* Strasbourg: Council of Europe Press.

Matthews, G. (1994). *Philosophy of Childhood*. Cambridge, Mass.: Harvard University Press.

Mautner, T. (1996). *A Dictionary of Philosophy*. Oxford: Blackwell.

Mazziotti, N. (1996). *La Industria de la Telenovela. La Producción de Ficción en América Latina*. Buenos Aires, Argentina: Paidós.

Mejía Barquera, F. (1998). "Del Canal 4 a Televisa," in Martínez, O. M. (ed) *Apuntes para una Historia de La Televisión Mexicana*: *Revista Mexicana de Comunicación*, pp 19-99.

Meyrowitz, J. (1985). *No Sense of Place: The Impact of Electronic Media on Social Behavior*. New York: Oxford University Press.

Meyrowitz, J. (1994). "Medium Theory,"in D. Crowley & D. Mitchell (eds) *Communication Theory Today*, Cambridge: Polity Press. pp 50-77.

Michael, J. (1998). "Teaching *South Park*," term paper, New York University, Masters program.

Miller, M. C. (1998). "It's a Crime: The Economic Impact of the Local TV News in Baltimore," project on Media Ownership, New York University, New York.

Miller, T. (1993). *The Well Tempered Self: Citizenship, Culture, and the Postmodern Subject*. Baltimore, Md.: Johns Hopkins University Press.

Miller, T. (1998). *Technologies of Truth: Cultural Citizenship and the Popular Media*. Minneapolis: University of Minnesota Press.

Mitchell, W. J. T. (1994). *Picture Theory*. Chicago: University of Chicago Press.

Moore, D. M. & Dwyer, F. M. (1994). *Visual Literacy: A Spectrum of Visual Learning*. Englewood Cliffs, N.J..: Educational Technology.

Morley, D. (1980). *The Nationwide Audience*. London: British Film Institute.

Morley, D. (1986). *Family Television: Cultural Power and Domestic Leisure*. London: Comedia.

Morris, J. (1980). *Destinations: Essays from* Rolling Stone. New York: Oxford University Press.

Moyal, A. (1984). *Clear across Australia : A History of Telecommunications*. Melbourne, Victoria: Nelson.

Mulgan, G. J. (1991). *Communication and Control: Networks and the New Economies of Communication*. Cambridge: Polity Press.

Musa, H. (1998). "Profound? No, Just Par for the Coarse," *The Australian*, 11 September 1998, p 15.

Nagel, T. (1979). "What Is It Like To Be a Bat," in T. Nagel *Mortal Questions*. Cambridge: Cambridge University Press, pp 165-180.

Nehemas, A. (1988). "Plato and the Mass Media," in A. Nehemas (ed) *Virtues of Authenticity*. Princeton, N.J.: Princeton University Press, pp. 279-299.

Newsday (2000). "Reality TV Ratings Success," *Newsday*, 30 June 2000.

*New York Daily News* (2000). "*Survivor* Changed TV Forever," *New York Daily News*, 18 February 2000.

Nightingale, V. (1990). "Women as Audiences," in M. Brown (ed) *Television and Women's Culture*. Beverly Hills, Calif.: Sage, pp 25-37.

Norris, C. (1998). "Welcome to South Park, Fat-Ass," *Spin*, March 1999, pp 66-75.

O'Connor, K. (1996). "Privacy and New Technology," University of Canberra Communication Seminars, 10 October 1996.

Olmas, A. (1998). "Del Canal 13 a TV Azteca," in Martínez, O. M. *Apuntes Para una Historia de La Televisión Mexicana: Revista Mexicana de Comunicación.* pp 99-143.

Oppenheimer, A. (1996). *Bordering on Chaos: Guerrillas, Stockbrokers, Politicians, and Mexico's Road to Prosperity.* New York: Little Brown & Company.

Page, B. (1996). *Who Deliberates? Mass Media in Modern Democracy.* Chicago: University of Chicago Press.

Palmer, P. (1986). *The Lively Audience: A Study of Children Around the Television Set.* Sydney: Allen & Unwin.

Peirce, C. S. (1965-6). *Collected Papers,* C. Hartshorne & P. Weiss (eds). Cambridge, Mass.: Belknap Press.

Perrott, C. (1988). *Classroom Talk and Pupil Learning.* London: Harcourt, Brace, Jovanovich.

Pettit, P. (1977). *The Concept of Structuralism: A Critical Analysis.* Berkeley, Calif.: University of California Press.

Pettit, P. (1992). *The Common Mind: An Essay on Psychology, Society and Politics.* New York: Oxford University Press.

Philosophy (1996-1997). *Advertising Booklet.* Barney's, New York. http://www.philosophy.com New York: Barney's.

Plato (1970). *The Republic.* Trans. B. Jowett. London: Sphere.

Poole, R. (1989 ). "Public Spheres," in H. Wilson (ed), *Australian Communications and the Public Sphere.* Melbourne: Macmillan, pp 6-26.

Poster, M. (1990). *The Mode of Information.* Chicago: University of Chicago Press.

Poster, M. (1994). "The Mode of Information and Postmodernity," in D. Crowley & D. Mitchell (eds): *Communication Theory Today.* Cambridge: Polity, pp 173-192.

Postman, N. (1982). *The Disappearance of Childhood.* New York: Delacorte Press.

Postman, N. (1985). *Amusing Ourselves to Death: Public Discourse in the Age of Show Business.* New York: Penguin.

Postman, N. (1988). *Conscientious Objections Stirring up Trouble about Language, Technology, and*

*Education*. London:Heinemann.

Postman, N. (1993). *Technopoly*. New York: Penguin.

Press, A. (1991). *Women Watching Television: Gender, Class and Generation in the American Television Experience*. Philadelphia: University of Pennsylvania.

Price, M. (1995). *Television: The Public Sphere and National Identity*. Oxford: Clarendon Press.

Priest, G. (1979) "Two Dogmas of Quineanism," *The Philosophical Quarterly*, vol 20, pp 289-301.

Priest, G. (1987). *In Contradiction*. Amsterdam: Martinus Nijhoff.

Pryor, G. (1991). "The Times They Are a'Changin,'" cartoon, *Canberra Times*, 22 February 1991.

Putnis, P. (1994). *Displaced, Re-cut & Recycled: File-Tape in Television News*. Brisbane: Centre for Journalism Research and Education, Bond University.

Quine, W.V. O. (1953). *From a Logical Point of View*. Cambridge, Mass.: Harvard University Press.

Quine, W.V.O. (1960). *Word and Object*. Cambridge, Mass.: MIT Press.

Quine W.V. O. (1974). *The Roots of Reference*. La Salle, Wisc.: Open Court.

Quiñones, S. (1998). "Telenovelas: Sexy Soaps Reflect a Changing Mexico," *US/Mexico Business*, December 1998, pp 41-45.

Radway, J. (1984). *Reading the Romance*. Chapel Hill, N.C.: UNC Press.

Rawls, J. (1972). *A Theory of Justice*. Oxford: Clarendon.

Ray, M. L. Sawyer, A. G., Rothschild, M. L., Heeler, R. M., Strong, E. C. & Reed, J. B. (1973). "Marketing Communication and the Hierarchy of Effects," in P. Clarke (ed): *New Models for Communication Research*. Beverly Hills, Calif.: Sage.

*Reforma*, (1997). "Encuentran sus 'miradas,'" 17 September 1997, p 9E.

*Reforma*, (2001). "Pácatelas! Los liberan," 26 January 2001, p 1.

Robbins, B. (1993). *The Phantom Public Sphere*. Minneapolis: University of Minnesota Press.

Romero, B. & Agudelo, M. (1998). *Mirada de Mujer* Mexico City: Plaza Janés.

Rorty, R. (1991). *Objectivity, Relativism, and Truth*. Cambridge, Mass.: Cambridge University Press.

Ross, A. (1998). *Real Love: In Pursuit of Cultural Justice*. New York: New York University Press.

Rushkoff, D. (1997). *Children of Chaos > \*[Surviving the End of the World as We Know It]*. New York: Flamingo.

Rushkoff, D. (1999). *Coercion: Why We Listen to What 'They' Say*. New York: Riverhead.

Russell, B. (1937). *The Principles of Mathematics*. London: George Allen & Unwin.

Samsung advertisement, Mexico City (1999). *Reforma*. 14 July 1999, p 27A.

Sandel, M. (ed) (1984). *Liberalism and Its Critics: Readings in Social and Political Theory*. New York: New York University Press.

Sartori, G. (1998). *Homo Videns*. Madrid: Taurus.

Schiffer, S. (1972). *Meaning*. Oxford: Clarendon Press.

Searle, J. (1969). *Speech Acts*. Cambridge: Cambridge University Press.

Sefton-Green, J. & Buckingham, D. (1996). "Children's Creative Uses of Multimedia Technologies," *Convergence*, vol 2, no 2, pp 47-79.

Shattuc, J. M. (1997). *The Talking Cure: TV Talk Shows and Women*. New York: Routledge.

Shirer, W. (1990). *A Native's Return, 1945-1988*. Boston: Little Brown & Company.

Shrensky, R (1997). "The Ontology of Communication," Ph.D. thesis, University of Canberra.

Sinclair, J., Jacka, E. & Cunningham, S. (eds)(1995). *New Patterns in Global Television: Peripheral Vision*. New York: Oxford University Press.

Skinner, Q. (1996). *Reason and Rhetoric in the Philosophy of Hobbes*. Cambridge: Cambridge University Press.

Slade, C. (1994). "Harryspeak and the Conversation of Girls," in D. Camhy (ed): *Children: Thinking and Philosophy*. Hamburg: Academia Verlag, pp 220-229.

Slade, C. (1995). "Analogy and Creativity: Reasoning in *Pixie*," in R. Reed & A. Sharp (eds): *Studies in Philosophy for Children, Pixie.* Madrid: Ediciones de la Torre, pp 232-242.

Slade, C. (1996). "Raisonnement et coopération," in M-F. Daniel & M. Schleifer (eds): *La Coopération dans la Classe.* Montréal: Editions Logiques, pp 125-150.

Slade, C. (1997). "Regulation and the Public Sphere," *Media International Australia.* vol 84, pp 102-111.

Slade, C. (1998). *The Reason and Media Web site.* University of Canberra, Canberra. http://communication.canberra.edu.au/Reason&Media

Solomon, R. & Higgins, K. (eds)(1993). *From Africa to Zen: An Invitation to World Philosophy.* Lanham, Md.: Rowman and Littlefield.

Spender, D. (1995). *Nattering on the Net: Women, Power and Cyberspace.* North Melbourne: Spinifex.

Splitter, L. & Sharp, A. (1995). *Teaching for Better Thinking: The Classroom Community of Inquiry.* Melbourne: ACER.

Steele, J. R. & Brown, J. D. (1995). "Adolescent Room Culture: Studying Media in the Context of Everyday Life," *Journal of Youth and Adolescence,* vol 24, no 5, pp 551-576.

Survivor http://www.cbs.com/primetime/survivor/show/concept/html

Sutel, S. (2000). "Simpson-matic," *Canberra Times, TV Guide,* 6 March 2000.

Tannen, D. (1991). *You Just Don't Understand: Men and Women in Conversation.* New York: Ballantine.

Tannen, D. (1998). *The Argument Culture: Changing the Way We Argue and Debate.* London: Virago.

Taylor, P. (1992). "Political Coverage in the 1990s: Teaching the Old News New Tricks," in *The New News vs the Old News.* New York: Twentieth Century Fund.

Thomas, C. (1999) "JFK Jr's Death Marked the End of Broadcast Journalism," *The News.* 30 July 1999, p 16.

Thompson, J. (1998). *Discourse and Knowledge: Defense of a Collectivist Ethics.* London: Routledge.

Thomson, J. (1992). *Justice and the World Order: A Philosophical Enquiry*. London: Routledge.

Thorne, B., Kramarae, C. & Henley, N. (1983). *Language, Gender and Society*. Rowley, Mass.: Newbury House.

Tichi, C. (1991). *Electronic Hearth*. New York: Oxford University Press.

Turkheimer, F. (1994). "Privacy and the Internet: The Next Step," *Computer Networks and ISDN*, vol 27, pp 395-401.

Turkle, S. (1995). *Life on the Screen: Identity in the Age of the Internet*. New York: Simon and Schuster.

Tyner, K. (1998). *Literacy in a Digital World*. Mahwah, N.J.: Lawrence Erlbaum.

Van Dijk, T. (1989). "Structures of Discourse and Structures of Power," in J. Anderson (ed): *Communication Yearbook* 12. Newbury Park, Calif.: Sage.

Venturelli, S. (1993). "The Imagined Transnational Public Sphere in the European Community's Broadcast Philosophy: Implications for Democracy," *European Journal of Communication*, vol 8, no 4, pp 491-518.

Wark, M. (1992). "Homer's Odyssey," *Family and Society*, vol 21, no 8, pp 48-51.

Whorf, B. (1956). *Language, Thought and Reality*. Cambridge, Mass.: MIT Press.

Williamson, J. (1981). *Decoding Advertisements*. New York: Marion Boyars.

Wilson, H. (ed) (1989). *Australian Communications and the Public Sphere*. Melbourne: Macmillan.

Wilson, R. (1996). "Soaps in Cyberspace," *Weekend Australian*, 31 August 1996, SYTE 3.

Windsor Jewelers (1997). *New York Times*, 26 April 1997.

Wittgenstein, L. (1961 [1921]). *Tractatus Logico-Philosophicus*. Trans D. F. Pears & B. F. McGuiness. London: Routledge & Kegan Paul.

Wittgenstein, L. (1953). *Philosophical Investigations*. Trans. E. Anscombe. Oxford: Blackwell.

Wittgenstein, L. (1956). *Remarks on the Foundations of Mathematics*. Trans. E. Anscombe. Oxford: Blackwell.

Young, I. M. (1990). *Justice and the Politics of Difference.* Princeton, N. J.: Princeton University Press.

Zamarripa, R. (2000). "Investigar del Villar a Televisión Azteca," *Reforma,* 10 April 2000, p 1.

# INDEX

# Studies in the Postmodern Theory of Education

*General Editors*
*Joe L. Kincheloe & Shirley R. Steinberg*

Counterpoints publishes the most compelling and imaginative books being written in education today. Grounded on the theoretical advances in criticalism, feminism, and postmodernism in the last two decades of the twentieth century, Counterpoints engages the meaning of these innovations in various forms of educational expression. Committed to the proposition that theoretical literature should be accessible to a variety of audiences, the series insists that its authors avoid esoteric and jargonistic languages that transform educational scholarship into an elite discourse for the initiated. Scholarly work matters only to the degree it affects consciousness and practice at multiple sites. Counterpoints' editorial policy is based on these principles and the ability of scholars to break new ground, to open new conversations, to go where educators have never gone before.

For additional information about this series or for the submission of manuscripts, please contact:

Joe L. Kincheloe & Shirley R. Steinberg
c/o Peter Lang Publishing, Inc.
275 Seventh Avenue, 28th floor
New York, New York 10001

To order other books in this series, please contact our Customer Service Department:

(800) 770-LANG (within the U.S.)
(212) 647-7706 (outside the U.S.)
(212) 647-7707 FAX

Or browse online by series:

www.peterlangusa.com